Assessing the Handicaps and Needs of Mentally Retarded Children

Assessing the Handicaps and Needs of Mentally Retarded Children

Edited by

BRIAN COOPER

Department of Epidemiological Psychiatry,
Central Institute of Mental Health,
Mannheim, FRG

 1981 · ACADEMIC PRESS

A Subsidiary of Harcourt Brace Jovanovich, Publishers
London · New York · Toronto · Sydney · San Francisco

ACADEMIC PRESS INC. (LONDON) LTD
24/28 Oval Road
London NW1

United States Edition published by
ACADEMIC PRESS INC.
111 Fifth Avenue
New York, New York 10003

British Library Cataloguing in Publication Data

Assessing the handicaps and the needs of mentally
retarded children.
1. Mentally handicapped children.
I. Cooper, B.
362.7'4   HV.891

ISBN 0-12-188020-6

LCCCN 81-66374

Printed in Great Britain

Contributors

P. Bächer *Department of Biostatistics, Central Institute of Mental Health, 6800 Mannheim 1, J5, FRG*

A.H. Bernsen *Paediatric Department, Municipal Hospital, Aarhus, Denmark*

J.A. Corbett *Consultant Psychiatrist, Hilda Lewis House, Bethlem Royal Hospital, 379 Wickham Road, Shirley, Croydon CR0 8DR, UK*

A. Dupont *Institute of Psychiatric Demography, Aarhus Psychiatric Hospital, 8240 Risskov, Denmark*

D. Eggert *Faculty of Education 1, University of Hannover, Bismarckstrasse 2, 3000 Hannover 1, FRG*

T. Fryers *Senior Lecturer in Community Medicine, Department of Community Medicine, University of Manchester, Stopford Building, Oxford Road, Manchester M13 9PT, UK*

Th. Gasser *Department of Biostatistics, Central Institute of Mental Health, 6800 Mannheim 1, J5, FRG*

J. Gould *MRC Social Psychiatry Unit, Institute of Psychiatry, De Crespigny Park, London SE5 8AF, UK*

M. Iivanainen *Department of Neurology, University of Helsinki, Haartmaninkatu 4, 00290 Helsinki 29, Finland*

L. Kebbon *Psychiatric Research Centre, Psychological Unit, University of Uppsala, Ulleråker Hospital, 75017 Uppsala, Sweden*

R. Kornmann *Department VI: Special Education, Heidelberg Teachers' College, Keplerstrasse 87, 6900 Heidelberg 1, FRG*

W.M. Lederer *Department of Biostatistics, Central Institute of Mental Health, 6800 Mannheim 1, J5, FRG*

M.C. Liepmann *Pirschweg 3, 6900 Heidelberg, FRG*

P. Mittler *Director, Hester Adrian Research Centre, University of Manchester, Manchester M13 9PL, UK*

J. Möcks *Department of Biostatistics, Central Institute of Mental Health, 6800 Mannheim 1, J5, FRG*

M. Ort *Department of Epidemiological Psychiatry, Central Institute of Mental Health, 6800 Mannheim 1, J5, FRG*

M. Oswin *Research Officer, Thomas Coram Research Unit, Institute of*

Education, University of London, 41 Brunswick Square, London WC1N 1AZ, UK

D. Preddy   Hester Adrian Research Centre, University of Manchester, Manchester M13 9PL, UK

N.V. Raynes   Hester Adrian Research Centre, University of Manchester, Manchester M13 9PL, UK

D.M. Ricks   Consultant in Charge of Children's Department, Harperbury Hospital, Harper Lane, Shenley, Radlett, Herts WD7 9HQ, UK

R. Verleger   Department of Biostatistics, Central Institute of Mental Health, Mannheim 1, J5, FRG

D. Wilkin   Research Fellow, Research Section, P.G.U. Building, Withington Hospital, Nell Lane, Manchester M20 8LR, UK

L. Wing   MRC Social Psychiatry Unit, Institute of Psychiatry, De Crespigny Park, London SE5 8AF, UK

Preface

Traditionally, the role of scientific research in medicine has been associated with the search for causes of disease and with the discovery and testing of new forms of treatment. While these remain today its primary functions, there is now a growing recognition of the value of research into many related aspects of health care; not least in defining the nature of the impairments and handicaps that may result from illness, and in establishing the special needs of handicapped persons for treatment, rehabilitation and social support.

Research of this kind is of great importance in planning services for the mentally retarded, a section of the population that more than almost any other in our society has suffered through being characterized by a single, catch-all label. There is now abundant evidence that persons to whom this label (or one or other of its analogues, such as mental deficiency or subnormality) is applied form a grouping so heterogeneous in composition, and so diverse in needs, as to invite comparison in both respects with those whom we call "mentally ill". Medical classification does not yet do justice to the diversity. Even in the most recent (ninth) revision of the International Classification of Diseases, of a total of 184 conditions listed as mental disorders, only five refer to mental retardation, and the diagnostic rubrics supplied for these five – mild, moderate, severe, profound and "unspecified" – are by any standards of low scientific and clinical utility.

Some improvement in this respect may follow on the introduction of multi-axial classification. Contemporary thinking in social medicine favours the classification of forms of illness-related impairments and handicap on axes separate from that of clinical diagnosis, and it seems likely that this approach will prove useful in defining the nature of mental retardation. However, progress in taxonomy will be of practical value only if it is accompanied and guided by systematic research on the biological, psychological and social concomitants of the condition, and their relationships with one another. The needs of individual mentally retarded children and adults – and, as a corollary, the sum of the needs represented by all such persons in a defined population – must be investigated in relation (a) to any specific impairments due to neurological damage or developmental anomaly; (b) to levels of intellectual performance and educational achievement, and (c) to patterns of adaptive or maladaptive behaviour and degree of social competence. Moreover, since (b) and (c) cannot be explained solely in terms of (a), but are always to some extent environmentally determined, an attempt must be made to distinguish 'primary' intrinsic handicaps from those 'secondary' handicaps caused by exposure to unfavourable conditions in the family and the local community, at school or in a residential institution.

The 18 previously unpublished contributions making up the present volume fit into this conceptual framework. They are based on papers read at a small colloquium held at the Central Institute of Mental Health in Mannheim, W. Germany, in March 1980, with the support of the Fritz Thyssen Foundation. The object of the meeting was to bring together clinical and scientific workers from a number of European countries, who are actively engaged in research into the handicaps and needs of the mentally retarded, in order to exchange information and to discuss common problems of method. Though drawn from the diverse specialist fields of paediatrics, psychiatry, neurology, clinical and educational psychology, biostatistics, sociology and special education, the participants had no difficulty in establishing a common frame of reference: largely because, with only one or two exceptions, their professional interests are focused on the problems of severe mental handicap (corresponding roughly to an intelligence quotient below 50 points). Problems associated with milder forms of retardation or educational subnormality, or with relatively circumscribed disabilities such as reading retardation, lay outside the scope of the meeting and are dealt with here only insofar as they relate to definition of the upper boundary of severe retardation. The questions touched on by the participants can be summarized as follows:

(1) What is the frequency of mental retardation among children in the general population, and how is it distributed? What differences between populations, and what temporal trends, can be detected in the incidence and prevalence of mental retardation?
(2) What is the nature of the specific or characteristic handicaps from which mentally retarded children suffer? How can these handicaps be identified and assessed by means of medical investigations, psychometric testing, informant interviews and other techniques?
(3) What family problems are associated with mental retardation, and what help do families require in coping with the added burden of care? How can the needs of families be analysed and measured?
(4) What methods are available for evaluating the services provided for mentally retarded children and their families, and for testing the

effects of innovation in these services?

(5) What are the present prospects for earlier recognition of mental handicap in young children and, more generally, for prevention of mental handicap through public health and social action?

It would not have been possible to deal systematically with all these questions and, in fact, no attempt has been made to do so. Instead, the contributors to this volume have either reported findings from their own research, or have picked out selected topics which seem to them important as growing points in their respective branches of research. It is hoped that the resulting book will provide a useful introduction to some contemporary issues in the scientific study of mental retardation and will help to stimulate further exchanges and collaboration between the different disciplines.

Many of the contributors, especially those from the United Kingdom, would wish to acknowledge the seminal influence on the field of mental restardation research of the late Professor Jack Tizard, who died while the Mannheim meeting was in preparation.

April 1981   *B. Cooper*

Contents

xii   Contents

Part 1
Estimating Needs for Care
in Defined Populations

1 Definition and identification of severe mental retardation

A. DUPONT

Institute of Psychiatric Demography, Aarhus Psychiatric Hospital, Denmark

There is a great need for clarification of the many unsolved problems related to mental retardation — not only during infancy and childhood, but also connected with the adult life of handicapped persons in modern communities with the problems of unemployment and fierce competition.

Although the ICD definition is well known — "Mental retardation is especially characterized by subnormality of intelligence and is of a nature or degree that requires or is susceptible to medical treatment or other special care or training of the patient" (WHO, 1974) — this definition is not always followed, either in daily practice or in many research papers.

The Swedish researcher Leif Wallin published a study in 1974 in which he reviewed the findings of the earlier prevalence studies. His paper summarizes the prevalence rates reported from these studies for "a medium and low grade" of mental retardation — that is to say, IQ below 50 — for the age groups 10–14 and 15–19 years in rural and urban areas, as shown in Table 1.

Summing up the papers cited here, Wallin stated that: "It is essential to achieve a reliable assessment at all age levels because a number of factors which influence prevalence in a community affect the various age-strata unequally". He also pointed out the need for surveys of urban populations, a task he himself undertook in the small industrial town of Mölndal outside Gothenburg (population 33 393). His method of epidemiological investigation was special and quite new. His first procedure was to examine a series of registers, archives and other sources of information in order to conduct a positive search for mentally retarded persons in the traditional way. In the second stage, his aim was to exclude severe mental retardation among the remainder of the population by means of a screening procedure for the assessment of every individual. The screening procedure, which was applied to the whole of the population, made it possible to exclude 91 per cent of the population from any suspicion of severe mental retardation.

Table 1 Prevalence in per cent of medium and low grade mental retardation in age groups 10–19 years in rural and urban areas (Wallin, 1974)

		Rural areas		Urban areas	
Author	Country	10–14	15–19	10–14	15–19
Lewis (1929)	England	0·56		0·37	
Lemkau *et al*. (1942B)	USA			0·33	
Goodman *et al*. (1956)	USA			0·36	
Kushlick (1961)	England			0·27	0·36
Goodman & Tizard (1962)	England			0·36	
Kushlick (1964)	England		0·38		0·35
Scally & Mackay (1964)	N. Ireland	0·36	0·40		
Imre (1968)	USA	0·47	1·39		
Innes *et al*. (1968)	Scotland	0·23	0·37		
Åkesson (1968)	Sweden		0·55[a]		
Birch *et al*. (1970)	Scotland			0·37[b]	
Flynn (1970)	Ireland	0·49			
Wing (1971)	England			0·37	
Brask (1972)	Denmark			0·37	

[a] Covering the age groups 10–20 years.
[b] Covering the age groups 8–10 years.

Wallin used the character of the person's work and other factors as exclusion criteria. In this part of the study, it was thus possible for him to incorporate the ICD criteria of definition which concern the person's level of social functioning. In his positive search for the mentally retarded, he went through many hospital and other records, and in any instance in which guidance from psychological case-reports or detailed psychiatric records did not enable him to reach an unequivocal decision as to the presence of significant mental retardation he made a personal examination. If an interview did not remove all doubts about this point, he also made a psychometric assessment. Hence, it was possible for him to include some persons irrespective of the criterion of impaired social functioning; indeed if we go through the case-histories it is possible to find at least two cases where mental retardation according to the full ICD definition is not clearly established. For instance, in case no. 33 the examination revealed that this person had an IQ of 45, but his social quotient — according to the description provided — was very high:

> He lives in his own apartment, situated in a house owned by his parents, and he himself attends to the cleaning work, clothing, personal hygiene and some preparation of meals. He lives on a pension he was awarded at 16 years of age. Since he was 19 years old he has worked mainly in a sheltered

workshop, but has worked in ordinary industry for some of the years. When he was 21, the pension was withdrawn, and subsequently he has been self-supporting.

It is typical that even in this very recent study, which is of high quality and uses a quite new technique, the criteria for "mental retardation" are still not firmly defined.

On the other hand, we know that studies of *registered populations* are based upon a different technique. Here only persons who for one reason or another need some kind of care or service are included — in this sense they all fulfil the social definition of mental retardation. The figures obtained from case-registers have always been subject to criticism: that the groups are very poorly defined and consist of all or nearly all moderately, severely and profoundly retarded adults, together with some severely and profoundly retarded children and an ill-defined group of mildly retarded of school age; that they reflect only the need for educational and social care, etc. However, case-register studies of the mentally retarded in two different countries, Denmark and Sweden, show many identical features. Comparing recently published figures from Sweden (Socialstyrelsen, 1979), with Danish figures (Dupont, 1980a) we find the results set out in Table 2.

A further analysis of residential patterns, schooling etc. also shows surprising concordance. This finding indicates that it is worthwhile to analyse the registered group of mentally retarded, since those persons who need special training, education, treatment and care are to be found here.

In the older approach used in prevalence studies the mental handicap was considered as a permanent attribute of the individual. In a dynamic system of classification, however, it becomes possible for a person to fulfil the criteria of mental retardation during one period of his life, but not at others. For instance, he may for educational reasons be classified as retarded during the school-age period, but later on, when he has been trained and may be earning a normal wage and living in a normal residence he need no longer be placed in this category. This flexibility is an advantage of the ICD type of classification.

In analysis of the distribution of mental retardation in a population, the

Table 2 Mentally retarded persons on record (Dupont, 1980a)

	Total prevalence %	N	Male/female ratio
Denmark (Dupont, 1978)	0·428	22 000	1·29/1
Sweden (Socialstyrelsen, 1975)	0·41	34 000	1·29/1

following factors are important: patterns of migration, the age-distribution and its relation to excess mortality in the different sub-groups of handicapped persons and, finally, the nature and severity of the associated handicaps.

The influence of migration is clearly shown by comparisons between the two Swedish studies by Wallin (1974) and Åkesson (1968). The population of the urban area (Wallin) is complementary to the rural area analysed by Åkesson; migration to industrial centres has reduced the age-groups 20–60 for both sexes in the rural population while the urban population shows a relative excess in these age-groups. The total prevalence of mental retardation in the urban population (all age-groups) is 0·24 per cent, compared with 0·61 per cent in the rural population. The residue population of areas with restricted communication— in particular of islands— showed a raised prevalence of mental retardation in a study of all Danish counties (Dupont, 1980a), when the present population was compared with all mentally retarded born in the county and still alive on the census day.

Comparisons of age-specific prevalence rates show a peak in the school-age period and a decline in the older age-groups (Dupont, 1975). The main reason for the decline in prevalence in the age-range 20–40 years is the ability of many adults, especially the relatively mildly retarded, to lead a fairly independent life with no need for special care. For the more severely retarded, especially after the age of about 40, there is an excess mortality leading to a decline in the prevalence rates (Åkesson and Forssman, 1971).

Differentiation of the groups subsumed under the term mental retardation is very difficult, and therefore many surveys of school-age children have been restricted to certain sub-groups. One approach has been to divide the mentally retarded into two main sub-groups, the "pathological" and the "subcultural", with a cut-off point for screening purposes in discriminating between severe or moderately severe retardation (usually pathological), on the one hand, and mild retardation (usually subcultural), on the other, roughly corresponding to IQ 50 (Cooper et al., 1979). The term "subcultural" does not necessarily imply an aetiological hypothesis, and it seems unlikely that there is a well-demarcated biological boundary dividing the pathological, severe from the subcultural, mild type of mental retardation.

Another sub-grouping is only indirectly related to the degree of the intelligence level, but is provided by the associated chronic handicaps: cerebral palsy, epilepsy, sensory handicaps, congenital malformations, speech and language disorders, etc. In a study of severe mental retardation in a Danish county, Bernsen (1980) found a single associated handicap in 39 per cent, two in 21 per cent, three in 17 per cent, four or more in five per cent. In all 82 per cent suffered from one to four handicaps in addition to their mental retardation. Cooper *et al.* (1979) showed that the frequency of severe associated handicaps increases with declining level of intelligence. The same trend has been found in a study of some 17 000 registered Danish cases (Table 3).

From the daily work with mentally retarded children it is a well-known experience that the training, education, and treatment of the multiply-handicapped with mental retardation present great difficulties. The complex nature of the disability caused by the mutual reinforcement of the intellectual defects and associated handicaps creates new demands.

For planners of special school facilities and services for care a sub-classification according to handicaps, behaviour and skills is most important. A special interview-schedule constructed for this purpose (Wing, 1975; Wing and Gould, 1978) has been used by a number of European research groups, and the findings are discussed later in this volume. From the results of the schedules, it is possible to classify the mentally retarded in sub-groups according to their burden upon the mothers or other caring persons. This approach has proved useful in a Danish study of families with a severely mentally retarded child living at home (Dupont, 1980b). Table 4 summarizes some of the findings of this study.

Detailed studies were performed of time-consuming aspects of the daily care and of detriments to the financial situation of the family caused by the handicapped child. This study is an example of an analysis of needs based on an epidemiological research with firm diagnostic criteria.

The final example of definition and identification to be mentioned here is based on aetiological diagnosis. The ICD (8th revision) provides a basis for grouping cases of mental retardation according to aetiological factors. Recent studies by Gustavson *et al.* (1977a, b) reflect developments in the

Table 3   Relationship between the IQ level (ICD diagnoses) and the number of associated handicaps (N = 17 622)

Number of associated handicaps	IQ range and ICD diagnostic category				
	68–85 (%)	52–67 (%)	36–51 (%)	20–35 (%)	<20 (%)
0	47·0	47·7	45·5	34·4	19·3
1	33·6	30·2	29·5	30·6	31·5
2	12·5	13·9	15·6	20·3	23·8
3	5·0	5·6	6·3	9·8	16·0
4 or more	2·0	2·6	3·1	4·9	9·4
Totals	100·1	100·0	100·0	100·0	100·0

Source: Danish Central Register of Mentally Retarded (Dupont, 1980a).

Table 4 Average time spent daily with children in four groups

	Group 1 (26–38[a])		Group 2 (15–38)		Group 3 (6–29)		Group 4 (1–10)	
	Hours	Minutes	Hours	Minutes	Hours	Minutes	Hours	Minutes
Night	0	16	0	20	0	2	0	0
Bedtime	0	11	0	20	0	12	0	2
Care	1	20	1	40	1	40	0	13
Clothes	0	55	0	51	1	15	0	4
Food	2	3	1	10	1	0	0	14
Occupation	2	17	2	15	2	53	0	20
Miscellaneous	0	40	1	2	1	6	0	12
Totals	7	42	7	38	8	8	1	5

Group 1: Totally non-mobile children in need of help for all daily activities.
Group 2: Hyperactive, destructive, non-communicating or passive, in need of much help.
Group 3: Mobile, not toilet-trained at night, often with epilepsy or other handicaps (of mild degrees), needing some help for daily activities.
Group 4: Manage daily life routines, with social interaction and skills corresponding to those of the normal child at a chronologically lower age (only 7% of total group).
[a] Weight load of symptoms.

diagnostic procedures. It is now possible to indicate the type of the underlying condition in all but about 10 per cent of children with severe mental retardation. The diagnostic category does not always identify a specific aetiology — for example "chromosomal disorder" or "a special prenatal damage". However, it is important to classify as many cases as possible for purposes of genetic counselling, for preventive measures, etc.

Comparisons of the distribution of diagnostic groups reported from earlier surveys with those of more recent studies using diagnosis based on the new methods in cytogenetics, biochemistry, etc. are obviously difficult. For instance, the figure for perinatal damage caused by obstetric complications consists of cases with damage to a normal foetus plus cases of abnormal — including microcephalic — foetus unable to withstand the stress of birth. Today some abnormal prenatal conditions, such as chromosomal anomalies, eponymous malformation syndromes and foetal alcohol syndrome, can be identified and diagnosed. Therefore, fewer cases of perinatal damage have been reported in the recent surveys, whereas the identification of prenatal aetiological factors and abnormalities has increased.

The epidemiologist working with severe mental retardation in child-hood is now able to give prevalence figures for many different diagnostic groups. In many countries, programmes for early case-finding, assess-ment and evaluation of risk-groups result in diagnosis before school age. Both in clinical practice and in prevalence surveys it is just as much an error to have "false negatives" as it is to have "false negatives" in the identification of mental retardation. Epidemiological criteria have not always been used carefully in earlier studies. Therefore new studies with better techniques of case-definition and case-identification are needed. In some surveys of mental retardation, case-finding is still restricted to special sub-groups of the population: persons on certain waiting-lists, persons included on hospital or special-school records, etc. However, it is a great advantage whenever possible to use a geographically-defined population as a basis for investigations of the needs for care and services. Otherwise, comparisons are difficult.

Why do we want to identify and classify the severely mentally retarded children?

(1) For scientific investigations — e.g. in order to measure the results of preventive measures.
(2) For comparisons between different regions, countries, etc.
(3) For planning purposes.

There is a need for statistics not only of the total population of mentally retarded, but also of many different sub-groups, classified:

(a) according to handicaps, behaviour and skills;
(b) according to diagnosis;
(c) according to the many different types of need: special education, special treatment, sheltered workshops etc., sheltered residence, institutions for the multiply-handicapped (especially for children with cerebral palsy and for blind children), nursing homes for the elderly mentally retarded, home visits, technical and financial aid and support.

Gruenberg (1977) has pointed to the failures of our health-care system: the raising pandemic of diseases with chronic mental illness, mental retardation and senile disorders. The "failures of success" in the struggle against these conditions now confront the industrialized countries and will very soon be a problem also for the developing parts of the world. The prevalence of such disorders will show a constant rise as the length of life for the severely handicapped persons continues to increase while the incidence remains stable or declines only slightly. There has been a tendency towards a pattern of new aetiological factors increasing as soon as well-known factors show a decline. The excess mortality of the mentally retarded is declining and therefore the prevalence of this group of disorders as a whole is increasing.

In Denmark, we spend about 1300 million Danish kroner a year on the national service for the mentally retarded (not including pensions, special education, and certain payments). This is about 10 per cent of the costs of the hospitals and about 0·4 per cent of the gross national product. Yet there is a need for much more money if care is to be provided according to modern standards. For instance, about 3000 of the Danish mentally retarded, multiply-handicapped are living in old institutions of a low quality without adequate space and without special staff (physiotherapists, speech-therapists, etc.). For the administrators, it has always been tempting to neglect the needs of these groups because it would be so expensive to provide care which would really meet their needs. It has always been thought more worthwhile to spend the money on the less handicapped groups and to leave the multiply-handicapped adults in old, overcrowded institutions (Ombudsmand's Report, 1975–77; Dupont, 1975) and the severely mentally retarded to the over-worked mothers (Dupont, 1980b; Wilkin, 1980).

Conclusions

(1) For all epidemiological studies it is still necessary to fix an upper level of IQ, such as an IQ of about 50.
(2) For all studies it is necessary to state explicitly whether or not the ICD diagnosis is the main criterion. If this is so, it is also necessary in all instances to exclude cases with adequate social functioning, whatever the IQ level, and therefore we need to determine not only the IQ but also a social competence quotient.
(3) It is now possible to use biological diagnostic criteria for epidemiological studies, e.g. studies of well-defined chromosomal anomalies.
(4) The Children's Handicaps, Behaviour and Skills Schedule or a comparable method of assessment is necessary for adequate description of the severely mentally handicapped — and often multiply-handicapped— child. If the planning of services and facilities is based only on estimates of need related only to the intellectual handicap, there will be gross underestimation of the problems.

Advances in diagnostic medicine (cytogenetic, biochemical, and clinical investigation), in social, psychological, and functional analysis and in the testing of handicaps, behaviour, and skills make possible a definition and identification of nearly all cases of severe mental retardation in early childhood. For the individual family, in need of advice for genetic counselling and in adjusting to life with the handicapped child, the advantages are obvious. Administrators planning preventive action and services for the handicapped also benefit from this progress.

References

Åkesson, H.O. (1968), *Severe Mental Deficiency in Sweden.* Läromedelsförlagen, Akademiförlaget: Stockholm, Göteborg, Lund.
Åkesson, H.O. and H. Forssman (1971), Mortality in patients with mental deficiency. *In* Primrose, D.A.A. (ed.): Proceedings of the Second Congress of the International Association for the Scientific Study of Mental Deficiency, Warsaw, 1970. Polish Medical Publishers: Warsaw, Swetz & Zeitlinger, N.V.: Amsterdam.
Bernsen, Alice H. (1980). Severe mental retardation among children in a Danish urban area. Assessment and Etiology. *In* Mittler, P. (ed.): *Frontiers of Knowledge in Mental Retardation.* Proceedings of the 5th Congress of IASSMD, Jerusalem, 1979. University Park Press: Baltimore, London, Tokyo (In press).
Cooper, B., M.C. Liepmann, K.R. Marker and P.M. Schieber (1979). Definition of severe mental retardation in school-age children: findings of an epidemiological study. *Soc. Psych.* **14**, 197–205.
Dupont, A. (1975) Mentally retarded in Denmark. *Danish Medical Bulletin,* **22**, 243–251.
Dupont, A. (1980a). Medical results from the Danish registration of the mentally retarded on record. *In* Mittler, P. (ed): *Frontiers of Knowledge in Mental Retardation.* Proceedings of the 5th Congress of IASSMD, Jerusalem, 1979. University Park Press: Baltimore, London, Tokyo (In press).
Dupont, A. (1980b). A study concerning the time-related and other burdens when severely handicapped children are reared at home. *In* Strömgren, E., A. Dupont and J.A. Nielsen (eds.): *Epidemiological Research as Basis for the Organization of Extramural Psychiatry.* Proceedings from the Second European Symposium on Social Psychiatry, Aarhus, 1979. *Acta Psychiatr. Scand.* **62**, suppl. 285, 249–257.
Folketingets ombudsmands beretning (Report by the Ombudsmand of the Danish Parliament) (1975) 347–352, 571–575, 631–635; (1976) 40–41, 64, 68–69, 399–404, 420–427, (1977) 52–55, 85–87.
Gruenberg, E.M. (1977). The failures of success. *Milbank Mem. Fund. Q./*Health and Society. Winter, 1977, 3–24.
Grunewald, K. and Wallner, T. (1979). Psykist utvecklingsstörda och deras livsvillkor i siffror (Facts and Figures on the Mentally Retarded and their Living Conditions in Sweden). *Socialstyrelsen redovisar* **5**.
Gustavson, K.-H., B. Hagberg, C. Hagberg and K. Sars (1977a). Severe mental retardation in a Swedish county. I. Epidemiology, gestational age, birth weight and associated CNS handicaps in children born 1959–70. *Acta Paediatr. Scand.* **66**, 373–379.
Gustavson, K.-H., B. Hagberg, G. Hagberg and K. Sars (1977b). Severe mental

retardation in a Swedish County. II. Etiologic and pathogenetic aspects of children born 1959–70. *Neuropädiatrie* **8**, 293–304.

Wallin, L. (1974). *Severe Mental Retardation in a Swedish Industrial Town.* Akademiförlaget, Scandinavian University Books: Stockholm, Göteborg, Lund.

Wilkin, D. (1979). *Caring for the Mentally Handicapped Child.* Croom Helm: London.

Wing, L. (1975). A study of language impairments in severely retarded children. *In* O'Connor, N. (ed.): *Language, Cognitive Deficits and Retardation.* Butterworths: London.

Wing, L. and J. Gould (1978). Systematic recording of behaviours and skills of retarded and psychotic children. *J. Autism Child. Schizo.* **8**, 79–97.

World Health Organization (1967). *International Classification of Diseases.* 1965 Revision, Vol. 1. WHO: Geneva.

World Health Organization (1974). *Glossary of Mental Disorders and Guide to their Classification.* WHO: Geneva.

2 Measuring trends in prevalence and distribution of severe mental retardation

T. FRYERS

Department of Community Medicine, University of Manchester, UK

Introduction

Severe mental retardation as a basis of classification has characteristics which pose serious problems for the epidemiologist. It is not unitary even in concept, composed as it is of many quite different pathological phenomena, the result of quite different aetiological processes operating at different times in the life cycle of the individual. These aetiologies often lead to other impairments besides severe retardation, which therefore has an important, but subtle and complex relationship with other expressions of neurological disorder, disadvantaging syndromes, and causes of early death.

The multiplicity of aetiologies are subject to many demographic, biological and social influences, including variations in health care and changes in mortality and survival, so the group as a whole is likely to be defined and observed differently in different communities and in the same community at different times.

In pursuing epidemiological research in severe mental retardation in Salford since the early 1960s, many methodological problems have necessarily arisen. It is the purpose of this chapter to discuss some of the most important of these problems and the possibility of overcoming them in applied research. This theme will be illustrated by some results of a study which has two main components: firstly, the measurement of the distribution and characteristics of the severely mentally retarded in one community since 1961; secondly, the evaluation and comparative analysis of secular and temporal trends of prevalence from studies reported in the literature over the last two decades. The results are to be found in detail in Fryers (1981) and Fryers and Mackay (1979a and b).

Salford is an industrial urban community within the Manchester conurbation in the North-West of England. The study area considered here, Salford County Borough, is now contained by the much larger Salford Metropolitan District. The County Borough was one of the most densely populated areas in the UK for most of the last 100 years, but its population fell from a peak of 247 000 in 1927 to 130 000 in 1971, and is still falling. Much of the population loss since the last war has been due to massive programmes of clearance of very poor 19th century houses and re-housing, often of young families, outside the boundaries of the old city. The population has relatively small proportions of occupational social classes I and II, and has consistently poor records for all indices of health and illness, including relatively high peri-natal and infant mortality rates. On the other hand, the community has shown great vigour in tackling its many problems.

The Salford Mental Retardation Register was started by Kushlick with an initial census on 1st January 1961. It was continued and developed by the present author, at first within the community Mental Health Service, where close working relationships were developed with child health, psychiatric, educational and social work personnel and records. It now collects data on all retardation service contacts by the 260 000 population of Salford Metropolitan District, including personal social, clinical, educational and residential information. Its principle purposes lie locally in planning and monitoring retardation services and, more broadly, in providing a base for research.

Problems of research method

Concepts of mental retardation

The complexity of the biological phenomena and their causes which we group together as severe mental retardation, and the wide range of disciplines involved in their study tends to lead to a confusion of concepts. The word retardation itself, implying some falling behind in norms of development, may not be inappropriate in paediatric, educational and psychological contexts; it has however been commonly assumed to imply a permanent reduction in intellectual function compared with population norms, particularly as measured by intelligence tests.

It has also apparently been assumed by many workers and writers that its expression in different communities will be similar, that is, that pre-valence ratios will be relatively constant in time and place, and any that are out of line with accepted norms must be methodologically suspect. Similarly, it is often assumed in the literature that the proportions within the whole of specific aetiological groups will remain constant. None of these assumptions is justified. With such a diverse collection of causes, processes and syndromes we must *expect* variations in incidence, pre-valence and diagnostic distribution, both by time and place. The difficulties are in standardisation of measurement, in measuring accurately and consistently so that comparison is possible, and in committing resources for long-term study. The sharing of realistic concepts is a prerequisite for such assessment and it is essential that the dynamic qualities of the prevalence of severe mental retardation be understood.

A major change over the last decade or so is the increase in our understanding of aetiologies and the precise diagnostic potential in everyday paediatric practice, involving neuropathological concepts and biological processes of causation. Concurrently, more emphasis has been placed upon the need to understand the precise functional disorders experienced by the mentally retarded which largely determine the nature of their daily lives and the specific assistance they require. This involves quite different concepts and a different approach to study. Neither functional limitations nor neuropathological lesions need correlate closely either with the general social disadvantage for the person and his family, or with his degree of retardation, and his classification, as determined by IQ.

Recently, a growing convention has arisen which helps to clarify these concepts, not least in mental retardation (Harris, 1971). Three terms are in use: (1) impairment; the basic biological fault in a tissue or organ; (2) disability; the limitation of function consequent upon impairment; and (3) handicap: the resulting personal and social disadvantage. There may of course be multiple impairments, disabilities or handicaps. Thus a brain-damaged child may have specific CNS impairments, disabilities including non-ambulation, incontinence, lack of speech and bizarre behaviour patterns, and gross and global handicaps since he is disadvantaged in every aspect of personal and social life. On the other hand, a child with Down Syndrome has a global impairment; his disabilities may include clumsiness, poor pronounciation and a reduced capacity for learning; his handicaps will depend upon his disabilities and the expectations of normal children of his age in his particular culture.

In mental retardation, studies of aetiologies and the potential for prevention are concerned with precise impairments and specific complexes of impairments, and must necessarily consider sequelae other than intellectual deficit alone. The importance of the work of Hagberg et al. (e.g. Hagberg, 1979) is in the concurrent study of cerebral palsy and epilepsy with mental retardation. The research reported by Iivanainen and by Gasser et al. (Part 2) attempts to give precise, detailed neurological and neurophysiological descriptions of impairments. In contrast, Wing and other workers employing her schedule are concerned to describe, define and classify syndromes of disability, important in assessing daily care needs. The study of relatively specific impairments and disabilities, which needs much greater emphasis in future epidemiological work, cannot be restricted entirely to severe retardation. The study of specific learning problems is also identifying disabilities and patterns of disability. The study of social disadvantage is even more difficult, since each person and his family are likely to present a unique multi-dimensional and changing profile. This fact is important to recognise in practice, as it implies the need for continuing professional contact with families to monitor changes and to assist them in living with their collage of handicaps.

The term severe mental retardation implies global personal disadvantage in terms of educational and other social inadequacy and dependency. As assessment and care services have become more sophisticated, such global concepts of handicap have become less useful. There are indeed dangers of generalisation; of assuming common patterns which don't exist and ignoring individual needs. Increasing understanding of impairments and functional disabilities may soon make the concept of global handicap implied by the traditional classification quite anachronistic. Yet in order to continue to study the group as a whole, and in the absence of better general categories for overall social, educational and health service provision, we will need to continue to use it for some time yet.

Definition of mental retardation

Scientific study requires standardisation of definitions and consistency in measurement. The definition of severe mental retardation has been endlessly debated in the literature, yet still gives rise to problems. The determination of criteria for a satisfactory definition depends ultimately on pragmatic objectives. Studies to assess family financial need, the demand for residential care, educational and medical needs, or the potential for prevention would each require different criteria. In most developed communities, the commonest administrative use of classification has been to determine special schooling and it has become generally accepted that a *sine qua non* should be a level of intellectual function equivalent to IQ below 50. This has undoubtedly improved the comparability of studies in the literature, but the use of intelligence and development tests, even where comprehensive, cannot be perfectly standardised when applied in different cultures by different people, to children of different ages in different environments. (cf. Gould, Part 3). We are forced to accept some looseness of definition around the borderline, and there is no doubt that this can affect prevalence ratios.

For the Salford study all available information relevant to classification was reviewed for each individual. Much of it, especially from earlier years, was incomplete, and a combination of IQ results, clinical data and educational performance over many years was necessarily used. Because of inevitable inconsistencies and conflicting objectives in different aspects of the study, a special "borderline" category was devised. This mostly included children with only slender intelligence test evidence, which would place them just outside the <50 IQ category, but who clinically and educationally were more appropriately placed amongst the severely retarded as confirmed by subsequent experience. This also allowed all children with Down Syndrome to be included if required for specific analyses.

Table 1 shows two five-year sequences of census counts of the severely retarded in Salford aged 5–9 years with the numbers under IQ 50 and the "borderline" group. It can be seen that there were very few "borderline" cases in early years but a significant number in later years. This is merely a product of more sophisticated and precise information being available for later cohorts of children: although the first column might appear more consistent, having a "strict" definition of IQ <50, this is spurious. Children falling into the border-line group in later years would, in earlier years, in the absence of professional assessment, have been allocated without qualm to the "severe" category, for example, any "bright" Down's children. The total in the final column is likely, therefore, to be more accurate.

It is perhaps ironic that as consistent IQ criteria have been increasingly accepted by research workers in mental retardation, psychologists have become less enamoured of intelligence testing itself, so that in many communities little testing is now done, and IQ data are not available for classification. In the future, paediatricians will be able to provide accurate

Table 1 Prevalence of severe mental retardation in Salford: children aged 5–9 years. Variation in numbers by definition

Year 1st Jan	IQ <50	Borderline Group	Total
1961	21	1	22
1962	25	1	26
1963	25	–	25
1964	28	–	28
1965	34	–	34
1971	56	8	64
1972	52	7	59
1973	53	7	60
1974	54	4	58
1975	50	6	56

pathological diagnoses with aetiological implications for most mentally retarded children and this will no doubt be a more satisfactory basis of classification for much scientific work. But it will be a different classification from the traditional one, and it may not prove very useful for planning educational or residential facilities. There seems little doubt that we will require several different definitions according to use.

Consistency in terminology

In spite of its long and honourable history, epidemiology has, as yet, failed to gain universal acceptance for some of its basic technical vocabulary. In particular, the terms *prevalence* and *incidence* are used confusedly even by trained epidemiologists themselves, and frequently by others. A universal consensus in the use of these terms would help us to avoid pitfalls of confused communication; there are some indications that we are moving in this direction. *Incidence* is a measure of the number of defined *events* in a *period* of time. Thus, new cases diagnosed in one year in a community is a measure of the incidence of a particular condition. Similarly, the numbers of admissions, discharges or births in a year are incidence type figures, and may be applied to defined categories of disorder. Deaths, being events, can only be described in incidence terms. Incidence figures are usually also related to a standard population (commonly "per 1000") but their governing characteristic remains that they measure events in a period of time.

   Prevalence is a measure of the number of defined *individuals* or *states* of "illness" or health care, present at a *point* of time. Thus the total number of severely retarded children in a community, aged between 5 and 9 years on the 1st January 1971, usually expressed as a ratio of the total population in that age group at the same point of time, is the age-specific prevalence of severe retardation. Any measure of "beds" occupied on a particular day, in hospitals or other residential care facilities, must necessarily be a prevalence type of measure. Complications arise because the point of time used need not be a point in "calendar time". It can be a point in "institutional time", such as at admission or discharge, or even "life time" of an individual, particularly at birth. Thus the number of Down Syndrome babies born in a community, per 1000 total births, independent of the period of time taken to produce 1000 babies, is a prevalence type of statistic. It is properly referred to as *prevalence at birth*, where *incidence* is the number of Down Syndrome babies (usually per 1000 *population*), born in a year. Because of the variability in births per year and birth rates, prevalence at birth is generally far more useful than incidence, for disorders present at birth. Of course, if birth rates are accurately known in the population, then prevalence at birth and incidence of specific disorders present at birth can be readily calculated one from the other. In many less developed communities, where population statistics, and therefore birth rates, are not accurately known, epidemiological study of births may proceed, if defined births are related to total consecutive births in which they are observed, allowing prevalence at birth to be calculated and comparisons undertaken.

The concept can be extended to any point in the life-time of individuals, so that we may legitimately describe, for example, the prevalence of Down Syndrome at age one year, meaning the number of Down Syndrome children reaching their first birthday, expressed as a proportion of all children reaching their first birthday in that population, during the period of study. (cf. Gustavson *et al.*, 1978).

Rather more philosophical objections may be made to the concept of incidence as applied to disorders observed at birth. The true "incidence" (the event of commencement) of many disorders would be at a much earlier stage of development. This may be illustrated again by Down Syndrome which is present at conception, and where spontaneous abortion significantly diminishes the numbers surviving to birth. At birth therefore, we are already seeing the end of a complex process which we should bear in mind. Nevertheless, the most useful measures we usually have are incidence of survivors at birth, the event recorded being the *birth* of an affected child.

Comprehensive identification of mentally retarded individuals

Comprehensive identification of the severely mentally retarded is a problem in many communities and is highly dependent upon the state of the child health services. The prevalence of severe retardation depends upon the age at which individuals are identified to be counted. Down Syndrome may be identified at birth but many others are progressively ascertained through a complex multidisciplinary assessment process. Thus any studies of the totality of severe retardation in the first few years of life must necessarily give incomplete answers. Hagberg (1978) illustrates a different problem when improved diagnostic techniques in neuropaediatrics identify finer and more subtle degrees of cerebral palsy than were previously recognised. At least in developed communities, we can expect nearly all severely mentally retarded children to be routinely identified by the age of six or seven, but it is the years before this which show the highest mortality and studies of specific impairments need to start from birth or even before.

Detailed denominators

Even the most sophisticated communities have problems in defining their populations in detail for demographic statistics. High mobility rates soon render census figures out of date. In Britain currently we are ten years from the last census, a decade of such social and demographic change that we can have little confidence in population projections. Moreover, changes in administrative boundaries have prejudiced demographic continuity. The Salford Register population ceased to exist as an entity in 1974 and it has proved difficult ever since to get good estimates of the current population. The problem was largely solved for children of school age by obtaining figures for school registrations from the Education Authority, which are collected each year from every school and which take into account cross-boundary transfers, children in private and special schools and children not currently attending school. I believe these figures to be as good as any from a new census and to have permitted a detailed description of population changes in these age groups. Figure 1 illustrates the subtle and complex changes in the population of two small age groups in an urban community over a period of 20 years. One of the most interesting features is that, in spite of a consistent and fairly dramatic fall in total population in Salford in this period, these two age groups changed very little and even rose slightly. We would not have assumed such a trend and without this sort of data our calculations of prevalence ratios could be quite erroneous. The

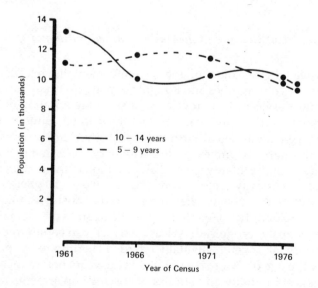

Fig. 1   Salford C.B. Population 5–9 yrs and 10–14 yrs, 1961–1977.

denominator for prevalence ratios is as important as the numerator and often needs almost as much effort to obtain. Yet the problem is often neglected, or ignored.

Even when detailed, accurate figures are known for each age group under study, temporal changes in prevalence ratios may be difficult to interpret in any but the most stable communities, because of the possibility of differential migration rates between families with retarded children and the rest of the population. In Salford this factor appears to have inflated prevalence ratios slightly throughout the whole period, but figures from Camberwell provided by Wing (1978) suggest that it has been of much greater significance there.

Table 2 uses numbers and age-specific prevalence ratios in Salford (at eight censuses since 1961), to show the mean changes over the last twenty years, by a comparison of the means for three sets of five consecutive annual cohorts. Death rates have varied, but mortality after the age of five has been low even for the severely retarded. The relatively few children fully ascertained later than five years have been added to the "cohorts". Rates of migration in and out have been surprisingly low with little overall effect on the figures. In the first two periods, there was a small net immigration, against the general flow of the Salford population. In the last period a net emigration was not sufficient to counter the effects of a more rapidly falling base population.

Thus differential migration does appear to have increased the level of prevalence ratios a little, particularly as seen in these "cohort" changes. But it appears to have produced this effect throughout the period of study and cannot explain the observed temporal changes in prevalence. If we use prevalence figures derived solely from Salford born children, the same general patterns emerge. Salford never seemed likely to attract much deliberate immigration of families with retarded children, as Wing has argued for Camberwell, as a response to relatively attractive services. Nevertheless it illustrates the importance and difficulty of understanding migration patterns.

For the study of aetiologies in relating affected children born, (e.g. Down Syndrome) to total numbers of babies born in the same period of time, details of the distribution of total births by maternal age are necessary, if sense is to be made of the statistics. In Salford the number of Down Syndrome children born fell dramatically between 1965 and 1970, but this is wholly explicable, within the limits of the small numbers, by the general reduction in birth rate and the differential reduction in birth rate by maternal age. Table 3 shows clearly the demographic changes which *must* significantly affect Down Syndrome births. In other cultures other demographic characteristics must be taken into account. For instance Narayanan (1981) describes the effects of high consanguinity

Table 2 Changes in "cohorts" of severely retarded children in five years

Mean "cohort" at 5–9			Mean "cohort" changes in 5 year period				Mean "cohort" at 10–14		
Years	Number	Prev. ratio/1000	Deaths	Late ascertainments	Emigrants	Immigrants	No.	Prev. ratio/1000	Years
(1961–65)	26·6	2·41	−1	+3·4	−1	+2·8	31·2	3·12	(1966–70)
(1966–70)	49·8	4·22	−6	+2·2	−2·8	+5·8	49	4·52	(1971–75)
(1971–75)	58·6	5·32	−3·8	+4·2	−6·4	+3·2	56·4	5·86	(1976–80)

Table 3   Salford total population: reduction of births between 1963 and 1973 by maternal age

Maternal age	Reduction in births
<20	7·1%
20–24	35·1%
25–29	48·6%
30–34	57·5%
35–39	70·6%
40–44	70·7%
45+	100%
All ages	43%

rates in some Indian communities upon the prevalence of certain types of severe mental retardation.

Age-specific prevalence

One of the difficulties presented by the published literature is the wide variety of age groups used to estimate prevalence of mental retardation. There are obvious problems in interpreting many published figures. In the first few years of life some causes have not yet operated and many affected individuals have not completed the prolonged process of assessment necessary, before they can be confidently ascertained as severely retarded. Therefore general prevalence ratios incorporating children in the first few years of life are of little value and cannot readily be compared with others.

Because of changes in known aetiological factors, and especially because of progressive changes in mortality and survival, different birth cohorts will have different survival rates at any particular age, and will reveal different distributions of diagnoses. These differences will be expressed in different prevalence ratios and characteristics in children of different age groups counted at the same census. It is extremely important that this dynamic relationship is appreciated. Very broad age bands, such as 0–19, are useless and even a 10-year span will mask potentially important differences within it. Since, however, in most surveys and case-registers the numbers for any one year tend to be too small for computation, a suitable compromise is a 5-year age group.

One terminological problem has arisen. These age groups of children progressing through school and community are not, strictly speaking, pure cohorts, since they may be added to by migration and occasional late causes or late ascertainments. In the absence of any term to describe these, I have resorted to using the word "cohort" in inverted commas.

In terms of aetiology we are most interested in events around the time of birth. The highest mortality is at the youngest ages and, moreover, cohorts of children born in most developed communities are increasingly affected by migration as they grow older. Therefore the youngest age group by which full ascertainment of severe retardation can be expected in such communities, that is, 5–9 years, is the most suitable for inter-community comparison. In these circumstances, the best population denominators available are likely to be for school age children, usually covering at least the range 5–14 years. The addition of a second age group, 10–14 years, will add a further dimension to the analysis, namely international comparisons of different "cohorts" of children in the same community. If more than one census is possible, temporal changes in these "cohorts" can be easily observed. Clues may then be gained of changes in aetiology and mortality even from prevalence studies alone. The later age group, 15–19 years, earlier favoured by Kushlick (1961), now has nothing to recommend it. More children will have died by this age and more have moved in and out of the community; moreover, this age group tends to be diluted by the addition of some mildly mentally retarded school leavers. Finally, by the time they are counted, they represent the remnants of a cohort of births between 15 and 20 years earlier.

The value of sequential prevalence studies in the two age groups 5–9

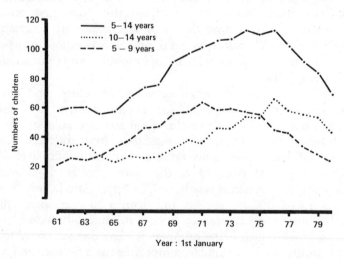

Fig. 2   Salford C.B. Prevalence of severely retarded children 5–14 years; numbers 1961–1980.

years and 10–14 years is demonstrated by the Salford data shown in Figure 2. The top line shows the total numbers in the broad age band, 5–14 years, increasing steadily to a peak between 1974 and 1976, then declining. Plotting figures for two separate five-year age groups clearly reveals a cohort phenomenon. The early peak in the 5–9 year group is reproduced five years later in the 10–14 year group, which relates to essentially the same "cohort" of children. We can even predict a little from such figures, since the 10–14 year group in the next five years will follow essentially the same pattern as the 5–9 year group in the last five years, unless some exceptional factors intervene dramatically to affect mortality or migration. If we also know the number of ascertained children in the 0–4 year group, we may get a clear indication of *trends*, though not absolute prevalence. We may then be able to predict what will happen in the next 5 years to the 5–9 year group. Adding this to the 10–14 year group projection allows us to plan and monitor school provision in a very practical way. In Salford, the evidence was that both 5 year groups would fall from 1977, producing a fairly dramatic diminution in the total number of mentally retarded children of school age, and this is being borne out in practice. Graphs for prevalence ratios show a similar pattern.

We can also relate the observed cohort phenomena approximately to years of birth. It can be seen from the figure that there was a threefold increase in the numbers of each 5-year group (between 1963 and 1971 for the 5–9 year age group, and between 1965 and 1976 for the 10–14 age group). The total group, however, showed only a two-fold increase, and here the peak is related to the "wrong" years because it is the sum of the others. Of course, in studies of very large populations — say of the order of 1 000 000 — single year groups would provide sufficient numbers and would allow even more precision. But the 5-year groups are usually the most pragmatic and potentially valuable.

Comparing prevalence ratios

Comparing prevalence ratios from studies done in different places at different times by different people is prejudiced by inconsistent methodologies and inadequate presentation of results. The problems are so great that Sorel (1971) commented, after detailed study, "Comparisons . . . are generally impossible", and they are indeed very difficult. Firstly, it is only possible to compare prevalence ratios directly for the same age group, since early mortality amongst the severely retarded is so great, though variable and diminishing, that different age groups must vary in the proportion surviving. In most developed communities virtually all severely retarded individuals are known by the age of 5 years and therefore the age group 5–9 will be the best for comparison, since it has suffered least from the ravages of high mortality (and the confusion of migration), and is the youngest group fully ascertained, and for which the base population is likely to be known.

However, even consistent use of similar age-groups would produce prevalence results difficult to interpret. If census dates of studies in different communities differ, as in most published work they inevitably do, then it is impossible by direct comparison to discriminate between secular and temporal variations. Most commentators in the literature appear to have escaped from this dilemma by assuming that one or other of these variations does not exist! We need some way of standardizing the prevalence ratios which will allow us to interpret comparisons in the context of likely common factors in aetiology and mortality which are the determinants of prevalence.

Prevalence ratios for particular age groups of children may be best related to one another by back-dating them to the years of birth from which the children arose. Thus children aged 5–9 years, counted on the

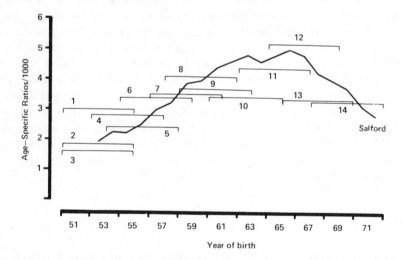

Fig. 3   Prevalence of severe retardation at 5–9 years, related to years of birth (from published studies and Salford, 1951–1972).
1. Middlesex, Goodman and Tizard, 1962; 2. London, Goodman and Tizard, 1962; 3. Salford, Kushlik, 1961; 4. Aarhus, Brask, 1972; 5. Wessex, Kushlik and Cox, 1973; 6. N. Ireland, Scally and MacKay, 1964; 7. N.E. Scotland, Innes et al., 1968; 8. Camberwell, Wing, 1976; 9. Sheffield, Bayley, 1973; 10. Aarhus, Bernsen, 1976; 11. Camberwell, Wing, 1976; 12. Eire, Mulcahy, 1975; 13. Sheffield, Martindale, 1977; 14. Manchester, Thomas, 1978.

The Salford figures are for IQ under 50 only, better to compare with published figures from elsewhere. The last three Salford figures are provisional.

1st January 1971, were born in the years 1961–65. Children aged 10–14 years, counted on the 1st January 1976, were born in the same 5 year period. They are therefore, a later expression of the same cohort of births: aetiological factors must have been largely the same but mortality will have had greater effect. On the other hand, children aged 5–9 at 1.1.76 were born between 1966 and 1970, and potentially subject to different factors. Although applying prevalence ratios to years of birth is somewhat artificial, in as much as they can include only survivors to later ages, nevertheless this gives us a means of direct comparison of one study with another, a way of discriminating between possible secular and temporal variations, and the hope of being able to relate such variations to known secular and temporal factors of potential aetiological or prognostic significance.

The results of such a procedure are shown in Fig. 3, with ratios for the 5–9 age group drawn from the published studies considered most reliable, and the Salford study. A small horizontal bracket expresses each published prevalence ratio applied to years of birth, in order to avoid any spurious hint of precision. For any one year, the dispersion of prevalence ratios vertically shows the range of secular distribution at that time, but the figure as a whole suggests general temporal changes over two decades. This is confirmed by the very close concordance with this general pattern of the Salford prevalence findings (for children with <50 IQ only), represented for clarity by single, mid-year points and a line graph. Such a generalized increase in prevalence of severe mental retardation as a whole (as well as for Down Syndrome and other categories separately) is most likely to be due mainly to increased survival at all ages, affecting all or most aetiological and clinical entities.

Studying aetiologies

Establishing true prevalence at birth is extremely difficult without large-scale prospective birth cohort studies. Indeed if we wish to study the sequelae of birth hazards we need to commence cohort studies before birth. Such studies have been done and have produced interesting and valuable results but they are expensive and time-consuming. There are also methodological dilemmas in defining beforehand both aetiological factors and clinical sequelae, in a field of such complexity and rapid change.

In retrospective studies there are serious difficulties in precisely relating recognised clinical effects to specific aetiological factors. Ascertained severely retarded children can now usually be given clear diagnoses with aetiological implications, but there will be other, similar children who died or migrated before recognition and assessment and, with some types of pathology, others who were still-born. On the other hand, some children may not fall within the definition of severe retardation, although the same causal processes are implicated. Some will be mildly retarded, others will suffer from cerebral palsy, epilepsy or various ill-defined conditions, and others again will exhibit a variety of congenital abnormalities. No aetiological study excluding these groups can be wholly satisfactory. Other children exposed to the same aetiological factors may die, or may recover without adverse consequences. Early foetal loss of affected individuals may also be important in determining prevalence at birth, as in Down Syndrome, and is difficult to take into account.

Retrospectively such problems can only partially be overcome. It is essential that diagnoses be confirmed accurately and consistently, but the available information may not be adequate and recently developed techniques may never have been applied to older children. Special research examinations on all children may be difficult to justify to parents, and very time-consuming. It should be possible now to get a firm diagnosis with aetiological implications for about 90% of children designated severely retarded.

In Salford, we wished to establish the prevalence at birth of the relevant syndromes. To do this, we perused all records of stillbirths, neonatal deaths and post-mortem examinations on children for the last twenty years. Usually these records have been scrupulously and comprehensively kept in hospitals, and very few children can have been missed in our search.

From these records we identified several groups of children. Some diagnoses irrevocably produce severe retardation in survivors, and these could be added to the ascertained children. We treated Down Syndrome in this way. Some, such as encephalitis, might have produced severe retardation had the child not died, but might not have done so, especially in an older child. These required some clearly defined criteria, such as age at death, to assist our judgement.

Other aetiologies, such as perinatal metabolic problems, could have resulted in any of a wide variety of neurological sequelae. Each case was assessed from the evidence and from clinical experience, as to whether or not the pathological processes would almost certainly have led to severe retardation, had the child not died. This rather uncertain procedure was more acceptable for some diagnostic groups than others. In particular, children who died from anoxic or hypoglycaemic syndromes at birth could not be included in our totals, because no outcome other than death could be presumed.

These investigations added a significant number of children to our

Table 4   Total "affected births" in Salford, 1961–1975

Year of birth	Mean annual numbers	Prevalence at birth, ratio/1000 total births			
		Neural tube defects	Down syndrome	Peri-natal metabolic	Totals
1961–65	32·4	3·95	1·70	0·50	10·2
1966–70	20·2	2·54	1·09	0·80	7·35
1971–75	12·8	2·52	0·84	1·05	6·75

ascertained cases, and gave us something approaching total prevalence at birth over 20 years, which we could use to explore the possibility of temporal trends. The most important results are indicated in Table 4. The total of affected births appears to have fallen significantly from the high figure of about 1% of births in 1961–65, but the results are in some ways particularly disappointing, since the conditions which have diminished are those largely beyond our control, while the potentially preventable conditions have increased. There had already been some concern about relatively high perinatal mortality rates, with efforts to improve antenatal and perinatal care, and in the last few years this trend has been reversed. The perinatal metabolic group has fallen considerably in prevalence at birth, since 1975. The total of "affected births" has also continued to fall, to little more than half the 1961–65 figure (Mackay, 1980). Though the prevalence at birth of neural tube defects and Down Syndrome has decreased since the 1961–65 cohort, the prevalence at later ages has increased with higher survival rates.

Incidentally, the figures in Table 4 illustrate the inadequacy of proportions of total morbidity as measures of incidence, although they are commonly used for this purpose. They may help to illustrate the nature of a local and immediate situation, but are of little value for comparison with any other study, since changes in the numbers of any one component will inevitably change the proportions of all. Attempting to compare proportions of aetiologies in different studies is usually merely confusing, and the figures should always be converted to prevalence ratios for each aetiological group separately.

Clearly what is needed is a study of much larger scope relating to all sequelae. To study these aetiological trends properly, we need a large-scale study, preferably prospective and in a variety of communities with different patterns of services. An international study might allow us to get to grips with the subtle details of the causes, with the potential for prevention of cerebral palsy and with the wider causes of perinatal and neonatal mortality, as well as of severe retardation.

Conclusion

The epidemiological problems described above are common ones. I have described some attempts to overcome them, in many cases far from satisfactory. However they demonstrate something of what can be done in one relatively small population with relatively slight resources. The *sine qua non* for such studies is a *prolonged* commitment to research in the same population. The long term temporal trends in prevalence of severe mental retardation are there, and their detailed elucidation should add to our potential for humane planning and effective prevention.

References

Bayley, M.J. (1973). *Mental Handicap and Community Care*. Routledge & Kegan Paul: London.

Bernsen, A.H. (1976). Severe mental retardation among children in the county of Aarhus, Denmark. *Acta Psychiatr. Scand*. **54**, 43–66.

Brask, B.H. (1972). Prevalence of mental retardation among children in the county of Aarhus, Denmark. *Acta Psychiatr. Scand*. **48**, 480–500.

Fryers, T. (1981). *Severe Mental Retardation: The Dynamics of Prevalence*. In preparation.

Fryers, T. and Mackay, R.I. (1979a). Down Syndrome — a 17 year study: prevalence at birth, mortality and survival, 1961–1977. *Early Hum. Dev*. **3**, 29–41.

Fryers, T. and Mackay, R.I. (1979b). The epidemiology of severe mental handicap. *Early Hum. Dev*. **3**, 277–294.

Goodman, N. and Tizard, J. (1962): Prevalence of imbecility and idiocy among children. *Br. Med. J*. **i**, 216–219.

Gustavson, K.H., Hagberg, B., Hagberg, G. and Sars, K. (1977). Severe mental retardation in a Swedish county. I. Epidemiology etc. *Acta Paediatr. Scand*. **66**, 373–379.

Hagberg, B. (1978). Severe mental retardation in Swedish children born 1959–1970: epidemiological panorama and causative factors. In: *Major Mental Handicap: Methods and Costs of Prevention*. Elsevier. Netherlands.

Harris, A. (1971). *Handicapped and Impaired in Great Britain*. H.M.S.O.: London.

Innes, G., Kidd, C. and Ross, H.S. (1968). Mental subnormality in North East Scotland. *Br. J. Psychiatry* **114**, 35–41.

Kushlick, A. (1961). Subnormality in Salford. In: Susser, M.W. and Kushlick, A. (eds.): *A report on the Mental Health Services of the City of Salford for the year 1960*. Health Department: Salford.

Kushlick, A. and Cox, G. (1973). The epidemiology of mental handicap. *Dev. Med. Child. Neurol*. **15**, 748–759.

Mackay, R.I. (1980). Personal communication.

Martindale, A. (1977). A case register as an information system in a development project for the mentally handicapped. *Br. J. Ment. Sub*. **XXII**, Part 2, No. 43.

Mulcahy, M. (1975). Prevalence of mental handicap in the Republic of Ireland. Paper presented in Dublin, Sept. 1975: personal communication.

Narayanan, H.S. (1981). A study of prevalence in rural and urban areas in Karnataka State of India. *Int. J. Mental Health*. (In press).

Scally, B.G. and Mackay, D.N. (1964): Mental subnormality and its prevalence in Northern Ireland. *Acta Psychiatr. Scand,* **40,** 203–211.

Sorel, F.M. (1974). *Prevalence of Mental Retardation.* Tilburg Univ. Press. Netherlands.

Thomas, A. (1978). A population study of children with severe mental handicap. Unpublished thesis, University of Manchester.

Wing, L. (1976). Services for the mentally retarded in Camberwell. In: Wing, J.K. and Fryers, T. (eds.): *Psychiatric Services in Camberwell and Salford: Statistics 1964–1974.* Inst. of Psych., London, and Dept. of Comm. Med. Univ. of Manchester.

Wing, L. (1975). Personal communication.

3 Mentally handicapped pupils and school-leavers: a survey in North West England

P. MITTLER and D. PREDDY

Hester Adrian Research Centre, University of Manchester, UK

Background

In 1971 education authorities in England and Wales assumed full responsibility for the education of all children of school age. Children could no longer be deemed "ineducable" or "unsuitable for education in school"; all children were included, no matter how severely, profoundly or multiply handicapped. Because virtually all children between five and sixteen years now attend schools, it is possible to conduct comprehensive population surveys of school-age handicapped children and to bring together information about the characteristics of the children, their progress and achievements during their school years.

The sample

In 1974 we embarked on a study in which we aimed to collect detailed information on all the children attending schools for severely educationally subnormal (ESNS) children within a 35 mile radius of Manchester. We also collected a considerable amount of information on the schools themselves, their staffing ratios, qualifications and experience of teachers and on visiting professionals. Three years later we conducted a second survey in order to assess changes in the intervening period.

Seventy out of a possible 77 day schools and ten out of a possible 12 hospital schools completed the first questionnaire. On the second occasion three years later 55 of the original 70 day schools and eight of the 10 hospital schools completed questionnaires on the schools and the children. The average number of pupils in each school was 65; there was an average of 9 teachers to a school, in addition to 9·5 classroom assistants: a ratio of one teacher for 7·2 children and of one classroom assistant for 6·8 children, or an overall ratio of one adult to 3·5 children.

Table 1   Sibship size and birth order of mentally handicapped pupils in day schools.

No. of sibs[a]	%	Birth order[b]	%
0	6·3	1st	18·0
1–2	55·2	2–3	55·1
3–4	25·2	4–5	18·8
5+	13·3	6+	8·1
Total	100·0		100·0

[a] No. of pupils, 2489. No information 288 (10·4%).
[b] No. of pupils, 1883. No information 894 (32·2%).

The schools co-operating with us in the 1977 survey provided information on a total of 3236 children. Of these, 86% were attending day schools and for the most part living at home but included 5% who were in some form of local community home or hostel and 1% living with foster families. 459 children (14% of the total sample) were living in hospitals for the mentally handicapped — in general, these children are much more severely handicapped in every way than those attending day schools (Bland, 1979). In the present paper we shall concentrate on children attending day schools; the number attending hospital schools is likely to become very small in the near future, mainly because hardly any children are now being admitted to hospitals for long term care in Britain (National Development Group, 1978).

We believe we have secured a comprehensive population sample of schools, teachers and children in the region; furthermore, the regional survey comprises approximately one in ten of all schools and pupils in the whole of England and Wales. However, sampling has been affected by a number of factors.:

(1) Lack of co-operation from about 30% of the sample schools in the second survey.
(2) A few mentally handicapped children may have been attending schools for the mildly educationally subnormal (ESNM) or even schools for normal children, though we suspect that the numbers were very small.
(3) Even schools who co-operated with us were unable to provide information on many important points. For example, less than half of those about to leave school had been psychologically tested during the whole of their school careers. We have therefore recorded a "no information" category and expressed this as a percentage of the total number of known children in the schools.

Results

We will limit ourselves in this paper to summarizing some basic information about the characteristics of the children attending or leaving ESNS schools, as reported by their teachers. The data has not been checked by personal interviews or clinical examination. A sample of the schools also completed a Gunzburg Progress Assessment Chart on each pupil but these data are not yet fully analysed.

We will first provide a "snapshot" of the abilities of all the children, regardless of age, but will then concentrate in particular on the characteristics of those children who were about to leave day schools. This after all is one way to judge the effectiveness of any educational system, whether for handicapped or non-handicapped children.

Sex ratio

The sex ratio of the sample was 56·8% boys to 43·2% girls. This is comparable with national statistics (DES, 1978) and with the results of other surveys (Leeming, Swann, Coupe and Mittler, 1979).

Family size and birth order (Table 1)

Information on the number of siblings was available for 90% of the children, though teachers could only give information on birth order for 68%. The data available suggests that many of the children came from large families, over a quarter having three or more older siblings. No doubt this is partly accounted for by the large number of Down's Syndrome children born to older mothers.

Social class (Table 2)

We used the Registrar General's Classification of Occupations to examine the frequency distribution of the five major social class divisions commonly used in the UK. We then compared the distributions found in our own sample of parents with those of the population in our own region (i.e. Manchester and South Lancashire) (Population Census, 1971), as well as those of all fathers of children aged 5–15 in the whole United Kingdom (General Household Survey, 1975).

The results suggest that the children of families in the lowest social class V are greatly over-represented — 19% compared with 10% in the region and 4% in the UK as a whole.

Table 2 Comparison of social class data with general population figures

Social class	Survey sample[a] (%)	Manchester & South Lancashire – all males[b] (%)	Great Britain – fathers of children aged 5–15[c] (%)
I	3·7	4·7	6·3
II	13·3	15·3	17·5
III	45·1	52·6	52·2
IV	18·8	17·6	19·8
V	19·1	9·8	4·2
Total	100·0	100·0	100·0

No. of children 1401. No information 1376 (49·5%).
[a] Day school children only.
[b] Source: Census, 1971.
[c] Source: General Household Survey, 1975.

The information on social class is difficult to interpret because of the low rate of reporting (50%) and because of possible lack of reliability in the teachers' descriptions of fathers' occupations; it is possible that descriptions such as "unskilled" or "labourer" were used when they were not sure of the work done by fathers. Nevertheless, these findings are of interest in view of the widely held view that severely mentally handicapped children are equally represented in all social classes, in contrast to the mildly mentally handicapped who are found predominantly in social class V. This was suggested by the comprehensive population survey in Aberdeen conducted by Birch and his associates (1970), by studies summarized in Carr (1974) and also by an earlier Schools Council survey of nearly 1400 children in 19 schools in North West England who were not included in the main sample reported here (Swann and Mittler, 1976; Leeming et al., 1979). In his last study the proportion of ESNS children in social class V was similar to that of the population as a whole.

Whatever the distribution of social class in the families of mentally handicapped children, it is of great interest that other studies seem to suggest that there is no relationship between social class and IQ or attainment scores in mentally handicapped children, in contrast to numerous studies on normal children which reflect very strong social class effects from an early age (e.g. Davie et al., 1972). For example, Carr (1970) failed to find differences in development on the Bayley mental and motor scales between middle and working class Down's Syndrome pre-school children; in the Schools Council study of 1400 mentally handicapped children attending 19 ESNS schools no significant differences between children from the five social classes could be detected on a series of language measures (Leeming *et al.*, 1979). However, these studies have been affected by lack of information on parental occupation and on other socio-economic data which would allow this kind of comparison to be made more accurately.

Aetiology (Table 3)

While information on aetiology and diagnosis is of doubtful value when collected by questionnaire rather than by clinical examination, we can at least estimate the number of children with Down's Syndrome and compare this with the large and heterogeneous group with other conditions. This has been done in Table 3.

The distribution reflects an interesting difference between children in day schools and those in hospital schools: the percentage of Down's children among the former is 30% compared with only 8% among the latter. These figures are comparable with the Schools Council survey of 1400 pupils, 34% of whom were Down's Syndrome children.

Epilepsy (Table 4)

Information on frequency of epileptic seizures is summarised in Table 4. About three-quarters of the children had no history of fits; less than 1·5% had daily fits. Although the frequency of fits is slightly greater in hospitalised children, hospital schools report a much greater proportion of children whose epilepsy seems to have been controlled by medication—34%,

Table 3   Proportions of children with Down's syndrome in day schools and hospital schools[a]

	Day schools (%)	Hospital schools (%)	Total (%)
Down's syndrome	30·1	8·1	27·0
Others	69·9	91·9	73·0
Total	100·0	100·0	100·0
No. of children	2777	459	3236

[a] "No information" category included as "others".

Table 4   Frequency of epileptic fits

	Day schools (%)	Hospital schools (%)	Total (%)
None	79·3	52·9	75·6
History of fits, but few or none observed	15·6	34·1	18·2
At least monthly	2·1	5·8	2·6
At least weekly	1·6	5·8	2·2
At least daily	1·4	1·4	1·4
Total	100·0	100·0	100·0
No. of children	2543	414	2957
No information	234 (8·4%)	45 (9·8%)	279 (8·6%)

compared with 16% in day schools. Some attempt was also made to obtain teachers' gradings of the severity of the fits — roughly one-third were graded as mild, one-third as moderate and one-third as severe.

Abilities and Characteristics of Day Pupils

In the following section we will summarize information made available by teachers on day pupils' mobility, use of arms and hands, visual and auditory handicaps and incontinence, as well as on receptive and productive language and intelligibility of speech and use of gesture. The data will be presented in two ways; first we shall consider day pupils of all ages, numbering 2777; secondly, we shall look particularly closely at 224* day pupils who had left the same schools at the age of 16 or over in the year immediately preceding the survey.

Mobility and use of limbs (Table 5)

Table 5 summarizes information on mobility and on use of arms and hands. Some two thirds of the total sample and over three quarters of the school-leavers had no difficulty; on the other hand, 8% of all ages and 2% of school-leavers were not only completely unable to walk but had no

---

* This is the highest number recorded in any single table. The missing data are mostly of the order of 3 or 4 children only, in addition to the children for whom we have recorded "no information". For this additional group we have returns from the teachers but nothing filled in for the specific item under discussion.

Table 5   Walking and use of arms and hands, children in day schools

	All ages (%)	School-leavers (%)
Walking		
No difficulty	66·4	77·8
Limps, unsteady	17·2	18·1
Needs help	4·1	0·4
Unable, but mobile	4·7	1·4
Unable, not mobile	7·6	2·3
Total	100·0	100·0
No. of children	2747	221
No information	30 (1·1%)	3 (1·3%)
Use of arms and hands		
Full use	81·4	86·9
Some help needed	10·0	9·0
Much help needed or no use	8·6	4·1
Total	100·0	100·0
No. of children	2720	221
No information	57 (2·1%)	3 (1·3%)

other means of getting about such as crawling. Differences in the two columns presumably reflect a combination of training and maturation.

Full use of arms and hands was available to over 80%; 13% of school-leavers still had some difficulties in this respect, compared with 18% of all pupils.

Sensory handicaps (Table 6)

Information on sensory handicaps is of doubtful reliability, since we do not know whether sensory functions have been expertly assessed — e.g. by audiologists or ophthalmologists — or whether opportunities exist for such examinations if requested. Information is summarised in Table 6.

Some degree of visual handicap is reported in about 15% of the children of all ages, and a similar proportion among the school-leavers. 12% of children wore glasses — a further 5% had glasses prescribed but did not wear them. Seven per cent of all pupils and 4% of school-leavers were reported as having some degree of hearing impairment; around two to

Table 6   Visual handicaps and hearing impairments, children in day schools

	All ages (%)	School-leavers (%)
Visual handicaps		
None	84·4	87·3
Some	11·0	9·1
Little useable vision	4·6	3·6
Total	100·0	100·0
No. of children	2421	220
No information	356 (12·8%)	4 (1·8%)
Hearing impairments		
None	92·7	96·4
Some	5·5	0·5
Severe/no useable hearing	1·8	3·1
Total	100·0	100·0
No. of children	2592	222
No information	182 (6·6%)	2 (0·9%)

three per cent were graded as severely impaired in this respect. Although a number of children are usually awaiting assessment of hearing functions, information was available on all but 1% of the school-leavers. Of the 73 children who had hearing aids prescribed, only 30 wore them.

Incontinence (Table 7)

Two-thirds of the children were reported never to be wet, whereas about one-fifth are wet daily. As expected, the figures for school-leavers are better: only 4% are wet daily and over 90% are rarely or never incontinent. Twelve per cent of all pupils but only 2% of school-leavers were reported as soiling daily; no problems in this respect were reported for nearly three-quarters of all pupils and for 94% of school-leavers (cf. Table 7).

Language and communication

The data in the following sections are based on teachers' responses to four groups of questions about the communicative abilities of the children in

Table 7   Incontinence, children in day schools

	All ages (%)	School-leavers (%)
Wetting		
Rarely/Never	67·2	90·9
Monthly	6·4	3·2
Weekly	5·9	1·6
Daily	20·5	4·3
Total	100·0	100·0
No. of children	2428	186
No information	349 (12·6%)	38 (16·9%)
Soiling		
Rarely/Never	73·6	94·0
Monthly	6·2	2·7
Weekly	8·3	1·1
Daily	11·9	2·2
Total	100·0	100·0
No. of children	2376	185
No information	401 (14·4%)	39 (17·4%)

their classes. These were concerned with speech reception, speech production, intelligibility and use of gesture.

Speech reception (Table 8)
Table 8 shows that just under half the pupils were able to follow complex commands or a simple story, the proportion rising to around 70% for school-leavers. On the other hand, around 20% of all pupils were functioning at relatively primitive levels of language comprehension — ranging from no response to sounds (6·7%), to linking single sounds or words to objects (7·8% and 6·2%). About a third were able to follow simple positive commands. The abilities of school-leavers were somewhat but not dramatically higher than this.

Speech production (Table 9)
Table 9 summarizes the information on ability to produce sounds, words and various levels of syntax. Only 18% of the total sample and one third of the school-leavers were rated as being able to speak in full or complex

Table 8 Receptive language, children in day schools

	All ages (%)	School-leavers (%)
Follows simple story	38·1	58·2
Follows complex commands	9·9	11·4
Follows simple positive commands	31·3	23·6
Links single words to objects	6·2	2·7
Links single sounds to objects	7·8	1·8
No response	6·7	2·3
Total	100·0	100·0
No. of children	2692	220
No information	85 (3·1%)	4 (1·8%)

Table 9 Productive language, children in day schools

	All ages (%)	School-leavers (%)
Complex sentences	17·9	33·1
One verb sentences	24·2	31·2
Restricted sentences	19·1	20·8
Single words	16·2	9·0
Babbles, cries only	20·1	5·4
No sound production	2·5	0·5
Total	100·0	100·0
No. of children	2714	221
No information	63 (2·3%)	3 (1·3%)

sentences; just under a quarter of the sample had not yet reached the level of using single words though only 6% of the school-leavers had not reached this stage.

Intelligibility (Table 10)
For those children who have started to speak, whether they are only at the one word stage or whether they are able to speak in sentences, the intelligibility of their utterances is clearly of the first importance to communication and also to their integration in the community. It is therefore a matter of great concern that half of all the children and one third of the school-leavers were graded as unintelligible or mostly unintelligible to a

Table 10   Intelligibility to strangers, children in day schools

	All ages (%)	School-leavers (%)	Schools Council (all ages) (%)
Intelligible	24·8	36·9	26·5
Mostly intelligible	26·2	29·0	34·8
Mostly unintelligible	21·0	20·7	23·7
Unintelligible	28·0	13·4	15·0
Total	100·0	100·0	100·0
No. of children	2581	217	911
No information	196 (7·1%)	7 (3·1%)	34 [a] (3·6%)

[a] Made up of children who had not started to speak.

stranger. These figures may represent a slight over-estimate, since there is evidence that some children who had not yet started to speak were graded as unintelligible.

Use of gesture (Table 11)
Since speech and language abilities are so limited in these children, we tried to obtain some information on the extent to which they communicated by some form of gesture. We hoped by this means to learn something about the means by which children tried to compensate for absence of speech and language by using alternatives to speech. We did not enquire about the use of formal sign languages, as these were only just being introduced into the schools.

The results indicate that 29% of the children either use no gesture (15%) or only very primitive gesture (14%); only 3% were described as having no speech but using a sophisticated gestural system and 5% as able to speak but preferring to gesture. A further 26% had some speech and used gesture to augment it. Figures for school-leavers reflect a higher level of functioning in the direction of a more "natural" combination of speech and gesture but still indicate around 10% with very limited ability to communicate either by speech or gesture.

The results of both the present and the Schools Council surveys reflect considerable degrees of impairment in the whole range of language and communication abilities of ESNS children; the cross-sectional study of language changes with age provides evidence of a long plateau in the middle years of childhood until about 15, when there is little or no change in the proportion of children reaching crucial stages of language development (Leeming *et al.*, 1979). Finally, the low levels of language

Table 11 Use of gesture, children in day schools

	All ages (%)	School-leavers (%)
Gesture and speech normal	38·4	56·5
Speaks, prefers gesture	5·0	4·7
Gestures augment speech	25·6	25·7
Sophisticated gesture only	2·6	1·4
Primitive gesture, no speech	13·5	2·8
No gesture, no speech	14·9	8·9
Total	100·0	100·0
No. of children	2638	214
No information	139 (5·0%)	10 (4·5%)

ability of older children about to leave schools give particular cause for concern.

On the other hand, interest in curriculum development in the field of language teaching has grown since these surveys were conducted and a number of other organisational and staffing developments have taken place in many schools. A further survey of language abilities some five years from now might reflect a less depressing picture of the language skills of ESNS children in general and older pupils in particular.

Contacts with other professionals (Table 12)

It is generally agreed that the wide range of handicaps and disabilities found in mentally handicapped children calls for a multi-disciplinary approach and that teachers working in special schools or classes would benefit from the advice of colleagues in other disciplines. In the following section we summarize the frequency of children's contacts with a number of key professionals — speech therapists, physiotherapists, educational psychologists and peripatetic teachers of visually and hearing impaired children, as well as a number of medical specialists. This information relates to the year 1977; it is possible that visits are now rather more frequent.

Table 12 summarizes the percentage of children in our total sample who were seen by one or more of these specialists, as well as the frequency with which they were seen. Once again, the information is limited by the large number of children for whom no information was given — between 30 and 50 per cent.

It seems that some 70% of the children were never seen by a speech therapist or physiotherapist, despite the large numbers with speech and motor disorders. On the other hand, a small minority seem to have regular sessions — about 14% saw a speech therapist and 23% saw a physiotherapist weekly or monthly. Just over half the children never saw an educational psychologist, while over a third saw one less than once each school term.

Peripatetic teachers of visually and hearing handicapped children are now visiting schools more frequently than formerly. The fact that 7% of the children were receiving visits from teachers of the deaf is consistent with the 7% of the children reported as having hearing impairments; on the other hand, the fact that less than 2% of children are visited even once a term by teachers of visually handicapped children does not seem to correspond to the information that 5% are reported as having no usable vision and a further 11% as having some degree of visual impairment.

Information on medical specialists is also not easy to interpret, since teachers do not seem to have distinguished very clearly between different types of specialist — in particular between paediatricians and medical officers working for the school health services. Although it is encouraging to note that about one-fifth of the children were seen each term by a doctor and a further 40% were seen less than once a term, it is still a matter of some surprise that 37% were reported as never being seen by a doctor and that for just under half the children in their care teachers were unable to say whether they had been seen by a doctor.

Other health personnel mentioned by teachers included psychiatrists (seen by only 18 children), health visitors (48) and ENT specialists.

We should also note an increasing tendency for visiting specialists to act as consultants to the school and to teachers, in contrast to working with individual children during their relatively infrequent visits to schools. For example, more psychologists are now concerned with training teachers to use a range of assessment techniques and to develop individual teaching programme plans. They are also implementing staff training schemes in behavioural methods of teaching (Foxen, 1978). Consultant and advisory work of this kind would not be reflected in our figures which are mainly concerned with contacts with the children.

Procedures for the placement of school leavers

Having summarized some information on the abilities and characteristics of school leavers in our sample, we will conclude with a brief account of the procedures used to assess these young people and to make decisions about their placement.

Table 12 Frequency of contacts between ESNS children in day schools and visiting professionals, children in day schools

	Speech therapists (%)	Physio-therapists (%)	Educational psychologists (%)	Teachers of blind (%)	Teachers of deaf (%)	Paediatricians (%)	Ortho-paedic surgeons (%)	Neurologists (%)
Weekly	9·4	13·8	0·2	0·0	1·0	0·7	0·1	0·1
Monthly	4·2	9·1	7·8	0·2	7·0	1·2	0·4	0·1
Once a term	4·1	2·0	2·0	1·7	1·0	19·8	10·4	1·2
Less than once a term	8·4	5·3	36·7	9·0	7·5	41·5	9·1	2·7
Never	73·9	69·8	53·3	89·1	83·5	36·8	80·0	95·8
Total	100·0	100·0	100·0	100·0	100·0	100·0	100·0	100·0
No. of children	1839	1834	1586	1740	1749	1488	1398	1303
No information	938 (33·8%)	942 (34·0%)	1191 (42·9%)	1037 (37·3%)	1028 (37·0%)	1289 (46·4%)	1379 (49·7%)	1474 (53·1%)

There has been much discussion in the United Kingdom on provision for young people leaving schools for the mentally handicapped. In particular, the report of a recent government committee of enquiry into the education of handicapped children and young people (DES, 1978a) stressed the importance of a full multidisciplinary assessment of children leaving all special schools (not just those for the mentally handicapped) in order to assess their strengths and needs and to make recommendations on how those needs could best be met within the locality. As far as ESNS children are concerned, it has been officially estimated (DES, 1978) that some 2000 pupils in ESNS schools reach the statutory leaving age of 16 each year. This corresponds to between five or six children per year for each total population unit of 100 000 people.

Because the range of opportunities for school-leavers is now beginning to expand, it is essential that each school-leaver should be comprehensively assessed so that decisions about future placement can be made in the light of individual need and local provision.

Information on procedures for the placement of school-leavers was accordingly sought from project schools in the second of the two main school surveys. We asked about:

(1) the extent to which a special assessment was carried out in the period before leaving;
(2) whether there was a case conference on each child;
(3) whether the results were made available to the next placement;
(4) the extent to which parents were involved in placement decisions.

Of the 55 schools who completed the questionnaire, 22 reported that they always carried out a special assessment, seven did so usually and a further seven occasionally. One third of the schools reported that such assessments rarely or never took place. Thirty-four schools had a member of staff with specific responsibility for liaison between the school and the next placement. About half the schools reported that case conferences were held to discuss future placement; whereas in one-fifth case conferences were never held on school-leavers.

Of the 38 schools who provided information, head teachers were always or generally available in 37; other personnel included Adult Training Centre (ATC) staff (30); social workers (28), educational psychologists (22), teachers with special responsibility for leavers (21), medical officers (21), careers officers (7), educational welfare officers (4) and advisers in special education (3).

Schools were also asked about the participation of parents in case conferences. Out of 38 schools, parents were reported as participating always or generally in 23 schools, occasionally in two and never in 13 (24%).

A preliminary analysis of data on procedures for assessment of school-leavers has been published elsewhere (Fleming, 1978). We are now engaged in further studies of a new cohort of school-leavers (Cheseldine and Jeffree, 1981).

Discussion

We have tried in this paper to summarize some basic information from a large-scale study of a total population of mentally handicapped children attending ESNS schools in North West England. Although our sample is large, our methods are necessarily crude and our data therefore of unkown reliability. In a large survey of this kind, undertaken by a two man research team, we have to depend on teachers not just responding to our questionnaires but doing so reliably and accurately. While we are reasonably satisfied on the first count, we cannot be confident on the second. Not only are teachers very busy and reluctant to fill in lengthy questionnaires on every child, but they often do not have the basic information which researchers want. For example, schools do not necessarily have access to a full medical diagnosis on each child, even if one has been made. School record systems are also very variable; vital information on the child's abilities and disabilities and his response to teaching are often unavailable or are recorded in a way which does not lend itself to objective analysis. The need for a comprehensive record system is often expressed both by teachers and by staff of adult services.

Nevertheless, in looking at our data certain broad trends emerge. One of the most obvious concerns the heterogeneity of the population. ESNS schools contain at one extreme children who are profoundly and multiply handicapped, with very limited physical, social and communicative skills. In this sample, 12% were unable to walk or were otherwise immobile and 8% had little use of arms and hands; 16% had some degree of visual handicap and 7% showed hearing impairments; about a fifth had very limited language comprehension; between a third and a fifth had not yet started to speak in single words; about half of those with some expressive language had articulation problems which rendered their speech largely unintelligible. At the other end of the ability scale we find children who, although almost certainly having IQs below 50, were fully mobile, continent, free of physical handicap or epilepsy and functioning at a reasonable level of social and linguistic competence.

We have chosen in this paper to look more closely at pupils at the school leaving stage because it is at this stage that we can begin to assess the extent to which the school system has been able to help the children to develop their abilities. We cannot of course determine the extent to which the higher abilities of the older pupils can be attributed to the teaching they have received either at school or at home or the extent to which these are merely a function of growth and maturation. More rigorous controlled studies are needed to examine such questions. What we can do is to provide a snapshot of the abilities of young people as they leave the school system in order to plan to meet their needs as adults.

In the United Kingdom virtually all children leaving ESNS day schools go to Adult Training Centres— 88% in the present sample. Adult Training Centres are now beginning to develop a broad and balanced curriculum in an effort to meet a wider range of needs than those concerned purely with work or industrial training (Whelan and Speake, 1977; Mittler and Whelan, 1979). Although there is no doubt that some mentally handicapped adults can be trained for both sheltered and open employment, virtually all are likely to benefit from a curriculum of social education which emphasises training in activities for daily living, leisure and recreation and further education, including literacy and numeracy training (National Development Group, 1977). In an impressive document prepared for the OECD study on handicapped adolescents, Tizard and Anderson (1979) make a strong plea for training in "significant living without work".

In a study carried out over 15 years ago, Marshall (1967) concluded that the abilities and attainments of young mentally handicapped people leaving the former Junior Training Centres corresponded on average to those of five and six year old normal children about to enter the educational system. This suggests that we should continue to make educational opportunities available for many years after the end of the normal period of schooling— not perhaps by compulsory raising of the school leaving age for handicapped children but by designing programmes to meet the wide range of individual need shown by this age group wherever they are.

Our own studies of school-leavers summarized in the present paper provide evidence of a population which varies greatly in abilities and needs. Over 90% are fully continent, 78% are fully mobile and 87% have full use of arms and hands, 87% and 96% are free of visual and auditory handicaps respectively and 97% are free of epilepsy. On the other hand, only 33% can speak in grammatical sentences and only one third of those with expressive language are intelligible to others. About 70% can understand enough language to follow complex commands or a simple story.

The information available to us is concerned only with the most obvious and superficial skills. But success as an adult for a mentally handicapped person depends to a large extent on a range of social, interpersonal and community living skills which are not dealt with in the data reported here. We are currently analysing Gunzburg Progress Assessment Chart records on the same sample of children and young people. In addition, a new and entirely separate research project on young mentally handicapped school leavers is currently under way in the Hester Adrian Research Centre conducted by Dorothy Jeffree and Sally Cheseldine. This project, which is broadly concerned with social and leisure skills, began with detailed interviews of 214 of the 240 families of children in Greater Manchester who were about to leave ESNS schools. The survey is particularly concerned with personal independence (including eating and drinking, domestic tasks, cleanliness and health, and selection and care of clothing) and social independence (e.g. giving and using information, notions of time, of money, use of amenities and freedom of movement). This survey reveals major gaps in social competence — particularly in knowledge of time, money and community resources— and considerable restrictions in social mobility and independence (Cheseldine and Jeffree, 1981).

Information about the abilities of school leavers from these and other surveys have a number of implications both for school curricula and for the design of services for adolescents and adults. As far as school curricula are concerned, it is clear that many young people are leaving special schools with only limited language and communication abilities, even though they may be more competent in other areas. Secondly, these findings point to a need to maintain continuity of educational programmes from school to adult services. This in turn underlines the importance of designing individual programme plans for handicapped persons of all ages (Mittler, 1979). Such plans are now mandatory in the USA and are increasingly being introduced into schools and service agencies for adults. Whether they can significantly increase competence as well as maintain a higher level of functioning is still an open question, but the attempt seems well worth making.

Acknowledgements

We are grateful to Diana Fowler for comments on an earlier draft of this paper. The study was supported by a grant from the Department of Education and Science.

References

Bland, G. (1979). Hospital schools for the mentally handicapped. *In* Craft, M. (ed.) *Tredgold's Mental Deficiency* (12th edn). London: Bailliere and Tindall.
Birch, H.G., Richardson, S.A., Baird, D., Horobin, G. and Illsley, R. (1970). *Mental Subnormality in the Community*. Williams and Wilkins: Baltimore, Md.
Carr, J. (1970). Mental and motor development in young mongol children. *J. Ment. Defic. Res.* **14**, 205–220.

Carr, J. (1974). The effect of the severely subnormal on their families. In Clarke, A. and Clarke, A.D.B. (eds.) *Mental Deficiency: the changing outlook.* (3rd edn.) Methuen: London.

Cheseldine, S. and Jeffree, D. (1981). A survey of ESNS leavers in the Greater Manchester area. *Special Education: Forward Trends* (Research supplement) (In press).

Davie, R., Butler, N., Goldstein, H. (1972). *From Birth to Seven.* Longmans: London.

Department of Education and Science (1978). *Statistics of Education* (Vol. 1: Schools). HMSO: London.

Department of Education and Science (1978a). *Special Educational Needs.* Report of Committee of Enquiry into the Education of Handicapped Children and Young People (Chairman Mrs. M. Warnock) Cmnd 7212. London: HMSO.

Fleming, I. (1978). Mentally handicapped school leavers — their assessment and placement. *Apex* **6,** 23–26.

Foxen, T. (1978). Pedagogic Devices Relevant to Staff Training in Specialist Techniques. In: Fink, A.H. (ed.): *International Perspectives on Future Special Education.* Reston, VA.: Council for Exceptional Children.

Leeming, K., Swann, W., Coupe, J. and Mittler, P. (1979). *Teaching Language and Communication to the Mentally Handicapped.* Schools Council Evans/Methuen Educational: London.

Marshall, A. (1967). *The Abilities and Attainments of Children Leaving Junior Training Centres.* National Association of Mental Health: London.

Mittler, P. (1979). Training, Education and Rehabilitation: An Overview. In: Craft, M. (ed.): *Tredgold's Mental Retardation* (12th edn). Bailliere and Tindall: London.

Mittler, P. and Whelan, E. (1979). Adult Education and Training. In: Craft, M. (ed.): *Tredgold's Mental Retardation* (12th edn).

National Development Group for the Mentally Handicapped (1977). *Day Services for Mentally Handicapped Adults.* NDG Pamphlet 5. Department of Health and Social Security: London.

National Development Group for the Mentally Handicapped (1978). *Helping Mentally Handicapped People in Hospital.* Department of Health and Social Security: London.

Swann, W. and Mittler, P. (1976). A survey of language abilities in ESNS children. *Spec. Educ. Forward Trends* **3,** 24–27.

Tizard, J. and Anderson, E. (1979). *Alternatives to Work for Severely Handicapped People.* Report to C.E.R.I. O.E.C.D.: Paris.

Whelan, E. and Speake, B. (1977). *Adult Training Centres in England and Wales: Report of the First National Survey.* National Association of Teachers of the Mentally Handicapped and Hester Adrian Research Centre: Manchester.

Part 2
The Neurological and Neurophysiological Basis of Handicap

4 Neurological examination of the mentally retarded child: evidence of central nervous system abnormality

M. IIVANAINEN

Department of Neurology, University of Helsinki, Finland

Introduction

Mental retardation refers to a reduced level of intelligence manifested during the developmental years, i.e., before 15 years of age. Mainly because of their deficiency in intelligence, mentally retarded persons are not able to take care of themselves as well as normal people. Although neuroscience has given evidence of brain abnormality as a cause of mental retardation, its origins remain largely unknown. Use of neuroscientific methods for establishing the aetiology of mental retardation has not become routine practice in all states and countries.

The assumption that the life of disabled persons should correspond to the life of normal persons as much as possible is called the normalization principle. Thus, for instance, the right to food, housing, education, and health care belongs to disabled individuals as well as to other people. The practical application of this principle is called integration. Despite these principles, opinions are still controversial as to whether the neurological investigation and prescription of treatment for the mentally retarded should be the same as that provided for other patients with brain symptoms. In order to clarify this issue, a series of 1000 patients admitted consecutively to an institution for the mentally retarded were examined neurologically according to the same principles applied to neurological patients with normal intelligence. The results appeared useful in determining the aetiology of mental retardation, in prescribing the treatment in each case, and in preventing new cases of mental retardation. Neuroradiological findings from 338 patients in the present series were reported earlier (Iivanainen, 1974). Basic principles for neurological examination of mentally retarded children and essential aspects of the experience obtained from this study are presented here.* It is hoped that many more mentally retarded children will be examined according to these principles than has previously been the case.

* A final report of the results from the whole series of 1000 subjects will be published elsewhere.

56   M. Iivanainen

The patient sample

One thousand patients admitted consecutively from 1943–1966 to the Rinnekoti Institution for the Mentally Retarded, Espoo, Finland, were selected for the present study. Detailed clinical histories and physical and psychiatric examinations were completed on 878 living patients residing in the Rinnekoti Institution, at home or elsewhere. Two others could not be contacted, and on one of these no data, except that of the sex, were available. Of 368 patients selected for neuroradiological examination, 30 (10%) could not be evaluated by this method because the guardians refused to give their written permission. Thus, 338 patients were investigated neuroradiologically (Iivanainen, 1974). The present sample includes these 338 individuals and the remaining 662, or the whole original series of 1000 subjects.

There were 584 males (58.4%) and 416 females (41.6%). Their mean age was 17 years, with a range of 1 to 60 years. Nearly half of the patients were 15 years old or younger (Table 1).

Methods of investigation

The procedure adopted was first to perform certain initial examinations, including collection of anamnestic data, physical and psychiatric examinations and laboratory screening tests, and thereafter, on the basis of the findings, to continue clarification of the aetiology of mental retardation by a number of supplementary tests according to the principles generally accepted in neurological practice. These initial examinations and supplemental tests are briefly reviewed here.

Table 1 Age and sex distribution of the patient sample

Age in years	Males	Females	Total	Per cent
≤5	44	29	73	7·3
6–10	99	68	167	16·7
11–15	133	93	226	22·6
16–20	134	92	226	22·6
21–25	95	66	161	16·1
26–30	42	41	83	8·3
>30	36	27	63	6·3
Unknown	1	–	1	0·1
Total	584	416	1000	100·0

Medical history

Anamnestic data were collected as completely as possible from all available sources. Previous medical records at maternal and other hospitals and at the Rinnekoti Institution were traced and inspected. This information was supplemented by interviewing patients and their relatives and guardians and, where this was not possible, by sending questionnaires to the relatives. All data obtained were eventually sorted and coded for computer analysis. In some instances, especially in those concerning developmental histories, the memories of the parents appeared to be inaccurate. (Usually, with handicapped children, the parents' memories are likely to be quite accurate, as they remember significant delays that alerted and alarmed them.)

Physical and neurological examination

All the 880 living patients, except for the two not contacted, were examined personally by the author. Corresponding findings, when available, were collected from the case records of the 120 deceased patients. Additional data were available from observations made by the author during the three years he was at the Rinnekoti Institution. All data obtained were sorted and coded for computer analysis. The patients were examined without reference to their previous medical records. In general, there was agreement between the observations made by the author and those recorded previously, except for the aetiological diagnosis. If the interpretation of the findings was difficult, a colleague examined the patient and the diagnosis was made jointly. The examination of each patient took at least an hour. Some physical abilities such as hearing and seeing are particularly difficult to test in mentally retarded persons. Thus, the visual ability of the patients was only crudely assessed. Confrontation perimetry by using fingers and hands was carried out routinely. Hearing ability was studied routinely by registering the patient's reaction to speech, whispering and other auditory stimuli. In cases of suspected hearing disability, auditory evoked potentials were ascertained (Dr Anna-Maija Seppalainen). Most of the severely retarded patients had no speech. Information concerning the children's speech and language development was provided by a speech therapist from the Rinnekoti Institution.

Inspection of the optic fundi in mentally retarded children is difficult. It was, however, usually successfully performed on the children in this series by playing with them and seeking their co-operation. When necessary, mild sedation was administered. In the most difficult cases, opthalmoscopy took more than an hour, but it was usually completed within 5 to 10 minutes. In addition, the optic fundi of all the 338 patients investigated neurologically were re-examined personally by the author just beforehand. If the interpretation of the findings was difficult, an ophthalmologist at the Rinnekoti Institution was consulted.

Sensory examination of mentally retarded children also presents difficulties, as only a few of the patients are capable of adequate co-operation during testing of the response to light and touch or testing of positional sense. Testing of deep sensory functioning and gesture functioning of mildly retarded subjects was successful. It was not possible, however, to test deep sensory functioning in severely retarded patients, although nearly all of them responded to sharp pin-prick and thus expressed their ability to feel pain.

Examining patients at their homes with the help of their parents proved to be the easiest method of examination. Patients who were selected for neuroradiological examination were admitted to the nearest central hospital or central mental hospital or the Rinnekoti Institution for about one week and, if necessary, further physical and neurological examinations were carried out there.

Where it was considered appropriate, the standard neurological examination of the Department of Neurology, University of Helsinki, was freely supplemented with other neurological techniques. Thus, the assessment of children with cerebral palsy included testing for responses such as Moro response, asymmetric tonic reflex, and the placing response. All physical data, such as measurement of height, weight and head circumference, were obtained personally by the author.

Assessment of functional handicaps

Information concerning the children's functional abilities (e.g., dressing, feeding, toiletting) was obtained from the nursing staff and, where possible, this information was re-checked by the author. Thus, at the time of the physical and neurological examinations the patients' skill in dressing and undressing was reassessed, and at mealtimes the nurses' reports concerning the patients' feeding skills were confirmed. Close personal contact between the children and the nurses made it more likely that information provided by the latter was reliable. However, it should be borne in mind that the nurses' reports about their patients' functional abilities may not always be accurate. Faced with the care of a large number of severely handicapped children, they may not realize that a particular child is capable, though slowly, of dressing himself and participating in feeding activities.

Psychological and psychiatric assessment

The intelligence level of the patients was assessed by a variety of tests, including: Terman-Merrill-Lehtovaara Intelligence Scale, Goodenough Draw-A-Man Test, Vineland Social Maturity Scale, Columbia Mental Maturity Scale, Wechsler Adult Intelligence Scale, Raven Progressive Matrices, and Bender Visual-Motor Gestalt Test. These tests were administered by the head psychologist in the Rinnekoti Institution (Harriet Lindgren, M.A.). In borderline cases, clinical observation of the patients' behaviour in different situations was taken into consideration. Final classification of intelligence level was decided together with the psychologist.

Detailed psychiatric examination of most patients was not possible because of their severe mental retardation. Thus, behavioural problems associated with other disturbances were analysed on the basis of what the doctor and other staff observed of the patients' behaviour in normal daily activities. Before the final psychiatric diagnosis was made, findings were discussed with the psychologist and child psychiatrist.

Laboratory tests

Laboratory screening tests were performed in an earlier study to detect any metabolic disorders that might have operated as causes of mental retardation (Palo, 1967). These included thyroid gland, liver, and kidney function tests, with determination of urine and/or serum amino-acids and carbohydrates. Determinations of serum calcium, phosphorus, potassium, and alkaline phosphatase concentrations, as well as per oral glucose tolerance tests, were performed in selected cases of convulsions. Routine tests of cerebrospinal fluid (CSF), including cell count, glucose and protein concentrations, colloidal reaction, electrophoretic fractioning of proteins and immunological syphilitic reaction were performed on patients who underwent lumbar puncture at pneumoencephalography (Iivanainen, 1974). Amino acid and carbohydrate concentrations of the CSF were also determined (Palo *et al.*, 1973).

Cytogenetic studies

Chromosome karyotyping was performed in patients who had one or more major or two or more minor malformations. Major malformation was defined as a structural anomaly associated with functional dis-turbance (e.g. cataract with visual defect), while this was not the case with minor malformation (e.g. clinodactyly). It was thought that chromosomal aberrations were the most likely common cause of malformations affecting various organs, including the skin, eyes, ears, nose, mouth, tongue, teeth, chin, heart, genitals, hands, feet, and brain. The final selection of patients for chomosome karyotyping was approved by the cytogeneticist.

Chromosome karyotyping was performed on peripheral venous blood samples by culturing lymphocytes and using an air-drying method (Moorhead et al., 1960). In suspected cases, chromosome karyotyping was also determined on skin biopsy. Tests to determine the presence of sex chromatin were performed in cases of gonadal infantilism, using cell samples taken from the mucous membrane of the inner wall of the cheek. The preparation was stained by the Feulgen method.

Clinical neurophysiological investigation

Electroencephalograms (EEG) were recorded from patients with epilepsy and other clinical signs of brain abnormality of unknown cause. Chloral hydrate or pentobarbital sodium was administered to anxious patients as a premedication, but the EEG could not be recorded in very restless patients. Auditory evoked potentials were ascertained in cases of suspected deafness by use of the EEG and a computer. Electromyograms and nerve conduction velocity were recorded in cases of suspected muscle disease with the aid of a 3-channel electromyograph (DISA 14 A 30).

Neuroradiological investigation

Neuroradiological examinations included skull X-ray films, echo-encephalography, cerebral angiography, pneumoencephalography, and radioisotope brain scanning. Computerized axial tomography (CAT) was not yet available. Technical details of the neuroradiological procedures have been described (Iivanainen, 1974).

Skull X-ray films were available on 356 of these mentally retarded patients with or without other clinical signs of brain abnormality of unknown aetiology. The most common indications for cerebral angiography and pneumoencephalography were focal cerebral symptoms and a progressive course of disease due to unkown cause. Increased intracranial pressure was a contraindication for pneumoencephalography. These are generally accepted principles in neurological and neuroradiological practice.

Neuropathological examination

The central nervous system of the deceased patients was examined macroscopically at autopsy. Microscopic examination of the brain was performed if the aetiological diagnosis of mental retardation was unclear or if the diagnosis of brain tumor needed further clarification. Skin and muscle biopsies were taken from surviving patients with suspected neurocutaneous or muscle disease. All microscopic examinations were rechecked by Dr Matti Haltia.

Findings of the survey

Medical history

The proportion of children born out of wedlock was significantly higher in the mentally retarded sample than in the general population (9·5% v. 4·7%; $p < 0.001$), as was also the proportion of children delivered without trained obstetric help (27·3% v. 2·0%; $p < 0.001$), that of children weighing 2500 g or less at birth (15·6% v. 4·5%; $p < 0.001$), and that of twins (3·2% v. 1·6%; $p < 0.01$). Abnormal maturity was found at birth in 142 children. Of these, 38 were dysmature (small for date of birth), 86 were premature (born more than two weeks before the calculated termination date), and 18 were postmature (born more than two weeks after the calculated termination date). Short gestation was considered to have had an aetiological significance in mental retardation in 11 cases (1·1%). Marked asphyxia immediately after birth (7·9% v. 3·7%; $p < 0.001$) and abnormalities during the neonatal period (49·1% v. 4·3%; $p < 0.001$) were also associated with mental retardation. Epilepsy had occurred in 442 (44·2%) of the patients. It was classified as focal in 89 (20·1%), as centrencephalic in 95 (21·1%), and as other unspecified type in 258 (58·4%) of the cases.

Physical and neurological examination

Distribution of patients according to their height and weight showed that 56·2% and 36·0% of them, respectively, were in the lower 2·5 percentile of a normal population. The head circumference was also in the lower 2·5 percentile of a normal population in 43·0% of the patients. However, small head circumference was found in only 24·9% when the values were related to height at the corresponding age and then compared with values

Table 2 Distribution of the different neurological syndromes

Type of neurological lesion	No. of cases	Per cent
Upper motor neurone lesion	370	37·0
Cranial nerve lesion	119	11·9
Extrapyramidal lesion	80	8·0
Cerebellar lesion	63	6·3
Miscellaneous abnormal findings	93	9·3

for a normal population. Flat skull (cephalic index 85·5 or more) was more common than in the general population (200/588 v. 111/1457; $\chi^2 = 153\cdot3$; $p < 0\cdot001$).

Major congenital malformations occurred more frequently than in the general population (15·95% v. 0·17%). Malformations were located most frequently in the eye and heart (7·5% and 5·4% of the whole series, respectively).

The patients were classified into sub-categories according to type of neurological abnormality (Table 2). Thus, a patient with accelerated reflexes, reduced muscle power indicative of a pyramidal lesion, and a positive Babinski sign was considered to have upper motor neurone lesions. In small babies a positive Babinksi is not reliable in this respect, but more attention should be given to the other signs mentioned above, especially clonic stretch reflexes. If a patient had involuntary movements, varying muscle tone or rigidity, and difficulty in maintaining balance, he was considered to have an extrapyramidal syndrome. Cerebellar syndrome, on the other hand, consisted of trunk and/or extremital ataxia, intentional tremor, and occasionally a positive Romberg test. In a few instances, these criteria were difficult to follow. Thus, for example, a child who had rigidity and accelerated reflexes, or signs of both extrapyramidal and upper motor neurone lesions, was placed in the sub-category of "miscellaneous abnormal findings".

Signs of upper motor neurone lesions were found in more than one-third of the patients (37·0%), signs of extrapyramidal lesions in 8·0%, and signs of cerebellar lesions in 6·3% (Table 2). In addition, it was impossible to exclude cerebellar lesions in 50 other patients with severe pareses.

Unilateral or bilateral optic atrophy was found in 89 patients, of whom one also had chorioretinitis. Chorioretinitis was also seen in eight other patients. Papilloedema was found in five patients, in two of whom the finding fluctuated. These two patients had so-called benign intracranial hypertension or pseudotumor cerebi. Blindness occurred in 4·1% and

Table 3 Distribution of spastic extremital paresis

Form of Paresis	No. of cases	Per cent
Diplegia	121	12·1
Tetraplegia	95	9·5
Paraplegia	54	5·4
Triplegia	26	2·6
Right hemiplegia	25	2·5
Left hemiplegia	13	1·3
Monoplegia	6	0·6
No paresis	660	66·0
Total	1000	100·0

deafness in 1·4% of the patients.

Spasticity was found in 34·0%, muscle hypotonia in 17·1%, dystonia in 1·1%, and rigidity in 0·4%. Reaction to painful stimuli was absent in 1·6% of the patients.

Symptoms of cerebral palsy (CP) were diagnosed in 412 patients (41·2%). The spastic form was the most common CP type (63·3%), while dyskinetic (14·8%), ataxic (2·9%), and miscellaneous forms (18·9%) were much less frequent. Of the spastic pareses, diplegia was the most common form (35·6%) (Table 3). This proportion included patients with spastic paresis belonging to both spastic and miscellaneous CP types. Tetraplegia and paraplegia were also rather common (Table 3). Movement disorder was detected in 126 patients (12·6%), including athetosis (40·5%), dystonia (10·3%), tremor (7·1%), and other or mixed forms (42·1%).

Disability in Daily Functioning

Speech was disturbed in most of the patients (84·6%). Inability to dress or undress, as well as poor control of bladder and bowel function, was also common (61·8%, 55·9% and 59·4%, respectively). Nearly half of the patients (44·2%) could not walk normally, while 20·4% could not walk at all and 13·9% could not sit up. More than one-quarter of the patients (28·9%) could not eat without help.

Psychological and psychiatric findings

About three-quarters of the patients were severely mentally retarded (IQ <35) (Table 4). Five patients currently appeared to be of normal intelligence, although previously in childhood they had been diagnosed as mentally retarded. They represent so-called pseudo-retardation. Cerebral palsy, deafness and stressful environmental circumstances (war-time) were primarily responsible for the pseudo-retardation of these subjects.

Psychotic signs were found in 81 patients (8·1%). These included restlessness in 37 (45·7%), autism in 28 (34·6%), and hallucinations in 16 (19·8%) of the 81 patients.

Laboratory findings

Most of the laboratory tests on serum and CSF showed abnormalities that were unrelated to the aetiology of mental retardation (Iivanainen and Kostiainen, 1971; Palo *et al.*, 1973; Iivanainen and Taskinen, 1974). The analysis of amino-acids and carbohydrates in the CSF during the acute stages of the disease may be important and may reveal significant findings, but the significance of these variables during the chronic stage of mental retardation appears to be small.

Infectious disease of the central nervous system had previously been diagnosed in 107 patients by conventional methods such as isolation of a microbe or follow-up of serum antibody titre. The Wassermann complement fixation test and Kahn flocculation test were positive in the CSF of a further three patients, although other syphilis tests of CSF and

Table 4 Degree of mental retardation

Degree	No. of cases	Per cent
Normal	5	0·5
Borderline (IQ about 68 to 85)	12	1·2
Mild (IQ about 52 to 67)	69	6·9
Moderate (IQ about 36 to 51)	165	16·5
Severe (IQ about 20 to 35)	231	23·1
Profound (IQ <20)	509	50·9
Unspecified	9	0·9
Total	1000	100·0

Table 5   Distribution of EEG abnormalities (N = 691)

EEG Abnormality	No. of cases	Per cent
Diffuse slow wave abnormalities		
slight	156	22·6
moderately severe	397	57·5
severe	77	11·1
Abnormal beta activity	159	23·0
Extreme spindles	3	0·4
Asymmetry or depression of background activity	84	12·2
Focal slow wave abnormalities		
slight	31	4·5
moderate	36	5·2
severe	7	1·0
Intermittent delta rhythms	17	2·5
Paroxysmal slow activity	216	31·3
Focal spikes and sharp waves		
sparse	61	8·8
abundant	45	6·5
Generalized irregular spikes and waves	69	10·0
Generalized regular 3 Hz spikes and waves	11	1·6
Rhythmical 2–2·5 Hz spikes and waves	27	3·9
Hypsarrhythmia	2	0·3
14 and 6 positive spikes	2	0·3
Other generalized bilateral changes	21	3·0
Normal or borderline EEG	40	5·8

serum, including the *Treponema pallidum* immobilization test and Reiter's test, were negative.

The findings of biochemical screening tests included cystinuria (three cases), peptiduria (two cases), hyperaminoaciduria (two cases), mucopolysaccharidosis (two cases), suspected renal glucosuria (one case), diabetes (one case), and isostenuria (one case) (Palo, 1967). Patients with peptiduria were later diagnosed as having aspartylglucosaminuria (Palo and Mattson, 1970; Autio, 1972).

The per oral glucose tolerance test showed an abnormally high and long-lasting response in two of the five epileptic patients studied. It is difficult to interpret this finding, as both patients had severe brain lesions. It is quite possible, however, that glucose intolerance was a contributing factor in the manifestation of convulsions. No insulomas were found. In one patient with muscle atrophy, low serum phosphorus concentration was normalized and osteoporosis cured after large doses of vitamin D were administered. This type of muscle atrophy was described by Dent and Harris in 1956.

Cytogenetic studies

Chromosome analysis showed an abnormal karotype in 136 of 372 patients studied. There were 124 cases of Down's syndrome, of which five had a translocation and one had a mosaic form. In addition, there were 32 other patients in the present series who had clinical features of Down's syndrome but did not undergo chromosome analysis. Aberrations of autosomal chromosomes other than G chromosome were diagnosed in eight patients [46,XY,5p− (2 cases); 46,XY,Bq+; 46,XX,Cq fragility; 46,XY,t(Cq−; Dp+); 46,XX,Er; 47,XX,9p−; 47,XX,mar+] and sex chromosome aberrations in four patients [45,X; 45,X/46,XXq−; 45,X/46,XXqi/47,XXqiXqi; 46,XXqi]. Two cases of mosaic form of Turner's syndrome were previously diagnosed by de la Chapelle (1962, 1963, 1966).

Clinical neurophysiological investigation

The EEG was normal or borderline in 40 (5·8%) of 691 patients, slightly abnormal in 136 (19·7%), and markedly abnormal in 515 (74·5%). Diffuse slow wave abnormalities were found in most of the patients (91·2%). Focal slow wave abnormalities occurred in 74 patients (10·7%) and focal spikes and sharp waves in 106 (15·3%) (Table 5). Localization of focal EEG

Table 6   Distribution of findings on skull X-ray films (N = 356)

Finding	No. of cases	Per cent
Asymptomatic anomaly	96	27·0
Congenital cranial deformity	42	11·8
Neoplasm or hematoma	7	2·0
Skull defect due to trauma	4	1·1
Asymmetry (small right-sided lesion)	19	5·3
Asymmetry (small left-sided lesion)	35	9·8
Infective changes (calcifications)	6	1·7
Miscellaneous pathological findings	69	19·4
Normal	78	21·9
Total	356	100·0

abnormalities of 211 patients was distributed as follows: temporal (30·8%), occipital (18·5%), frontal (10·0%), parietal (6·6%), and other or multiple (34·0%). Focal EEG abnormalities were lateralized slightly more frequently on the right than on the left (42·2% v. 40·3%). Bilateral localization occurred in 10·0% and fluctuating asymmetry in 7·6% of the 211 patients with focal EEG abnormalities. Results of electroneuromyography and auditory evoked potentials have been reported (Iivanainen, 1974). Myotonic paroxysms after mechanical stimulation and a typical myotonic pattern along with normal motor nerve conduction velocity were compatible with the clinical diagnosis of myotonic dystrophy in two patients. A normal electroneuromyograph has been reported in a case of muscle atrophy (Dent and Harris, 1956). The auditory evoked potentials did not give any additional information on the aetiology of mental retardation.

Neuroradiological investigation

About half of the skull X-ray findings were abnormal (Table 6). Cerebral angiography showed abnormal findings in 64 (74%) of 90 patients studied (Table 7). Pneumoencephalographic findings were abnormal in 301 (90%) of 334 patients studied (Table 8). The details of these findings have been reported elsewhere (Iivanainen, 1974).

Table 7   Distribution of the main findings at cerebral angiography (N = 90)

Findings	No. of cases	Per cent
Displacement of cerebral vessels due to a nonexpansive process	42	46·8
Dysplasia of cerebral vessel	8	8·9
Subdural hematoma	4	4·4
Arterial aneurysm	2	2·2
Cerebral angiopathy	2	2·2
Cerebral neoplasm	2	2·2
Occlusion of cerebral vessels	2	2·2
Miscellaneous pathological findings	2	2·2
No definite pathological findings	26	28·9
Total	90	100·0

From Iivanainen, 1974.

68   M. Iivanainen

Table 8   Distribution of the main findings at pneumoencephalography (*N* = 334)

Finding	No. of cases	Per cent
Symmetrical macroventriculy	84	25·1
Asymmetrical macroventriculy	38	11·4
Hemimacroventriculy	45	13·5
Temporal horn dilatation	31	9·3
Other localized ventricular dilatation	6	1·8
Cortical atrophy or dysplasia	13	3·9
Cerebral malformation	52	15·5
Intracranial expansion (neoplasm)	3	0·9
Cerebellar atrophy or dysplasia	20	6·0
Miscellaneous pathological findings	5	1·5
Insufficient gas filling	4	1·2
No definite pathological findings	33	9·9
Total	334	100·0

From Iivanainen, 1974.

Table 9   Brain weight by age groups

Age group (years)	Sex	Present series Mean ± S.D.	(*n*)	Controls[a] Mean ± S.D.	(*n*)
1–14	Male	920 ± 422[b]	19	409 ± 137	147
>15	Male	1120 ± 288[c]	24	1502 ± 119	313
1–14	Female	956 ± 337[d]	21	1209 ± 194	16
>15	Female	1022 ± 178[e]	13	1357 ± 105	116

[a] From Lehti, 1971. [b] $p < 0.001$ ($t = 10.5$). [c] $p < 0.001$ ($t = 13.1$). [d] $p < 0.05$ ($t = 2.7$). [e] $p < 0.001$ ($t = 10.0$).

Neuropathological examination

At autopsy, the organs were weighed and the cause of death, as well as the cause of mental retardation, was determined as accurately as possible. Brain weight was significantly reduced in mentally retarded subjects (Table 9). The brain size was classified as abnormally small in 62, abnormally large in three, and normal in 13 of the 78 autopsied patients. The size of the cerebral ventricles was found to be increased in 37 and normal in 27 patients. In addition, one patient had abnormally small ventricles (so-called microventriculy), another had local ventricular enlargement, two had deformed cerebral ventricles, while in ten cases the size of the cerebral ventricles was not recorded. Descriptions of cortical gyri included atrophy or dysplasia (27 cases), flattening (14 cases), microgyria (six cases), defect of gyri (three cases), macrogyria (one case), heterotopia (one case), hard gyri (one case), and normal gyri (25 cases). Hemispheral cerebral defect was detected in 33 patients. Three patients had a midline defect, and seven had an atrophic or dysplastic brain stem. There was a cyst in the brain stem of one patient. Cerebellar atrophy or dysplasia was detected in 19 patients and malformed cerebellum in one patient. The spinal cord was atrophic in two patients.

Microscopic examination of the brain was performed in five patients post mortem and in two surviving patients by biopsy. The brain biopsies revealed astrocytoma in both patients. The neuropathological diagnoses of the other five patients were astrocytoma, microencephaly, mild diffuse fibrotic gliosis in white matter, several ectopic nerve cells in white matter and cortical dysplasia. The microscopic diagnoses of skin biopsy of five patients were pseudoxanthoma elasticum, congenital ichthyosis, xeroderma pigmentosum, tuberous sclerosis, and anhydrotic cutaneous dysplasia.

Aetiological classification of mental retardation

When all the anamnestic and biographic data had been collated with the results of the various examinations and tests, the cause of mental retardation was assessed separately in each case. The aetiological diagnosis was made without knowledge of any previously recorded diagnosis. After a diagnosis had been made, the results were compared with the previous case records. On the basis of findings from the neuroradiological examinations and other studies, the aetiological

Table 10   Aetiological classification of developmental brain disorders of 1000 patients according to the time of insult

Aetiological category	No. of cases	Per cent
Prenatal	512	51·2
Perinatal	117	11·7
Postnatal	156	15·6
More than one category	34	3·4
Indeterminable	181	18·1
Total	1000	100·0

diagnosis of mental retardation had to be changed in 43% of the 338 patients examined neuroradiologically. The most significant changes in ascribed causes of mental retardation were: (1) a decrease of birth injuries; (2) an increase in prenatal factors; and (3) an increase of unknown cause with structural reaction in the classification system of Heber (1961). Individual cases were discussed with paediatric and neurological colleagues when the diagnosis presented difficulties. The patients were classified in two main ways: (1) according to the time of the insult or the onset of the process, using the criteria laid down by Yannet (1945, 1956) and modified by Iivanainen (1974), and (2) according to the aetiological categories of the World Health Organization (1967).

Classification According to the Time of Insult

The operative time of the causative factor of mental retardation was the prenatal period in more than half of the patients (Table 10). In about one-fifth, however, the operative time could not be determined. Also, the aetiological factors had operated more frequently after birth than perinatally (about 16% and 12%, respectively).

The WHO Classification

The cause of mental retardation was thought to be an unknown prenatal factor in about one-fifth (21·7%) of the sample (Table 11). Patients in this group had various types of morphological maldevelopments without any clearly defined cause (90 cases), malformation syndromes associated with chromosomal aberrations were also rather common (16·8%). Thus, prenatal factors constituted the largest category in this system of classification. The proportion of infections and intoxications was 14·8%, or 148 cases, of which 57 were prenatal. Trauma and other physical factors were also aetiologically significant, occurring in 11·9%. Mechanical and hypoxic birth injury were among the most frequent factors in this group.

The proportion of metabolic disorders in the aetiology of mental retardation was 4·5%. Spielmeyer-Vogt's disease (juvenile neuronal ceroid lipofuscinosis), gargoylism, and Brader-Willi's syndrome were most common among this group. Phenylketonuria was diagnosed in one patient only, but aspartylglucosaminuria was found in three patients.

Among gross brain diseases, tuberous sclerosis was the most common (11 out of 29 cases). Brain neoplasm was diagnosed in three cases; all had astrocytoma. Down's syndrome was the most common among chromosomal aberrations (156 out of 168 cases). Other autosomal

Table 11 Aetiological classification of brain developmental disorders of 1000 patients according to the WHO classification (1967)

Aetiological category	No. of cases	Per cent
Infections and intoxications	148	14·8
Trauma or physical agents	119	11·9
Disorders of metabolism	45	4·5
Gross brain diseases	29	2·9
Unknown prenatal influence	217	21·7
Chromosomal aberrations	168	16·8
Prematurity	8	0·8
Major psychiatric disorder	17	1·7
Psycho-social deprivation	1	0·1
More than one probable cause	50	5·0
Other and unspecified causes	198	19·8
Total	1000	100·0

aberrations were found in eight patients and sex chromosome aberrations in four patients. An unknown prenatal factor was thought to be the most frequent primary cause of mental retardation in patients with more than one probable cause. Hypoxia at birth, toxaemia of pregnancy, and postnatal infections were other common causes in this group. One chromosomal aberration (47,XX,mar+) belonged to this category of multiple causes.

Discussion

The present study indicates that the use of a thorough neurological examination, including current developmental-neurological techniques, makes it possible to determine the aetiology of mental retardation in about 90% of affected patients. Although this rate (90%) must depend to a considerable extent on the patient sampling and examination methods used, it appears to be realistic in the context of a hospital sample. This figure is compatible with the corresponding figures obtained from autopsy of mentally retarded patients (Malamud, 1954; Freytag and Lindenberg, 1967). Most previous clinical investigations, however, have shown surprisingly few abnormal findings, especially those suggesting prenatal origins and vascular disorders (e.g., Halperin, 1945; Dupont and Dreyer, 1968). This contradiction is understandable, as mentally retarded children have seldom been examined by all available investigational methods. If the most sensitive diagnostic methods are not used, aetiological diagnosis of mental retardation remains more or less unreliable. In the past this has often been the case. For instance, neuroradiological examinations have rarely been done, and generally they have had no connection with carefully planned, dynamic developmental-neurological examination of the patient. Thus, for example, vascular brain diseases have remained unrecognized (Isler, 1971). This view is in agreement with the earlier finding among 338 patients that the aetiological diagnosis of nearly every second patient had to be changed on the basis of the neuroradiological and other findings (Iivanainen, 1974). The present study of 1000 subjects, including those selected for neuroradiological examinations as previously reported, is even more representative of the aetiological distribution of mental retardation. The findings were also helpful in the daily treatment and rehabilitation of the patients. Therapeutic difficulties were most frequently encountered in the cases of epilepsy (Iivanainen et al., 1977). Therefore, the need for careful investigation of mentally retarded patients with epilepsy is emphasized.

In the physical examination, it is extremely important that the physician has good contact with the patient. When examining mentally retarded patients, especially children, one has to play games with them. Thus, the technique is basically the same as that used in paediatric neurology (Paine and Oppe, 1966; Amiel-Tison, 1976; Prechtl, 1977; Touwen, 1979).

The collection of anamnestic and biographic data should be as complete and as reliable as possible and cover all essential information on the health of the patients and their relatives. Childhood diseases and development should be recorded. It is necessary to know the developmental milestones of the normal child for comparison (Touwen, 1976). A progressive course of disease is typical in many cases of metabolic disorder, brain tumour and chronic central nervous system infection (Craft, 1979a, b).

The importance of a complete neurological examination of mentally retarded children has been emphasized (Zappella, 1964). A variety of mental retardation syndromes may be recognized on the basis of typical clinical features. External facial characteristics and typical findings of the skin, circulatory system and abdominal organs should be recorded. Special attention should be paid to the shape (craniosynostosis) and size (macrocephaly, microcephaly) of the head, as well as to the forehead (hypertelorismus, prominent forehead bossing), the face (cleft lip, cleft palate, flat face, loutish face, wide face, receding chin), the ears (malformed) and the eyes (nystagmus, prominent inner eye fold, slanted eyes, squint) (Craft, 1979a). In the physical neurological examination, the function of the whole nervous system, including motor movements, coordination, muscle power, reflexes, sensibility and cranial nerves should be examined in the same fashion as for other neurological patients. Ataxia, deafness, epilepsy, spasticity, dystonia and muscle hypotonicity are principal diagnostic features of central nervous system abnormality. Localization or extension of the lesion in the central nervous system is assessed on the basis of the findings.

Psychological aspects and psychiatric disorders must also be considered (O'Gorman, 1967). Psychosis may cause mild retardation. In such cases psychosis has prevented the child from having contact with his environment, a necessity for normal mental development. Treatment of psychiatric disorders may improve the child's mental performance. Many autistic children have later been found to have normal intelligence levels, which had not been possible to demonstrate previously because of contact disturbance. Some children who had been diagnosed as mentally retarded behaved normally after their epileptic seizures were controlled (Blaw and Torres, 1967). Such cases represent so-called pseudo-retardation, as in the case of sensory defects. It will subside when the contact disturbance is corrected. A new aspect in the relationship between psychotic disturbance and mental retardation is described by the observation of a temporal lobe lesion, often left-sided, in autistic children (Iivanainen, 1974; Hauser et al., 1975). In such cases the speech disturbance is aphasia, which prevents the child from making contact with other people.

In recording the clinical history, a differential diagnosis should be made on the basis of information revealed by physical and other examinations. Thus, the collection of historical data, physical and psychiatric examinations and laboratory screening tests are the basic sources of information and should be applied to every mentally retarded child as early as possible. Supplementary studies should be done according to certain indications and contraindications, as in neurological practice on other patients with brain symptoms. An EEG is needed if the cause of the disease is unknown or if the patient has epileptic seizures. Indeed, the present trend is to use the EEG as a diagnostic tool in as many cases as possible, since, for instance, subclinical forms of epilepsy are otherwise difficult to recognize. Chromosome analysis is primarily indicated in mentally retarded patients with malformations. Computerized axial tomography and other neuroradiological methods are used in cases where there are signs of focal or diffuse brain lesion or a progressive course of disease without known cause. With the CAT method, it is possible also to reveal abnormalities in patients with demyelinating diseases (Arimitsu et al., 1977), which was not possible by previous neuroradiological techniques. Since the use of CAT, pneumoencephalography, which is more inconvenient for the patient, has become rare. This, of course, is a step forward. Thus, the CAT technique is now especially useful and necessary for investigating large populations of mentally retarded children. Cerebral angiography is necessary for the examination of the shape and course of cerebral vessels. Such findings may even be pathognomonic in the diagnosis of certain cerebrovascular diseases such as moyamoya disease. In some degenerative diseases, brain biopsy may be needed for necessary information on the course of the disease.

A responsible well-grounded neurobiological diagnosis is extremely important in all cases of mental handicap. An incorrect diagnosis may cause unnecessary and irreparable damage to the child and the family. To begin with, the diagnosis of mental retardation should be fully justified. All the causes of possible pseudo-retardation, including, for example, impaired vision, hearing disorders, speech abnormalities and locomotive disability, as well as an isolated living environment, should be taken into consideration. One must remember that all physical disorders disturb mental function. For instance, mental retardation may be seen in hospitalized children due to the contributing effects of chronic illness, malnutrition, and institutional confinement.

There are differing opinions as to whether neuroradiological examinations should be done on all mentally retarded children or only on selected cases. The former opinion is supported by the observation that neuroradiological methods have revealed some abnormalities even when other methods have failed to do so (Valk, 1975). However, this practice may not be easy to carry out. The latter opinion is reinforced by the commonly accepted neurological practice that neuroradiological and other special methods are used only in cases where there is a clearly defined need for further clarification of the results of previous examinations and at the same time where there are no contraindications. Thus, the neurological examination makes its progress step by step in order to arrive at the correct diagnosis. The overall situation is reassessed when the results of each new step are available. So the character of the neurological examination is very dynamic. This commonly accepted principle was followed in the present study.

Conclusions

On the basis of the experience obtained in the present study, the following general conclusions can be drawn.

(1) By the current diagnostic principles, a fairly accurate aetiological diagnosis of mental retardation is possible in about 90% of patients.

(2) The diagnosis of mental retardation should be as accurate and as complete as possible, and every available modern technique of investigation, such as chromatography, cytogenetics, neurovirological tests and neuroradiological studies, including computerized axial tomography, should be used when indicated.

(3) These investigations should be performed as early as possible to ensure that they are of the greatest possible benefit to the patient.

(4) Better understanding of the causes of mental retardation and knowledge of the pathological changes in the brains of mentally retarded subjects are helpful in the choice of optimum treatment and rehabilitation of the patients, for the parents, other relatives and guardians in relating to these problems, and in the work of preventing mental retardation.

(5) Consequently, the neurological investigation and prescription of treatment for the mentally retarded should be the same as that of patients suffering from other cerebral symptoms. This means that the so-called normalization-integration principle is fully applicable to and indicated in the care of mentally retarded patients.

References

Amiel-Tison, C. (1976). A method for neurologic evaluation within the first year of life. *Curr. Probl. Pediatr.* **7**, 1–50.

Arimitsu, T., Di Chiro, G., Brooks, R.A. and Smith, P.B. (1977). White-gray matter differentiation in computed tomography. *J. Comput. Assist. Tomogr.* **1**, 437–442.

Autio, S. (1972). *Aspartylglucosaminuria. Analysis of Thirty-four Cases. J. Ment. Defic. Res.*, Monograph Series No. 1, National Society for Mentally Handicapped Children: London.

Blaw, M.E., Torres, F. (1967). Treatment for pseudoretardation associated with epilepsy. *Mod. Treat.* **4**, 799–816.

Chapelle, A. de la (1962). Cytogenetical and clinical observations in female gonadal dysgenesis. *Acta Endocrinol.* (Copenh) **40** (Suppl. 65).

Chapelle, A. de la (1963). Sex chromosome abnormalities among the mentally defective in Finland. *J. Ment. Defic. Res.* **7**, 129–146.

Chapelle, A. de la, Wennstrom, J., Hortling, H. and Ockey, C.H. (1966). Isochromosome-X in man. Part I. *Hereditas* **54**, 260–276.

Craft, M. (1979a). The neurology of mental retardation. In: M Craft (ed.), *Tredgold's Mental Retardation* (12th edn), pp. 43–48. Bailliere Tindall: London.

Craft, M. (1979b). The psychiatry of mental retardation. In: Craft, M. (ed.): *Tredgold's Mental Retardation* (12th edn), pp. 144–156. Bailliere Tindall: London.

Dent, C.E. and Harris, H. (1956). Hereditary forms of rickets and osteomalacia. *J. Bone Joint. Surg.* [Br]. **38**B, 204–226.

Dupont, A. and Dreyer, K. (1968). Mentally retarded patients classified according to AAMD system. *Dan. Med. Bull.* **15**, 18–24.

Freytag, E. and Lindenberg, E. (1967). Neuropathologic findings in patients of a hospital for the mentally deficient. A survey of 359 cases. *Johns Hopkins Med. J.* **121**, 379–392.

Halperin, S.L. (1945). A clinico-genetical study of mental defect. *Am. J. Ment. Defic.* **50**, 8–26.

Hauser, S.L., De Long, G.R. and Rosman, N. (1975). Pneumographic findings in the infantile autism syndrome — a correlation with temporal lobe disease. *Brain* **98**, 667–688.

Heber, R. (1961). *A Manual on Terminology and Classification in Mental Retardation* (2nd edn). *Am. J. Ment. Defic.* **66**, Monograph Suppl.

Iivanainen, M. (1974). *A Study on the Origins of Mental Retardation*. Clinics in Developmental Medicine No. 51. Spastics International Medical Publications, William Heinemann Medical Books: London, and JB Lippincott: Philadelphia.

Iivanainen, M. and Kostiainen, E. (1971). Changes in the electrophoretic pattern of the lumbar cerebrospinal fluid during fractional gas encephalography. *Acta Neurol. Scand.* **47**, 91–105.

Iivanainen, M. and Taskinen, E. (1974). Differential cellular increase in cerebrospinal fluid after encephalography in mentally retarded patients. *J. Neurol. Neurosurg. Psychiatry* **37**, 1252–1258.

Iivanainen, M., Viukari, M. and Helle, E.P. (1977). Cerebellar atrophy in phenytoin-treated mentally retarded epileptics. *Epilepsia* **18**, 375–386.

Isler, W. (1971). *Acute Hemiplegias and Hemisyndromes in Childhood*. Clinics in Developmental Medicine Nos. 41/42. Spastics International Medical Publications, William Heinemann Medical Books: London, and J.B. Lippincott: Philadelphia.

Lehti, A. (1971). Normal weights of human organs. A post mortem study on cases of death from external causes. Dissertation, University of Helsinki.

Malamud N: Recent trends in classification of neuropathological findings in mental deficiency. *Am. J. Ment. Defic.* **58**, 438–447, 1954.

Moorhead, P.S., Nowell, R.C., Mellman, W.J. Battins, D.M. and Hungerford, D.A. (1960). Chromosome preparations of leucocytes cultured from human peripheral blood. *Exp. Cell Res.* **20**, 613–616.

O'Gorman, G. (1967). *The Nature of Childhood Autism*. Butterworth: London.

Paine, R.S. and Oppe, T.E. (1966). *Neurological Examination of Children*. Clinics in Developmental Medicine Nos. 20/21. Spastics International Medical Publications, William Heinemann Medical Books: London.

Palo, J. (1967). Prevalence of phenylketonuria and some other metabolic disorders among mentally retarded patients in Finland. *Acta Neurol. Scand.* **43**, 573–579.

Palo, J. and Mattson, K. (1970). Eleven new cases of aspartyglucosaminuria. *J. Ment. Defic. Res.* **14**, 168–173.

Palo, J., Savolainen, H. and Iivanainen, M. (1973). Free amino acids and carbohydrates in the cerebrospinal fluid of 305 mentally retarded patients: a screening study. *J. Ment. Defic. Res.* **17**, 139–142.

Prechtl, H.F.R. (1977). *Neurological Examination of the Full-term Newborn Infant* (2nd edn). Clinics in Developmental Medicine No. 63. Spastics International Medical Publications, William Heinemann Medical Books: London, and J.B. Lippincott: Philadelphia.

Touwen, B. (1976). *Neurological Development in Infancy*. Clinics in Developmental Medicine No. 58. Spastics International Medical Publications, William Heinemann Medical Books: London, and J.B. Lippincott: Philadelphia.

Touwen, B.C.L. (1979). *Examination of the Child with Minor Neurological Dysfunction* (2nd edn). Clinics in Developmental Medicine No. 71. Spastics International Medical Publications, William Heinemann Medical Books: London, and J.B. Lippincott: Philadelphia.

Valk, J. (1975). Neuroradiology in the research of mental retardation. In: DAA Primrose (ed.): *Proceedings of the Third Congress of the International Association for the Scientific Study of Mental Deficiency*, pp. 259–262. Polish Medical Publishers: Warsaw.

World Health Organization (1967). *The International Classification of Diseases*. WHO: Geneva.

Yannet, H. (1945). Diagnostic classification of patients with mental deficiency. *Am. J. Dis. Child.* **70**, 83–88.

Yannet, H. (1956). Mental deficiency. *Adv. Pediatr.* **8**, 217–257.

Zappella, M. (1964). Postural reactions in 100 children with cerebral palsy and mental handicap. *Dev. Med. Child. Neurol.* **6**, 475–484.

5 The EEG patterns of mildly retarded children: clinical and quantitative findings

TH. GASSER, R. VERLEGER, J. MÖCKS, P. BÄCHER and W.M. LEDERER

Department of Biostatistics, Central Institute of Mental Health, Mannheim, FRG

Summary

Preliminary results of a neurophysiological study with 25 mildly mentally retarded children and a matched control group of normal children indicate that this dimension could — in conjunction with psychometric test scores and sociodemographic variables — help in gaining an understanding of the phenomenology of mental retardation and in identifying subgroups. The retarded children have statistically significant differences as compared with the control group both with respect to a standardized clinical rating of the EEG and with respect to computerized EEG parameters (broad band spectrum analysis).

Introduction

The group of mentally retarded and severely educationally subnormal children is heterogeneous and there is no clear picture of its composition. Such an understanding, however, is vital for case definition, for administrative policy, for therapeutic intervention and in planning programmes designed to develop skills of the children. A cross-sectional study of the kind reported here is close to the problems formulated above, and the organic nature of the variables recorded should not hide its phenomenological rather than aetiological orientation.

A widely accepted case definition of mental handicap is based both on intelligence test scores and on the degree of social competence (Grossmann, 1973, p. 11). These behavioural criteria may or may not relate to some kind of brain dysfunction. A commonly accepted view, following Lewis (1933) focuses on the distinction between an organic and a sociocultural group, largely corresponding to the groups of severe (IQ < 50) and mild ($50 \leqslant$ IQ < 70) mental retardation respectively, as these are specified in the ICD criteria. For our first neurophysiological study, we chose a group of mildly retarded children (IQ 50–70), a group for which a verifiable organic disorder or an immaturity in terms of developmental physiology is disputed. The sample was based on an epidemiological investigation of mentally retarded children in Mannheim (Liepmann, 1979).

Work on the EEG in mental retardation has tended to concentrate on the more severe cases (Iivanainen, 1974). In the work of Gibbs (Gibbs *et al.*, 1960; Gibbs and Gibbs, 1964), a distinction was made between mildly and severely retarded persons and between different age-groups, but the sample was based on clinic admission and psychometric criteria were rather vague. Others concentrated on precisely defined aetiological groups, in particular Down's syndrome (Tangye, 1979). Epilepsy was often a major theme of these studies.

The overall conclusion to be drawn from the literature is as follows: retarded children have a higher frequency of pathological EEG signs than non-retarded children, and more so if they are severely retarded. The signs are highly variable and are not specific for mental retardation. With the exception of one recently published paper (Baird *et al.*, 1980), the available data are all based on clinical rating of the EEG paper trace. Baird and his co-workers studied groups of "achievers" and "under-achievers" at school, both epileptic and non-epileptic. In addition to a clinical rating, they extracted computerized EEG parameters ("broad band spectrum parameters"), as we did in our study. Interestingly enough, more differences could be found in the computerized EEG parameter between the healthy achievers and under-achievers than between the healthy achievers and the epileptic achievers.

Because of the scarcity of normative and epidemiological data for the EEG, we used a matched control design. Experience in clinical electroencephalography, as well as the findings of the large developmental study undertaken in Gothenberg (Petersen and Eeg-Olofsson, 1971; Matousek and Petersen, 1973), led us to hypothesize that retarded children show, in terms of clinical rating, more frequent paroxysms, more abundant grapho-elements, a less mature EEG, a less prominent rhythm and a higher amplitude than normal controls. Regarding the computerized EEG parameters, we conjectured that the retarded children would have significantly different values from the control groups on those indices which show drastic changes during development (Matousek and Petersen, 1973). We also expected to find a less differentiated topographical organization of the brain-wave patterns in the retarded group. The expected heterogeneity of the mildly retarded group should result in a wider variance: note that we can compare variances of the computerized EEG indices based on interval scales, whereas psychometric data refer only to ordinal scales and therefore do not allow comparisons of variability. This first stage of our study should also lead to the generation of hypotheses to be validated with another sample.

Subjects and methods

Subjects

Out of a group of 35 children with IQ 50–70 identified in an epidemiological study (Liepmann, 1979) the parents of 26 agreed to their participation in the present study. Since one girl was not cooperative, we finally had a group of 25 mildly retarded children (50 ≤ IQ < 70), aged 10–13*. They attended either a school for the mentally retarded (14) or a school for educationally subnormal (11), the level of intelligence used as a guideline in allocation to these different types of school being at IQ < 60. The control group was individually matched for sex (11 male, 14 female) and age (± 3 months), and across the sample for social class. The mean age was 12 years 6 months in both groups, with a standard deviation of 10 months. The social class status, as measured by a prestige score (Treiman, 1975; Statistisches Bundesamt, 1971) is somewhat higher in the control group; the medians of the two groups are 31 and 38 and both values are typical of the lower social class, which has a range lying between 18 and 46.

Recordings

There are 8 unipolar leads at F_3, F_4, C_3, C_4, C_z, P , O_1, O_2 (10/20 system) with connected earlobes as reference electrodes. To discriminate the influence of eye-movements in the EEG from genuine slow cerebral waves, the electro-oculogram was recorded from the right eye vertically bipolar. We registered both on paper and on analog magnetic tape; the latter was digitized for computer-analysis. The recording session lasted for about an hour. The different neurophysiological modalities were recorded in the following order: Spontaneous EEG (200–300 sec); eyes opening/closing (3 × 10 sec each); contingent negative variation (CNV) paradigm "Discrimination" (200 sec); contingent negative variation paradigm "Learning" (280 sec); visual evoked potentials (120 sec). The results reported here refer to the spontaneous EEG; for those relating to the CNV, compare Verleger et al. (1980).

* Because a computerized EEG-analysis implies the processing of mass data (13 million numbers for each proband in our study) samples have to be fairly limited in size.

Psychometric and social data

In a separate session we applied the Columbia Mental Maturity Scale, CMM (Burgemeister *et al*., 1954), in a standardized German version (Bondy *et al*., 1969) and the vocabulary subtest of the Wechsler Intelligence Scale for Children (WISC) (German version: HaWIK, Hardesty and Priester, 1966). Because of "ceiling" effects of the CMM, a further test (Prüfsystem für Schul- und Bildungsberatung, PSB; Horn 1969) was given to the control group. Data on social competence, motor, speech and sensory defects and neurological signs were gathered in the preceding epidemiological study. We also checked the handedness of the children.

Clinical rating and computerized EEG-analysis

The EEG paper traces were clinically evaluated, according to a standard 'blind' procedure, by a neuropaediatrician, who gave each child a rating on each of a series of simple 3-point scales (cf. Table 1). Differences between the retarded and control groups were then tested by applying the χ^2-test to 2×3 contingency tables. Since some of the cells had small expected frequencies, we also applied an exact multinomial test for a 2×2 table by combining item levels 2 and 3 (Freeman and Halton, 1951).

The methodology of biosignal analysis has become quite sophisticated (Dumermuth, 1973; Gasser, 1977), and it seems inappropriate to go into details here. The computer program developed in our group proceeded roughly as follows: selection of the quietest epoch of 20 sec out of 120 sec with respect to eye movement energy; computation of the power spectrum for these 20 sec and parametrization of the brain activity in terms of absolute and relative power in the following (commonly used) frequency bands:

$\delta(1\cdot5-3\cdot5\,\text{Hz}),\theta(3\cdot5-7\cdot5\,\text{Hz})$, $\alpha_1(7\cdot5-9\cdot5\,\text{Hz})$, $\alpha_2(9\cdot5-12\cdot5\,\text{Hz})$, $\beta_1(12\cdot5-17\cdot5\,\text{Hz})$, $\beta_2(17\cdot5-25\cdot0\,\text{Hz})$.

Six broad band spectrum parameters were computed for epochs of 20 sec, judged by an algorithm to be the quietest 20 sec, for the EEG at eight topographical locations, and also for the electro-oculogram (EOG).

Results

The clinical rating

Some of the results of the standardized and blind clinical ratings are

Table 1   Results of the clinical EEG rating: mentally retarded children and matched controls (*n* = 25)

Item	Normal	Border-line	Deviant	2 × 3 χ^2 test	2 × 2, exact test, 1-sided
Overall assessment					
retarded children	8	6	11	$p < 0.001$	$p = 0.023$
control	16	9	0		
Maturity					
retarded children	12	9	4	$p < 0.05$	$p = 0.019$
control	20	5	0		
Paroxysms					
retarded children	17	4	4	$p < 0.1$	$p = 0.037$
control	23	2	0		
Grapho-elements Θ					
retarded children	3	17	5	$p < 0.1$	$p = 0.048$
control	9	15	1		
Prominence of rhythm					
retarded children	12	10	3	$p < 0.1$	$p = 0.074$
control	18	7	0		

summarized in Table 1. There is a clear shift towards more deviant EEG characteristics for the group of mentally retarded children as compared to the control group. The *a priori* hypothesis regarding a larger amplitude for the retarded children could not be confirmed.

Broad band spectrum analysis

Hypotheses on differences between retarded and non-retarded children in the computerized parameters with respect to frequency bands and topographical locations were derived from the large normative study (*N* = 401) undertaken in Gothenberg (Matousek and Petersén, 1973, Table 2): whenever an EEG-parameter decreases (increases) drastically with age, we postulate a larger (smaller) average value for the retarded children. The significance of the differences between the group of mildly retarded children and the matched controls (*n* = 25) was checked by matched Wilcoxon tests, performed separately for each location and each frequency band. Because we know on what side the difference should lie, if there is one, we computed one-sided *p*-values. In Table 2 only those *p*–values are given which are smaller than or equal to 5%, otherwise there is a blank. The heavy lines indicate the topographical locations and the frequency bands where we expected significant differences— to a higher degree than for other parameters— in case of large developmental varia-

Table 2 Broad band spectrum parameters of the EEG: mentally retarded and matched controls, $n = 25$ (p-values of matched Wilcoxon-tests given, if significant at 5% or below)

Loca-tions: eye	Absolute band power						Relative band power					
	δ	Θ	α_1	α_2	β_1	β_2	δ	Θ	α_1	α_2	β_1	β_2
F_4	1%	2·5%	5%		2·5%	5%						
F_3	1%	2·5%	5%		2·5%	1%						
C_4	1%	0·5%			2·5%					0·5%		
C_3	1%	0·5%			5%	5%				2·5%		
C_z	2·5%	2·5%										
P_z	1%	2·5%					−	−			1%	
O_2	−	5%					1%	1%			2·5%	
O_1	−						2·5%	1%			2·5%	

tion (as measured by correlation with age by Matousek and Petersén). The findings conform rather well to our expectations. The slow waves (δ,Θ) are all significantly different in absolute power, except in the occipital region. Notable are the differences in absolute β-power in the fronto-central region. The differences in relative power are concentrated on the parieto-occipital region: more fast α-activity — a typical developmental parameter — and less slow activity for the control group. Since eye-movements may enhance the EEG-activity, in particular the slow one, it is important that no significant differences could be found in the electro-oculogram. Figure one shows a norm chart for one of the parameters, the absolute power in the Θ-band at the central location C_3 (as a normalizing transformation we took logarithms). The age-standardized norms are based on a sample of $n = 31$ children attending normal schools. There is a clear tendency for larger values than normal, in particular for the children attending a school for the mentally retarded: there are eleven children with values beyond the 95th percentile (with only two attending a school for the educationally subnormal), and five children beyond the 99th percentile (with only one attending a school for the educationally subnormal).

As simple measures of topographical differentiation we have used ratios of broad band spectrum parameters both inter- and intrahemis-pheric. The picture that evolves is rather distinct: The ratios of EEG-parameters for the retarded children from one hemisphere to the other are not statistically different from the control group. whereas the anterior-posterior and central-posterior ratios are larger for the control group for almost all frequency bands (Table 3); a further statistical

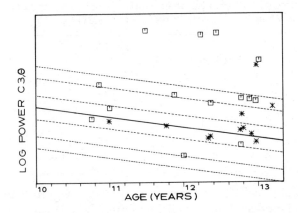

Fig. 1. Age-standardized norms (1%, 5%, 25%, 50%, 75%, 95%, 99% percentile) for power in Θ-band at location C_3; values for mildly retarded (squares) and educationally subnormal children (stars).

analysis showed that these differences are primarily due to the 14 children who were attending a school for the mentally retarded. Table 4 gives the ratios of variance for the controls and the retarded children in the spectrum parameters for three topographical locations. Despite the fact that our group of mildly retarded children covers a narrow IQ-range, the variability of neurophysiological parameters is on the average much higher than that of the control group. This is a clear indication of heterogeneity of the group of mildly retarded children in neurophysiological terms, of the existence of subgroups.

Multidimensional scaling (MDS) is a method which allows a reduction in dimensionality while preserving the rank order in terms of distances

Table 3 EEG-topography, measured by quotients of broad band spectrum parameters: mentally retarded and matched controls, $n = 25$ (p-values of matched Wilcoxon-tests given, if significant at 5% or below)

Broad band parameters	Interhemisph. symm. locations			Interhemisph. anterior/ posterior locations					
	$\dfrac{F_4}{F_3}$	$\dfrac{C_4}{C_3}$	$\dfrac{O_2}{O_1}$	$\dfrac{F_4}{C_4}$	$\dfrac{C_4}{O_2}$	$\dfrac{F_3}{C_3}$	$\dfrac{C_3}{O_1}$	$\dfrac{F_4}{O_2}$	$\dfrac{F_3}{O_3}$
δ	5%	2·5%			5%		5%		
Θ					2·5%		5%	5%	
α_1					0·5%		0·5%	0·5%	2·5%
α_2				2·5%	2·5%		0·5%	0·5%	0·5%
β_1					2·5%		0·5%	0·5%	2·5%
β_2					2·5%		2·5%	0·5%	2·5%

Table 4 Neurophysiological variability: ratio of variances of broad band spectrum parameters of controls v. mentally retarded ($n = 25$)

Parameters	Location		
	F_4	C_4	O_2
δ	1:16	1:22	1:8
Θ	1:33	1:10	1:6
α_1	1:19	1:9	1:15
α_2	1:4	1:1	1:2
β_1	1:3	1:3	1:1
β_2	1:5	1:1	1:0·3

between individuals in the best possible way. Figure 2 gives a two-dimensional representation of all 50 children, based again on broad band spectrum parameters (48 dimensions); most subjects lie in one main cluster, but four mildly retarded children (three of them attending a school for the mentally retarded) lie well outside it. Closer to the cluster, there is still a tendency for retarded children to have deviant MDS-values.

Table 5 contains correlations between selected EEG-parameters (absolute power in the band δ, at topographical locations F_4, C_4, O_2, in the band Θ at locations F_4, C_3, in the band α_1 at locations F_4, C_4 and in the band β_1 at location F_3) and psychometric test scores (Columbia Mental Maturity Scale, CMM; Prüfsystem für Schul- und Bildungsberatung, PSB; verbal subtest of Wechsler Intelligence Scale for Children, WISC). As was to be

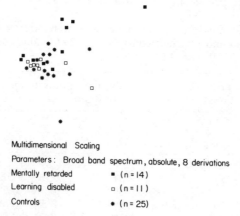

Multidimensional Scaling

Parameters : Broad band spectrum , absolute, 8 derivations

Mentally retarded   ■ (n = 14)

Learning disabled   □ (n = 11)

Controls   ✳ (n = 25)

Fig. 2 48 EEG-dimensions reduced to two by multidimensional scaling: pattern for 25 controls, 14 mildly retarded and 11 educationally subnormal children.

expected, these correlations are low for the control group, but substantially higher for the retarded group; they are, however, low enough in general to indicate that the EEG parameters represent a dimension distinct from intelligence test scores.

Discussion

Our results are preliminary in two respects: first, statistical analysis of the present findings and their comparison with other results reported in the literature are not yet completed; secondly, a further study of neurophysiological aspects of mental retardation, based on a larger sample and including more severely retarded children, is now in progress and will be completed in the near future. As in the present study, this investigation is based on an epidemiological survey of mentally retarded children in Mannheim, and to that extent the findings will be representative.

A "blind" standardized clinical rating showed a significant difference between the retarded children and the controls for items relevant for the diagnosis of functional disorders of the brain and/or of a general immaturity. The percentage of retarded children showing paroxysms in their EEG was of the same order as that reported by Gibbs *et al.* (1960). In agreement with the literature generally, we found clinically significant pathological signs less frequently among the less severely retarded children. The notion of a sub-clinical epilepsy (i.e. paroxysms in the EEG-trace without epileptic attacks) is somewhat vague, and the same is true of its postulated association with learning difficulties; nevertheless, the work of Hutt *et al.* (1978) has provided some empirical support for such speculations. For subclinical EEG-deviations, however, a computerized EEG-

Table 5 Correlations of psychometric tests with EEG-parameters: for mentally retarded children and matched controls separately ($n = 25$)

Test	EEG-Parameter: location band							
	F_4/δ	F_4/Θ	F_4/α_1	F_3/β_1	C_4/δ	C_4/α_1	C_3/Θ	$0_2/\delta$
CMM (retarded children)	0·01	–0·45	–0·37	–0·08	–0·11	–0·39	–0·48	–0·22
CMM (control)	–0·03	–0·20	0·15	–0·03	0·12	0·14	0·04	0·06
PSB (control)	–0·20	–0·18	–0·09	–0·06	–0·17	–0·20	–0·21	–0·25
WISC (retarded verbal children)	–0·25	–0·39	–0·30	0·22	–0·43	–0·33	–0·57	–0·26
WISC (control) Verbal	–0·10	–0·36	–0·28	0·05	–0·04	–0·24	–0·29	–0·03

88 Th. Gasser *et al.*

analysis seemed to us superior to a clinical rating.

Since there was quantitative agreement between the retarded and the non-retarded children with respect to EOG-parameters, differences found in the EEG cannot be attributed to eye movements. A number of hypotheses about differences between the retarded children and the controls could be verified by matched Wilcoxon-tests, and further differences could be found *post hoc*. They can always be interpreted as developmental delays (Matoušek and Petersén, 1973), but some of them could also be signs of brain pathology. It is rather striking that retarded children lagged behind controls in intrahemispheric, but not interhemispheric, brain differentiation. There is clear evidence that the neurophysiological differences are accounted for by a sub-group of the 25 retarded children and that the group as a whole is heterogeneous in neurophysiological terms, despite the fact that it was restricted to children with mild retardation: the variance of the EEG-parameters is much higher for the retarded group than for the non-retarded, and the norm-chart (Fig. 1) as well as multidimensional scaling show a sub-group of about eight retarded children whose EEG patterns have extreme properties. This suggests that the simple identification of mild mental retardation (IQ 50–70) with sociocultural deprivation may not hold. It is hoped that a second and larger study to be completed soon will shed more light on the question of sub-groups within the population of retarded children as a whole.

Correlations between EEG-parameters and intelligence test scores are low for the control group; our preliminary interpretation is that a lagging in brain development leads on the average to a somewhat lower test score. The correlations are markedly higher for the retarded children, which means that some brain damage or some functional disorder of the brain may be an important factor for low test scores at least for a sub-group of children. The size of the correlations indicates that the EEG-parameters provide information beyond that contained in intelligence test scores.

Acknowledgment

This research project was funded by the Deutsche Forschungsgemein-schaft as part of Sonderforschungsbereich (Special Research Programme) 116, "Psychiatrische Epidemiologie" at the University of Heidelberg.

References

Baird, H.W., John, E.R., Ahn, H. and Maisel, E. (1980). Neurometric evaluation of epileptic children who do well and poorly in school. *Electroencephalogr. Clin. Neurophysiol.* **48**, 683–693.

Bondy, C., Cohen, R., Eggert, D. and Lüer, G. (1969). *Testbatterie für geistig behinderte Kinder* (TBGB). (Hrsg. K. Ingenkamp) Beltz-Verlag, Weinheim.

Burgemeister, B.B., Blum, L.H. and Lorge, I. (1954). Manual, Columbia Mental Maturity Scale. Yonkers-on-Hudson, New York.

Dumermuth, G. (1973). Numerical spectral analysis of the electroencephalogramm. *Handbook of EEG Clin. Neurophysiol.* **5A**, 33–60.

Freeman, G.H. and Halton, J.H. (1951). Note on an exact treatment of contingency, goodness-of-fit and other problems of significance. *Biometrika* **38**, 141–149.

Gasser, Th. (1977): General characteristics of the EEG as a signal. In: A. Rémond (ed.): *EEG Informatics*, pp. 37–56. Elsevier: Amsterdam.

Gibbs, E.L., Rich, C.L., Fois, A. and Gibbs, F.A. (1960): Electro-encephalographic study of mentally retarded persons. *Am. J. Ment. Defic.* **65**, 236–247.

Gibbs, F.A. and Gibbs, E.L. (1964). *Atlas of Electroencephalography*, Vol. 3, pp. 146–151. Addison-Wesley Publishing Company: Reading.

Grossman, M.D. (1973). *Manual on Terminology and Classification in Mental Retardation*. AAMD Special Publication. Series No. 2. American Association on Mental Deficiency: Washington.

Hardesty, F.P. and Priester, H.J. (1966). *Handbuch für den Hamburg-Wechsler Intelligenztest für Kinder*. Huber: Bern.

Horn, W. (1969). *Prüfsystem für Schul- und Bildungsberatung PSB*. Hogrefe: Göttingen.

Hutt, S.J., Newton, J. and Fairweather, H. (1977). Choice reaction time and EEG activity in children with epilepsy. *Neuropsychologia* **15**, 257–267.

Iivanainen, M. (1974). *A Study on the Origins of Mental Retardation*. Spastics International Medical Publications: London.

Lewis, E.O. (1933). Types of deficiency and their social significance. *J. ment. Sci.* **79**, 298–304.

Liepmann, M.C. (1979). *Geistig behinderte Kinder und Jugendliche*. Huber: Bern.

Matoušek, M. and Petersén, I. (1973). Frequency analysis of the EEG in normal children (1–15 years) and in normal adolescents (16–21 years). In: Kellaway, P. and Petersén, I. (eds): *Automation of Clinical EEG*. pp. 75–102. Raven Press: New York.

Petersén, I. and Eeg-Olofsson, O. (1971). *Internationale Standard-Klassifikation* children from age one through 15 years: non paroxysmal activity. *Neuropädiatrie* **3**, 277–304.

Statistisches Bundesamt Wiesbaden (1971). *Internationale Standard-Klassifikation der Berufe*. Kohlhammer, W.: Stuttgart.

Tangye, S.R. (1979). The EEG and incidence of epilepsy in Down's syndrome. *J. Ment. Defic. Res.* **23**, 17–24.

Treiman, D.J. (1975). Problems of concept and measurement in the comparative study of occupational mobility. *Soc. Sci. Res.* **4**, 183–230.

Verleger, R., Gasser, Th., Bächer, P. and Weingärtner, O. (1980). Analysing poor performance by recording event-related potentials of the EEG. In: Mittler, P. (ed.): *Frontiers of Knowledge in Mental Retardation*. Proceedings of the 5th Congress of IASSMD, Jerusalem, 1979. University Park Press: Baltimore, London, Tokyo (In press).

Part 3
Methods of Assessing
Mental Handicap

6 Psychometric tests — their uses and limitations

J. GOULD

MRC Social Psychiatry Unit, Institute of Psychiatry, London, UK

General overview

There are two separate but equally important aspects of assessment of cognitive skills in severely retarded children. These are, first, the measurement of the overall level of intellectual function and, second, the exploration of the individual child's impairments and abilities. In this section the values and limitations of both types of assessment will be considered in relation to test procedures.

Estimates of overall intelligence are traditionally used in comparative studies of prevalence both for research and for planning services. In clinical and educational work they are useful as part of the initial screening of children who are presenting behavioural or learning problems. The results provide part of the information needed in order to make recommendations concerning education and management and to give a prognosis for adult life.

In epidemiological studies the use of standardized tests has obvious advantages, since they allow comparisons to be made within and between populations. In work with individual children, the use of such tests avoids possible subjective biases which might affect judgement of a child's ability based on informal observations (Warren, 1977).

However, many problems arise when testing mentally retarded children. First, intelligence tests are constructed on the assumption that the abilities measured are normally distributed. The intelligence quotient is calculated from the degree of deviation from the average score for the relevant chronological age. None of the commonly used intelligence tests have included mentally retarded children in the normative samples. If a child's score falls outside the expected range, his IQ has to be calculated by extrapolation, which is a most unreliable procedure.

Second, an even more serious disadvantage arises from the use of a single numerical index to give an indication of a child's level of intelligence. This is an over-simplification even when applied to normal children. Some mentally retarded children have very marked discrepancies between different types of skills. In these children, an intelligence quotient based on the average of the sub-tests covers up the variability of performance.

Third, additional handicaps of, for example, hearing, vision or motor skills can have marked effects on test performance. Children with multiple physical as well as mental handicaps are particularly difficult to assess. Although many such children are profoundly retarded in intellectual development, there are some with higher levels of intelligence. Because of the physical handicaps it is impossible to pick out such children on the results of intelligence testing alone. Observation by people who know the child very well may give the only indication that he or she has intellectual abilities hidden behind the handicaps.

Lastly, retarded children may be difficult in behaviour and not motivated to carry out the tasks. In practice, this tends to occur in children with severe language problems affecting all forms of communication, non-verbal as well as verbal. The lack of motivation and the difficult behaviour during testing are then often due to poor understanding of the instructions. In some cases, the tests may underestimate the child's abilities. In others, a child may perform very well on one sub-test but refuses to do all the others. The tendency will then be to over-estimate the general level.

What tests can be used to assess overall intelligence?

There is no easy answer to this question. There are a variety of standardized test-batteries available (see the following major section), but they all suffer from the disadvantages mentioned above. The choice has to depend upon the individual child and his pattern of handicaps. For more severely retarded children it is easier to hold their attention with tests involving brightly coloured toys and objects of the right size for them to handle. The Merrill-Palmer Scale is one example of a test the children tend to enjoy, but it is by no means suitable for all types of children.

The lack of a universally applicable test poses a particular problem in research on groups of children. In an epidemiological study of severely retarded children aged under 15 years, living in Camberwell, London, several tests were used for each child, covering visuo-spatial, language and self-care skills (Gould, 1976). From the results it was possible to derive a very approximate estimate of the intelligence quotient — more precisely referred to as an age-related quotient. Because of the basic unreliability of this kind of procedure, children were placed in very broad groups, corresponding to the mild, moderate, severe and profound levels of mental retardation as defined in the 8th edition of the International Classification of Diseases (WHO, 1967). This was used to make very simple comparisons with findings from other areas and other countries.

The results from the separate tests were all grouped in the same way. This highlighted the difficulty of calculating a single IQ score, since some children classified, for example, as severely retarded on a test of language level were moderately or mildly retarded on visuo-spatial or self-care skills. Discrepancies were found in a significant proportion of the children in the study (Gould, 1977).

Workers in some countries have tackled the problem of compiling and standardizing test-batteries specifically for mentally retarded children. In West Germany, the "Testbatterie für geistig behinderte Kinder" (Bondy *et al.*, 1971) has been developed and widely used for this purpose. In the USA Schopler and Reichler (1979) and DeMyer (1979) have produced tests for children with severe language and learning problems. All these batteries of tests produce profiles rather than single scores.

Analysis of individual profiles

The second and more important stage of psychological assessment is the detailed analysis of each child's pattern of skills and handicaps. This is essential for planning a programme of education and is often of relevance for the management of behaviour problems. For this aspect of assessment, a more flexible approach can be used than when following the standard procedures of formal psychological testing. Because of the wide variety of patterns of handicap found among mentally retarded people, it is necessary to be familiar with a range of tests so that a whole battery or some sub-tests can be selected as appropriate. The results of testing should be supplemented with information from people who know the child well and also by direct observation of his behaviour in his own familiar environment.

The aim is to examine the levels reached in different functions. These include gross and fine motor skills, self-care, practical and domestic tasks, visuo-spatial abilities, comprehension and use of verbal and non-verbal communication, the development of symbolic, imaginative activities, social behaviour and finally the quality of the child's social interaction.

Formal tests are available for some of these functions (see the following major section), but others are not covered at all. For example, there are no standardized tests of non-verbal communication; that is, gesture, vocal intonation, facial expression and so on, although impairment of these skills constitutes a severe handicap. It is therefore necessary to use methods other than psychological testing; for example, structured interviews with informants who know the child well.

Sometimes it is helpful to invent tests to explore specific problems; Churchill (1978), for example, has devised a simple artificial language consisting of nine objects representing "words" which he uses to examine concept formation in children with severe language problems. Various methods of testing through teaching have also been described (Taylor, 1976; Mittler, 1976).

Service planning and research

The assessment of large groups of children as a guide in planning services presents special problems, since it is usually impossible to spend the time needed for detailed testing. In such work it is essential to give extensive details of the tests that have been used. However, as already emphasized in this chapter, even if this is done, comparisons are still difficult because of the very different profiles of handicaps and skills in children who may have identical overall scores. These profiles are not just of academic interest. They are important because they are clearly linked to overt behaviour and this, in turn, affects the types of services needed.

In research, comparisons based on several different aspects of functioning have more meaning than overall scores, but pose difficult problems in practice, partly because there are so many different skills and behaviours that could be measured and partly because of the difficulty of deriving a system of classification from complex profiles.

In the end, the choice both of functions to be examined and of tests to be used, and the way in which the resulting patterns are grouped, must all depend on the purpose of the individual study.

To summarize, intelligence testing has a role to play in research, service planning and individual assessment, but the stage has now been reached when it is necessary to try to develop a variety of different ways of classifying mentally retarded people each of which is relevant for a specific purpose, such as planning education, behaviour management and future occupation.

Psychometric tests and assessment scales that can be used for severely retarded children

Most of the tests described in this section are for use with children in the normal range of intelligence and who are within a specified chronological age-range. However, when testing severely retarded children, it is the mental rather than the chronological age which must determine the choice of tests. Using a test designed for young children for someone who is physically much older is far from ideal, but is often the best compromise available.

Tests of intellectual development

The Bayley Infant Scales of Mental and Motor Development (Francis Williams and Yule, 1967; Bayley, 1969)
These scales can be used for very young or very retarded children. They were standardized on infants aged one month to 2 years 6 months. Separate mental and motor quotients are obtained. The former include non-verbal and verbal items. These scales are more suitable for children with even profiles of development than for those with marked discrepancies between different types of skills.

The Merrill-Palmer Scale of Mental Tests (Stutsman, 1931)
The Merrill-Palmer Scale can be used with children whose mental ages are between 18 months and 72 months. It consists of a collection of sub-tests which are arranged in increasing order of difficulty. Some of them require varying levels of understanding and use of speech, while others are tests of performance which can be demonstrated without using words. The tests requiring language include, for example, simple questions such as "What does the birdie say?", "What is your name?", for the younger children, and, for the older ones, more difficult questions such as "What hops along?" "What writes?". The performance tests include fitting pegs into boards, assembling picture puzzles and matching shapes, which do not require logical reasoning and therefore can be done even by children who do not have any system of symbols for communication.

The majority of the items are of the "performance" kind. The scale is constructed in such a way that the tester can make allowances for items which are omitted or which the child refuses to try, so that he is given full credit for those which he does complete. This is a great advantage when testing children who are unable to do any of the verbal items, or with disturbed children whose attention can be held only long enough to complete a few of the sub-tests. The test materials are interesting even to the most withdrawn or difficult child. All the items are packed in different, brightly coloured boxes of varying sizes and since there is no definite order of presentation the child can choose what he wants to do next.

The Merrill-Palmer Scale contains, among other items, the test known as the Seguin form board, consisting of a wooden board with different shaped holes into which wooden pieces can be fitted. It is a particular favourite with children with severe language problems who may be able to complete this with speed and skill even though their abilities in other areas may be at a much lower level.

The main disadvantage of the Merrill-Palmer Scale is that the limited age-range makes it unsuitable for use with older children who have good non-verbal skills. Another disadvantage is that the scoring depends on speed as well as accuracy of performance. Some children are slowed down because of their motor disabilities and others because of their repetitive rituals, for example, one child insisted upon licking, smelling and tapping twice upon each piece of equipment before placing it correctly. These problems are, however, outweighed by the usefulness of the scale for younger and also for severely retarded children.

The scale gives a mental age, but the calculation of an IQ is not appropriate for statistical reasons related to the design of the test.

The Wechsler Tests (Wechsler, 1949; 1955; 1967; 1974)
The Wechsler Tests include the Wechsler Pre-school and Primary Scale of Intelligence (WPPSI) for the age range 4 to 6½ years and the Wechsler Intelligence Scale for Children (WISC) for the age range 5 to 15 years 11 months. (There is also a Wechsler Scale for Adults which will not be discussed here). The original Wechsler Tests were developed in America but the WPPSI has now been standardized on a British sample of children and various modifications have been made (Yule *et al.*, 1969).

The disadvantage in using the Wechsler tests with children who have severe language problems is that the distinction between the verbal and the so-called performance items is somewhat dubious. In particular, the picture completion, picture arrangement and coding tests do not call for a spoken response, but the ability to reason logically in words or in some other system of symbols, whether in silent thought or aloud, is essential for their completion. The high correlation between verbal and performance scales found when testing large groups of non-handicapped people underlines the fact that there is a large overlap between the two. Certain children may therefore obtain very different scores when given the truly non-verbal items of the Merrill-Palmer Scale and the performance items on the WPPSI.

The Wechsler scales each give a verbal IQ, a performance IQ and an overall "full scale" IQ score. They are suitable only for administration to a small minority of severely retarded children, their chief value being that they give a profile of skills.

Raven's Progressive Matrices (Raven, 1956; 1960)
The standard form of the progressive matrices consists of 60 designs. Each design has one piece missing and the appropriate piece to complete the design has to be selected from a number of possible choices. The designs are arranged in five groups of 12. Within each group the designs gradually increase in difficulty but the principle remains the same throughout. The test can be used for children of 8 years upwards and for adults. There is also a version using coloured patterns which is described as suitable for normal children aged from 5 to 11 years, for old people, for those who for reasons of background or disability cannot understand or speak English and for mentally retarded children and adults.

The Columbia Mental Maturity Scale (Burgemeister, Hollander, Blum and Lorge 1972)
This scale with age-range 3 years to 10 years was developed primarily for use with cerebral palsied children, and consists of a set of cards each bearing a series of drawings in bright colours or a series of written words. The task is to choose the one item in each set which does not fit in. The early ones are simple; for example, a series consisting of two red circles and a yellow square in which the odd one out is distinguished both by colour and shape. The later ones are much more difficult; for example a series of pictures of things in motion, only one of which is animate. Some of the series are printed words; for example "car, bus, train, river".

The earlier, simpler series can be used for training in order to ensure that the child grasps the idea of the task. The problems in using the scale with some children arise from the inclusion of written series as well as pictorial ones, and from the combination of increasing visual complexity together with increasing complexity of concepts, many of which require logical reasoning to resolve. Because of this mixture of dimensions of difficulty, the hierarchy of difficulty laid down in the test is often not appropriate for severely retarded children who may be able to do some of the supposedly harder, later items but fail on the earlier ones.

The usefulness of the scale lies in the clues it can give to the types of concepts an individual child is able to handle and those which he cannot grasp. A mental age and IQ can be calculated from the scores.

The Leiter International Performance Scale (Leiter, 1952)
The Leiter Scale was developed for use with deaf children. The materials consist of a series of picture cards and sets of small wooden cubes each with a picture on one face. The picture cards are displayed in turn in a frame. The child has to match the pictures on the blocks with those on the cards and then place the blocks in the holes provided in the frame, adjacent to the appropriate picture on the card. The instructions are given

entirely by demonstration and do not require any words at all. The items cover the age range 2 to 18 years.

The earlier items include matching by colour, shape, design and number. Some depend on matching by analogy. Later items in the scale involve the ability to visualize in three dimensions.

The absence of verbal instructions makes this test suitable for children with severe language problems. As with the Columbia Scale it is interesting to see which concepts are intact and which are not. The scale gives a mental age and an IQ.

Scales of social development

A child's ability in self-care skills and the way he interacts with other people can develop at a different rate from his intellectual skills, especially if he has some handicapping condition.

The Vineland Social Maturity Scale (Doll, 1953)

Just as tests of intelligence assign a mental age, so it is possible to give a child a social age by measuring his practical and social achievements and comparing them with a sample population of normal children.

The widely used Vineland scale assesses the child's ability to look after his own practical needs. It covers eight different areas. These are general self-help, eating, dressing, locomotion, occupation, communication, self-direction and socialization. The person who knows the child best is interviewed in order to elicit the information necessary for making a rating on each particular item. There is no set list of questions to be asked, but the booklet gives, for each item, a series of examples of behaviour that should be present in order to say that the skill has been achieved. The age range covered is from under one month to over 25 years.

Some children may score lower on this scale than on truly non-language dependent intelligence tests because many of the items depend on the comprehension and use of language both for social communication and for thinking and planning ahead. It is therefore more informative to look at the pattern of scores for the individual child than at his overall social age, which can be calculated from the child's total score on the scale.

Although not ideal, the Vineland Scale can give some clue as to the level of development of a child who is functioning as very severely retarded and who appears to be unable to cope with any of the more formal tests, even with preliminary training.

The Gunzburg Progress Assessment Chart (Gunzburg, 1974)
This, as its author states, is *not* a test but a chart for recording the stages reached by individuals in self-help skills (eating, mobility, toilet training, washing and dressing) communication, socialization and occupation. The items under each heading can be rated as present or absent and marked on the chart accordingly. This gives a profile of skills and deficiencies in a readily assimilated pictorial form. Later assessments can be compared with earlier ones and progress, or lack of it, can be easily seen.

The chart was designed specifically for mentally retarded children and adults of all ages. Its biggest deficiency is the absence of any rating of the behavioural abnormalities which are often of importance in planning treatment and rating progress.

The American Association on Mental Deficiency (A.A.M.D.) Adaptive Behaviour Scale (Nihira et al., 1969; 1974)
This scale examines adaptive behaviour which has been defined as "the effectiveness with which the individual copes with the natural and social demands of his environment" and is thought to be a separate dimension from measured intelligence. The scale has been designed to provide a quantitative description of the coping behaviour of the mentally retarded.

The scale is divided into two parts. The first covers levels of development in 10 areas of function, such as language, socialization and independence. The second is concerned with maladaptive behaviours under 14 different categories, including, for example, violence and destructiveness, hyperactivity, antisocial behaviour and stereotypies.

The scale allows a profile of skills and behaviour problems to be constructed for each individual.

The MRC Handicaps, Behaviour and Skills (HBS) schedule (Wing and Gould, 1978)
This schedule, which is described in Chapter 4, has been designed to distinguish the cognitive and behavioural problems of early childhood psychosis from those found in other forms of mental handicap.

Of the above instruments only the Vineland Social Maturity Scale allows the calculation of a social age and age-related social maturity quotient. The others give individual profiles and should not be regarded as psychometric tests.

Test of language development

Testing the level of language development and looking for language abnormalities is a crucial part of the psychological assessment of severely retarded children.

The Peabody Picture Vocabulary Test (Dunn, 1959)
This test is presented in the form of a booklet. Each page has four pictures. The tester says a word and the child has to point to the corresponding picture. The number of correct responses is counted and the child is also rated for rapport, speed of response, verbalization, attention span, attentiveness, guessing and for pauses before responding. It should be noted that the child has only four different pictures from which to choose, so if he guesses he has a one-in-four chance of being correct. The test covers the age range 2 years 6 months to 18 years. There are alternative forms so that the test can be repeated at a later date without very much effect due to practice.

The original Peabody Test was standardized on American children and many of the words do not have the same frequency in an English vocabulary. An English version has been produced consisting of two tests, one for the age-range 5 years to 8 years 11 months and one for 7 years to 11 years 11 months. There is also a pre-school supplement for the age range 3 years to 4 years 11 months (Brimer and Dunn, 1966).

This test measures the size of the vocabulary of words understood by the child and not his spoken vocabulary or his ability to use language. In normal children language skills and vocabulary size usually develop together, so that the Peabody score does give some idea of general language skills. This may not be the case for mentally handicapped children, some of whom may have good vocabularies, but very limited ability to use the rules of grammar or to use language for thinking and planning. The Peabody Test therefore has only a limited place in assessing handicapped children (see Mittler, 1976).

The scores can be used to calculate mental age and IQ.

The Reynell Developmental Language Scale (Reynell, 1969)
These scales have been developed with English children and cover the age range 5 months to 6 years 1 month. The test materials consist of a set of miniature objects including small dolls, furniture, clothing, domestic and farmyard animals, plus a set of five pictures taken from the Ladybird book series illustrating the everyday activities of a family.

The scales attempt to measure two fundamental aspects of language; firstly, the process of interpreting what is heard (receptive language; comprehension) and, secondly, the ability to express ideas in words (expressive language). These are often referred to as "central" processes, meaning that they depend on the higher levels of brain activity and are *not* simply a question of hearing and speaking words.

The verbal comprehension scale, version "A", is divided into nine sections, which follow the normal pattern of development of understanding of language. Reynell has also developed a second comprehension scale "B". This was designed for physically handicapped children and requires a minimum of response from the child. It follows the same developmental stages as Scale A but it is slightly easier at the upper end of the test. Separate norms are provided for this scale.

The expressive scale is divided into three sections; these are language structure, vocabulary, and content.

The Reynell Scales gives a language age for comprehension and another for expression. A new revised edition of this test is now available (Reynell, 1977), covering the age range 5 months to 7 years.

The Illinois Test of Psycholinguistic Abilities (Kirk, McCarthy and Kirk, 1968)

The age range covered by this test is from 2 years 3 months to 9 years 3 months. It has been standardized on American children so that some of the items are unfamiliar to children in the United Kingdom. The material consists of picture-cards and a few miniature objects. The idea behind the test is that language ability can be broken down into different skills, each of which can be tested separately.

The author's method of breaking down language is arguable, but it can be useful in some children with special language problems, and as a basis for a programme of language training. However, the test can be completed only by a small proportion of severely retarded children because of its complexity.

The Illinois Test gives a language age for each sub-test and an overall language age can be calculated from the sub-test ages.

Tests of symbolic development

Mary Sheridan technique

Mary Sheridan developed a technique for making observations of the play behaviour of young children aged from 12 months to 4 years, which provides information on the acquisition of "inner language" (Sheridan, 1969).

The materials consist firstly of a series of common objects such as brush and comb, cup and spoon, and some commonly used toys; secondly of a set of miniature baby dolls, domestic animals, household objects and furniture, and a car, ship and plane.

The common objects can be used from 12 months of age onwards. The child's spontaneous reactions and manipulations of the objects are observed to see if he understands their purpose. The miniatures are used

104   J. Gould

from about 21 months of age. They are presented one by one and the child's reactions, verbalizations or gesture and miming noted. His ability to understand instructions involving prepositions, to carry out a sequence of commands and to invent and describe make-believe situations is then tested using the miniatures. The procedure cannot be used to derive any kind of score, but it is a good way of obtaining information about the development of the use of symbols.

The Symbolic Play Test

Lowe and Costello (1976) have devised a test which adopts a similar approach to that used by Sheridan, but has been standardized on normal children aged 12 to 36 months. It is therefore possible to assign a "symbolic play" age from the results of the test. It is of considerable interest to observe how elaborate is the child's play as well as the level of his understanding of the nature of the miniature objects.

(The details of psychological tests given above are based on material published in M.P. Everard (Ed.) *An Approach to Teaching Autistic Children* Oxford: Pergamon (1976), and appear by kind permission of Pergamon Press.)

References

Bayley, N. (1969). *Bayley Scales of Infant Development*. Psychological Corporation: New York.
Bondy, C., Cohen, R., Eggert, D. and Lüer, G. (1971). *Testbatterie für geistig behinderte Kinder* (TBGB). (Hrsg. K. Ingenkamp). Beltz: Wernheim.
Brimer, M.A. and Dunn, L.M. (1966). *English Picture Vocabulary Test* (2nd edn). National Foundation for Educational Research: Windsor.
Burgemeister, B.B., Hollander Blum, L. and Lorge, I. (1972). *Columbia Mental Maturity Scale* (3rd edn). Harcourt Brace Jovanovich: New York.
Churchill, D.W. (1978). *Language of Autistic Children*. Winston and Sons: Washington.
DeMyer, M.K. (1978). *Parents and Children in Autism*. Winston and Sons: Washington.
Doll, E.A. (1953). *The Measurement of Social Competence. A Manual for the Vineland Social Maturity Scale*. Educational Test Bureau: Washington.
Dunn, L.M. (1959). *Peabody Picture Vocabulary Test*. American Guidance Services: Minneapolis.
Francis-Williams, J. and Yule, W. (1967). The Bayley infant scales of mental and motor development: an exploratory study with an English sample. *Dev. Med. Child Neurol.* **2**, 391–401.
Gould, J. (1976). Language, development and non-verbal skills in severely retarded children: An epidemiological study. *J. ment. Defic. Res.* **20**, 129–146.
Gould, J. (1977). The use of the Vineland Social Maturity Scale, the Merrell-Palmer Scale of Mental Tests (non-verbal items) and the Reynell Developmental Language Scales with children in contact with the services for severe

mental retardation. *J. ment. Defic. Res.* **21,** 213–226.

Gunzburg, H.C. (1974). *The Primary Progress Assessment Chart of Social Development.* S.E.F.A. Publications: Birmingham.

Kirk, S.A., McCarthy, J. and Kirk, W.D. (1968). *Illinois Test of Psycholinguistic Abilities* (revised edn.). University of Illinois Press: Urbana.

Leiter, R.G. (1952). *Leiter International Performance Scale.* C.H. Stoelting Co.: Chicago.

Lowe, M. and Costello, A.J. (1976). *Manual for the Symbolic Play Test (experimental edn).* National Foundation for Educational Research: Windsor.

Mittler, P. (1976). Assessment for language learning. In: Berry, P. (ed.) *Language and Communication in the Mentally Handicapped,* pp. 5–35. Edward Arnold: London.

Nihira, K., Foster, R., Shellhaas, M. and Leland, H. (1969). *AAMD Adaptive Behaviour Scale.* American Association on Mental Deficiency: Washington.

Nihira, K., Foster, R., Shellhaas, M. and Leland, J. (1974). *AAMD Adaptive Behaviour Scale, Revision.* American Association on Mental Deficiency: Washington.

Raven, J.C. (1956). *Standard Progressive Matrices* Revision. H.K. Lewis: London.

Raven, J.C. (1960). *Guide to using the Coloured Progressive Matrices.* H.K. Lewis: London.

Reynell, J. (1969). *Reynell Developmental Language Scales.* National Foundation for Educational Research: Windsor.

Reynell, J. (1977). *Reynell Developmental Language Scales (Revised).* National Foundation for Educational Research: Windsor.

Schopler, E. and Reichler, R.J. (1979). *Individual Assessment and Treatment for Autistic and Developmentally Disabled Children (Vol. 1), Psychoeducational Profile.* University Park Press: Baltimore.

Sheridan, M.D. (1969). Playthings in the development of language. *Health Trends* **1,** 7–10.

Stutsman, R. (1931). *Mental Measurement of Pre-School Children.* World Book Company: New York.

Taylor, J. (1976). Language problems and a method of assessment and teaching. In: Everard, M.P. (ed.): *An Approach to Teaching Autistic Children,* pp. 99–119. Pergamon: Oxford.

Warren, S.A. (1977). Using tests to assess intellectual functioning. In: Mittler, P. (ed.): *Research to Practice in Mental Retardation, Vol. II, Education and Training,* pp. 3–11. University Park Press: Baltimore.

Wechsler, D. (1949). *Wechsler Intelligence Scale for Children.* The Psychological Corporation: New York.

Wechsler, D. (1955). *The Manual for the Wechsler Adult Intelligence Scale.* The Psychological Corporation: New York.

Wechsler, D. (1967). *The Manual for the Wechsler Pre-School and Primary Scale of Intelligence.* The Psychological Corporation: New York.

Wechsler, D. (1974). *The Manual for the Wechsler Intelligence Scale for Children – Revised.* The Psychological Corporation: New York.

Wing, L. and Gould, J. (1978). Systematic recording of behaviours and skills of retarded and psychotic children. *J. Autism Child. Schizo.* **8,** 79–97.

World Health Organisation (1967). *Manual of the International Statistical Classification of Deseases, Injuries and Causes of Death. 8th Revision.* WHO: Geneva.

Yule, W. Berger, M. Butler, S., Newham, V. and Tizard, J. (1969). The W.P.P.S.I.: An empirical evaluation with a British sample. *Br. J. Educ. Psychol.* **39,** 1–13.

7 Psychometric tests and the need to assess abilities in planning special educational programmes for the mentally retarded

R. KORNMANN

Heidelberg Teachers' College, Heidelberg, FRG

Ysseldike and Salvia (1974) differentiate between two theoretical models, which build the basis for diagnostic–prescriptive teaching in special education:

(1) the ability training approach, and
(2) the task analysis viewpoint.

The results of psychometric tests are particularly important for the first approach. I for my part have worked with this approach over a relatively long period of time: however, during recent years, I have found it necessary to reconsider this concept. I should like to discuss three theoretical aspects of special education which bear upon the question. The second is based upon the first, and the third upon the second:

(1) a general definition for the word "handicap";
(2) goals and methods of advancing development;
(3) the diagnostic axioms and methods.

A new concept of the definition of handicap

The word "handicapped" is generally used today as a label which defines negative deviations of individual characteristics from certain norms. This meaning can also be found in most modern scientific treatises. Certainly such definitions are not wrong: they are indeed very pragmatic, but by the same token also quite problematic. A whole series of controversial questions present themselves. For example:

(1) which individual characteristics were chosen to describe the state of being handicapped? Why were these characteristics chosen instead of others? Who stipulated the selection of these terms? Whose interests are promoted by such selection?

The theoretical and practical justification of these questions can more easily be understood if we consider the following anomaly: in the Federal Republic of Germany we find some forms of handicap which are unknown in many countries.

(2) How are norms and their cut-off positions determined? For what reason were these cut-offs set at a particular level?

Obviously it is of great importance whose interests are served by decisions. Again an example can serve to clarify this point. Within the last few years we find here in the Federal Republic that an ever increasing number of persons with severe forms of retardation are schooled and trained, whereas in former years these same persons would have been considered nursing cases, totally dependent on care, for whom logically no steps could be taken, either pedagogically or in a therapeutic context, to alleviate the situation.

These examples illustrate the point that it is very necessary to search for satisfactory theoretical definitions. I for my part find a better alternative in the marxist concept of special education as postulated and developed in the Federal Republic especially by Jantzen (1978; 1979).

For the problems which are taken into consideration in this chapter I find the following postulates of fundamental importance:

(a) The word "handicap" is to be defined as a deranged relationship between a person and his material and social environment.

(b) An equitable relationship exists between a person and his environment, when the individual is in a position to take action in order to realize certain personal goals.

(c) Active intercommunication with nature is a specific human characteristic. Among all creatures only human beings are capable of changing and modifying their environment by means of planned activity with individual aims. These variations must be considered products. Their manifold forms (such as tools, cars, techniques, literature, mathematics, art, principles) develop slowly over a period of time in the history of mankind and were handed down from generation to generation, where they were developed and augmented. They are accepted as "social knowledge" or "cultural heritage".

(d) All people are confronted again and again with parts of this cultural tradition in their real environment. Considering the catalogue of learning possibilities, we find here all learning opportunities for each and every individual, so to say programmed: an individual can learn only that with which he is confronted.

(e) Personal development in the ontogenetic sense can progress only if stimulation and new experiences are constantly provided. An individual alters through each newly developed ability, with every unfolded skill and every new assimilated knowledge he gains. These changes are not discernible as isolated characteristics and cannot be understood as such. On the contrary, they are changes in the individual's relationship to his environment. With growing competence in abilities, skills and knowledge the individual gains a position from which he can master new, more difficult tasks. In this manner he wins more and better possibilities to control and direct his environment, his situation in life, reality as it presents itself to him. Thus he gains greater freedom from external pressures, he becomes less dependent on others, in short: his personality can — as, indeed, is prescribed in the constitution of the Federal Republic — be freely developed.

(f) On the other hand a deranged relationship between an individual and his environment can be defined as a discrepancy in the act of learning or in learning processes. Jantzen preferred here the term "isolation": that is, isolation from the principally available possibilities to assimilate a cultural heritage.

(g) Isolating configurations, handicaps in learning, occur where the individual is permanently confronted with tasks which conform neither to his needs nor to the level of his abilities, skills, and knowledge. In particular there are three characteristics of tasks which can — in conjunction with the personality of the individual — lead to handicaps in the process of assimilation.

  (i) The content of the task remains obscure to the individual; he is not able to grasp the situation; he finds no meaning for himself in the task and can fathom neither its results nor the significance it may have for him.

  (ii) The task is too difficult for the individual. He can use previously acquired abilities, skills, and knowledge neither on his own nor with the help of others. He is completely overwhelmed and unable to derive benefit in terms of learning.

  (iii) The task is too easy for the individual. Its mastery requires abilities which he has long had at his disposal and can use without effort; which can be considered almost automatic. He is posed no challenge and lacks the necessary stimulus to acquire new skills.

This interpretation of the term "handicap", which defines it in relation to given tasks, and this always in relation to the level of individual development, make the questions noted at the beginning of this chapter meaningless. Some of Jantzen's critics (e.g. Bleideck, 1978) appear to think that specific influences — as for example organic noxae, or aspects of the social macro- or microenvironment— have not been taken into consideration. This interpretation is totally false. The effects of these influences concern not only the individual, but also the complex relationship which develops between a person and his real-life situation. Such relationships can be recognized, comprehended and analysed. Here we have the source of direct and practical concepts for pedagogic and therapeutic work, which will be dealt with in the following section.

Alternative goals and methods of prescriptive teaching

According to the traditional understanding of the term "handicap", we find that the goals of prescriptive teaching were derived from the comparison of individual characteristics with standard norms. Some institutions, for example, follow a concept by which a handicapped individual is trained specially in those skills in which he shows little disparity compared with so-called normal people, with the aim of making the handicapped person relatively normal in respect of certain characteristics. Other institutions prefer to concentrate on those skills which appear to be extremely weak when compared with intra- and inter-individual norms; in this way they attempt to achieve a broader, more general level of ability. Such theoretical approaches, which are based on traditional interpretation of the term "handicap", provide no indication as to which *methods* of education are required.

Such goals are questionable and the theoretical basis for the methodical procedure is inadequate. Jantzen's theory is not affected by this kind of inadequacy. The theory proposes that the learner be confronted with tasks which enable him to master independently the concrete problems of everyday life. The learning activities should lead to results which are of direct use to the individual. The learner should be able, even before the act of learning begins, to anticipate how and why and for what reasons these skills are important to him and how he can apply them. Further, after he has completed a learning process, he should be able to experience in a concrete situation that he can master that situation and thus that what he has learned is useful to him. Practical application and control of acquired skills represents the most effective form of training.

These facts have been recognized not only by marxist-oriented scientists (Galperin, 1969); psychologists such as Piaget (1966) and Bruner (1971) developed similar concepts. According to their theories of development the comprehension of objects and circumstances occurs step by step. The lowest step deals with activities with concrete objects— that is to say activities which can be directly observed and therefore are called "outer activities". "Inner activities", which would be the highest step in a learning process, include those which deal with symbols and thought processes: that is to say, they can be recognized only through their results. This developmental model appears to be valid for ontogenesis as well as phylogenesis in human development. Probst (1978) has shown how the various steps or levels of psychical representation described by these different authors relate to one another (cf. Table 1).

Activities on a higher step or level of a psychical representation can only be successful when the activities carried out on the directly preceding step were fully mastered. For prescriptive teaching this implies that the difficulty of the chosen task must be directly proportional to the level of intellectual development. However, this is only one essential point.

The other point, which Probst (1979) particularly stresses, deals with the grade of complexity of a problem: tasks with simple structures are easier to solve than tasks with more complex structures. Probst's (1979) scheme for the progression of individual cognitive development includes both these aspects as shown in Fig. 1.

Much of the content of learning and teaching can be understood in terms of the tasks. Usually both dimensions, i.e. representational level and grade of complexity, are manifest. This type of task-analysis permits successive steps in learning, which neither overwhelm the individual nor are too easy for him. The tasks must lie within the "zone of next

Table 1 Steps of psychic representation of objects and circumstances

Steps	Bruner	Galperin
Symbolic–abstract	Symbolic representations by language, concepts, rules, systems of symbols, digital signs	Intellectual activities with inner, shortened, speechless language Outer language for itself, inner, yet unfolded speaking
Perceptual, pictorial, representational, outer language	Iconic representation by graphics, models, pictorial mental images	Outer language, spoken during activity
Concrete acting	Enactive representation, the object being represented by corresponding acts and movements	Materialized acting, concrete handling and manipulations with the object

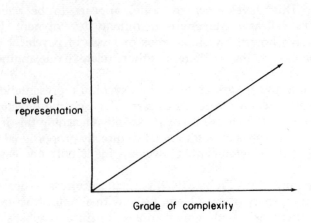

Fig. 1. Progression of individual cognitive development.

development", neither beneath it nor above. As a rule, the "zone of next development" circumscribes those tasks which the pupil cannot master alone— that is, without the help of a teacher or a model— despite the fact that he possesses all prerequisites. Tasks which meet the criteria set by the "zone of next development" avoid learning handicaps. Accordingly the teacher or therapist must ascertain the developmental level of the learner in relation to the object of learning. This point is further discussed in the next section.

Modern concepts and methods of diagnosis

Traditional psychometric diagnosis in the field of special education and therapy is used to define individual deviations in certain personality characteristics. It not only offers a definition for, it actually produces handicaps as a result of the interpretation of the term "handicap" as one understands it today (see the first section of this chapter). The theory which is the basis of this type of diagnosis deals with human abilities, skills, and knowledge and their development, isolated from the concrete demands with which an individual is confronted in his lifetime. This has two important practical consequences.

(1) Even with tests known to have a relatively high validity, it is in individual cases by no means certain that the tasks specified by the test really correspond to those demands which the person under investigation fails to meet in his real-life situation. On the basis of

such test results, he could be trained in skills which in fact would be of little value in meeting the demands of everyday life, whereas precisely those skills and abilities which are of primary importance for the individual's adjustment to his social environment would not be assessed by the test procedure and hence would not be catered for in the remedial programme.

(2) Even if the requirements of the test procedure do in fact correspond more or less to the individual's real-life situation, the results do not in themselves provide any information as to why certain specific tasks can be achieved and others not. Precisely this information, however, is essential in the planning of remedial measures for the individual.

Contradictions of this type become more clear, when traditional methods are compared with alternative diagnostic concepts, based upon the performance of realistic tasks and activities. Perhaps the first diagnostic concept of this type is nearly fifty years old, though still relevant and modern. The author is the Göttingen emeritus for psychology, Kurt Gottschaldt (1933), a gestalt psychologist of the "Berlin School". In his book "Der Aufbau des kindlichen Handelns" (the construction and development of child activity) he depicts the planning, carrying out, and results of psychological examinations of mentally retarded and normal children. His work aimed at the following two goals.

> firstly . . . to develop methods, which permit the recognition of the particular intellectual qualities of normal and psychically abnormal children, secondly . . . to show the essentials of primitive intellectual events and their singular structure as well as their individual causal dynamics (p. 20).

Based on his "Kritik der Testmethodik" (criticism of test methods), which can easily serve as basic knowledge for students today, the author reaches the following conclusions:

(1) The test situation should be set up in such a manner that childish needs and wishes can be met. The child himself should not merely "submit to the will of the examiner nor to his instructions" (p. 6).

(2) In the test situation the child should work productively. The situation must allow the child to act according to his own needs and goals (e.g. to build a tower with blocks, to set up a row of bricks so that they overcome a barrier, or to use tools).

(3) The test situation should allow systematic recording of the following data: which demands arise in a certain situation, to what extent these demands have already been encountered and what they signify for the child's own productive activity.

(4) Particular attention should be paid to the process and the products of activities. In particular, one can gain important insights by observing how the child proceeds.

(5) A test situation must be altered when activities are unsuccessful: for example, one may be able to help the child by adding some new components or by excluding some of the original components. Such variations in the test arrangement can demonstrate to the tester which circumstances lead the child to a successful conclusion. In projective diagnosis this methodical device is known and practiced as "testing the limits" (Klopfer and Kelley, 1942). Within the past few years it has found widespread application in the evaluation of performance tests (Schmidt, 1969; Kornmann, 1977, 1980; Schmidtke, Schaller and Becker, 1978).

Gottschaldt's concept leaves out of account some important therapeutic and pedagogical issues. For example, in which fields and with which methods can children be brought to a higher level of intellectual development? In the meantime, diagnostic techniques have been developed which are designed to promote the development of skills. This approach, known in English-speaking countries as "task analysis" (Gold, 1969), has been outlined as follows:

> This analysis divides each activity into the steps the learner must accomplish in order to be successful in the activity. All aspects of the program are directed to answering these questions:
>
> (1) What are the skills necessary to perform any given learning activity?
> (2) In what sequence must the skills be performed to be successful in the learning activity?
> (3) Can any of the skills be subdivided into further component skills?
> (4) At what level is each child successful?
> (5) How may we best help each child to move to the skill level necessary to be successful in the learning activity?
>
> (Rothenberg, Lehman and Hackman, 1979, p. 72).

To my knowledge German publications have not even begun to deal with these issues. Though I do not claim to be familiar with all existing literary sources, it is my impression that so far pragmatic points of view have predominated in relation to "task analysis", whereas the theoretical aspects have tended to be neglected.

In the Federal Republic two authors have come, on the basis of marxist personality theory, to conclusions similar to those postulated by the representatives of "task analysis". Schnotz's (1979) concept "Lerndiagnose als Handlungsanalyse" (learning diagnosis as activity analysis) is based on Hacker's (1973) Activity Regulation Theory. Elements of this concept are identical to elements of the theory which Miller, Galanter and Pribram (1960) advocate. Although Schnotz's concept is most interesting, it cannot be further considered here. Beyond the fact that it was not conceived for work with handicapped persons, it is quite similar, formally and in content, to Probst's (1979) concept, which I have already outlined. Hence one finds the following practical consequences for developmental diagnostics:

(1) Tasks which a child should master are to be structured according to representational levels and complexity, i.e., ordered in a hierarchical manner.
(2) In this structure each particular element can also be regarded as a task. Furthermore, it can be formulated as an item for the test examination.
(3) The child is examined on these items. Items or tasks which he masters without help represent abilities, skills and knowledge already learned. The "zone of next development", the next goal to be promoted, or next step in development, is derived from those items in the hierarchical structure immediately above the last item on the highest representation and complexity level which can be mastered.

How can the "zone of next development" be attained? The higher and more differentiated the development of certain abilities, the more useful and the more economical they are for an individual in the mastery of corresponding tasks. It can be assumed that many children notice this for themselves and that they make efforts to further their own advancement. A task should offer children scope to carry out certain activities on their highest possible individual level of development. The teacher or therapist should carry out the same procedure as the child, but on the next higher level, corresponding to the child's "zone of next development". For example, when a child is solving a puzzle, the therapist can voice his accompaniment (higher representational level), or he can solve the same puzzle form, using however a greater number of pieces (higher grade of complexity). In practice this usually suffices to bring about the desired effect, as various reports show (e.g. Mann, 1978).

How objective, reliable and valid are the diagnostic data which build the basis for this procedure? It is obviously not easy to evaluate a qualitative diagnostic procedure of this type by quantitative measures. In general, it must suffice to be able to note a constant advancement in development. In such instances the diagnostic approaches, methods, and results have most assuredly proven themselves not to be false.

The structure-oriented concept does disregard to some extent the questions: with which tasks is a child confronted in his everyday life?; which of these tasks has he already mastered and which not? Using this approach one can define which abilities, skills and knowledge the child should acquire next (see Kornmann, 1979). Further data are necessary for this purpose. Appropriate methods include observations in real-life situations and appropriate reports from relatives and peers and from the child himself.

References

Bleidick, U. (1978). *Pädagogik der Behinderten*. 2. Auflage, Marhold: Berlin.
Bruner, J.S. (1971). Über kognitive Entwicklung. In: Bruner, J.S. Oliver, R. and Greenfield, P. (eds): *Studien zur kognitiven Entwicklung*. Klett: Stuttgart.
Galperin, P.J. (1969). Die Entwicklung der Untersuchungen über die Bildung geistiger Operationen. In: Hiebisch, H. (Hrsg.) *Ergebnisse der sowjetischen Psychologie*. Klett: Stuttgart.
Gold, M.W. (1969). *The Acquisition of a Complex Assembly Task by Retarded Adolescents*. Children's Research Center: Urbana, Illinois.
Gottschaldt, K. (1933). *Der Aufbau des kindlichen Handelns*. Barth: Leipzig.
Hacker, W. (1973). *Allgemeine Arbeits- und Ingenieurpsychologie*. Volk & Wissen: Berlin.
Jantzen, W. (1978). *Persönlichkeitstheorie, Behindertenpädagogik, Therapie*. Pahl-Rugenstein: Köln.
Jantzen, W. (1979). Materialistische Behindertenpädagogik und Therapie. In: Probst, H. (Hrsg.): *Kritische Behindertenpädagogik in Theorie und Praxis*. Jarick: Oberbiel.
Klopfer, B. and Kelley, D.M. (1942). *The Rorschach Technique*. World Book Company: Yonkers, New York.
Kornmann, R. (1977). *Testbatterie für entwicklungsrückständige Schulanfänger* (TES). Beltz: Weinheim.
Kornmann, R. (1979). Diagnostische Handlungsperspektiven im Rahmen einer materialistischen Behindertenpädagogik. In: H. Probst (Hrsg.): *Kritische Behindertenpädagogik in Theorie und Praxis*. Jarick: Oberbiel.
Kornmann, R. (1980). *Diagnose der Testbedingungen — ein Ansatz zur Erklärung schwacher Testleistungen und zur Indikation von Förderungsmaßnahmen*. In: Stevens, L., Groot, R. and van Waesberghe, B.T.M. (eds). Verslag van het congres ter gelegenheid van het 75-jarig bestaan van de vereniging O & A, gehouden te Amsterdam mei 1978. Wolters & Noordhoff: Groningen.
Mann, I. (1978). *Schlechte Schüler gibt es nicht*. Urban & Schwarzenberg: München.
Miller, G.A., Galanter, E. and Pribram, K.H. (1960). *Plans and the Structure of Behavior*. Holt, Rinehart & Winston: New York.
Piaget, J. (1966). *Psychologie der Intelligenz*. Rascher: Zürich.
Probst, H. (1978). *Neue Ansätze zur Diagnose individueller Fähigkeiten*. Unpublished MS: Heidelberg.
Probst, H. (1979). Strukturbezogene Diagnostik. In: H. Probst (ed.): *Kritische Behindertenpädagogik in Theorie und Praxis*. Jarick: Oberbiel.
Rothenberg, J.J., Lehman, L.B. and Hackman, J.D. (1979). An individualized learning disabilities program in the regular classroom. *J. Learn. Dis.* **12**, 496–499.
Schmidt, L.R. (1969). Testing the Limits im Leistungsverhalten: Empirische Untersuchungen mit Volk- und Sonderschülern. In: Irle, M. (ed.): *Bericht über den 26. Kongreß der Deutschen Gesellschaft für Psychologie*, Tübingen 1968. Hogrefe: Göttingen.
Schmidtke, A., Schaller, Sylvia and Becker, P. (1978). *Coloured Progressive Matrices* von. J.C. Raven, J. Court and J. Raven Jr. Beltz: Weinheim.
Schnotz, W. (1979). *Lerndiagnose als Handlungsanalyse*. Beltz: Weinheim.
Ysseldyke, J.E. and Salvia, J. (1974). Diagnostic-prescriptive teaching: two models. *Except. Child.* **41**, 181–185.

8 Test procedures and other techniques for the assessment of mental handicap: problems of method

M.C. LIEPMANN

Heidelberg, FRG

As part of a combined cross-sectional and longitudinal study of mentally retarded children of school age, our research group in Mannheim is now investigating the nature and severity of physical and psychological handicap and behavioural disorder as well as of social and family problems known to influence the children's degree of handicap.

In addition to medical and psychological examination of each child, two semi-structured interviews are carried out with the parents or other primary care-givers. One of these is a German translation of the schedule for assessment of children's handicaps, behaviour and skills (HBS), developed by Wing and Gould (1978) for the British Medical Research Council, the other a family interview specially constructed for the present investigation. The decision to use this kind of research method confronted us with a number of problems which, we believe, are of more general relevance for research in this field. I shall therefore attempt to discuss some of these practical problems in a broader theoretical framework.

Nowadays, three main criteria are used to define and describe mental retardation: learning difficulties, subaverage intellectual functioning and problems of social adaptive behaviour. For the assessment of these criteria a number of different research methods may be applied, notably:

(1) psychometric tests;
(2) learning tests;
(3) direct observation;
(4) informant interviews.

Each of these approaches will be discussed briefly, in turn.

Psychometric tests

The contributions in this volume by Gould (Chapter 6) and Kornmann

(Chapter 7) deal in some detail with the advantages and limitations of psychometric test procedures. I shall therefore limit myself to two points of immediate practical relevance.

First, a large proportion of severely retarded children simply cannot be assessed by means of the available intelligence tests. This fact is hardly surprising, since the tests have been constructed in order to differentiate within the normal intelligence range and since, in the calibration, scores derived from ordinal scales are transformed in an arbitrary way to fit the model of a normally distributed variable.

Secondly, the value of IQ scores in relation to diagnosis and prognosis is relatively limited: a fact now widely recognized both among clinicians and in the field of special education.

As regards clinical diagnosis, it is important to remember that the medical classification of mental retardation on the basis of IQ scores has not produced a satisfactory standard of reliability for comparative studies, although progress is now being made in this direction. The definition of mental retardation is still based primarily on subnormal intelligence, operationalised in the psychometric criterion of the IQ and measured by the so-called intelligence tests. Among the tests most widely used for this purpose are the Stanford-Binet Intelligence Scale (Terman and Merill, 1960), Wechsler Adult Intelligence Scale (WAIS) (Wechsler, 1955), Wechsler Intelligence Scale for Children (WISC) (Wechsler, 1949), Progressive Matrices Test (PMT) (Raven, 1938, 1941, 1956) and Columbia Mental Maturity Scale (CMM) (Burgemeister et al., 1954).

The main arguments in favour of the application of psychometric tests can be summarized as follows: feasibility (in contrast, for example, to direct observation techniques); standardization and reference to population norms; objectivity and reliability. With these advantages are bound up hopes for uniformity of research techniques and for direct comparibility between the findings of different studies. This aim has not yet been achieved, because many different psychometric tests have been employed and because there is no general agreement as to where cut-off points should be fixed in differentiating between severe and mild mental retardation, or between mental retardation and learning backwardness. Comparison of frequency rates drawn from studies in different countries, for example, could lead to false conclusions.

On the basis of our research findings in Mannheim, we concluded that IQ and other psychometric tests provide no evidence of a "natural" boundary between the mildly and severely retarded groups, but that when a guideline for classification is required — as in case-identification in epidemiological surveys — the best "cut-off" seems to be at about IQ 50 (Cooper et al., 1979).

Apart from the problem of a meaningful cut-off score and the use of diverse test procedures, the chief criticism offered against reliance on intelligence tests, particularly from clinicians and remedial teachers, relates to the over-emphasis of a single score, in the form of an intelligence quotient, and to the dubious prognostic validity of such a measure (Wolfensberger, 1967; McClelland, 1967; 1973).

From the theoretical side has come the objection that the psychometric approach assumes a unimodal distribution of variables; the psychologically relevant characteristics are assumed to be stable over time and independent of the external situation. The basic axiom is that the individual's score on a test represents the sum of a "true" score and a random error. One always assumes that the tests are adequately standardized, that the scales constructed can be treated as interval scales and that the scores obtained conform to a normal distribution. In practice this may mean that a normal distribution must be forced somewhat arbitrarily onto the data (Dietrich, 1973; Gasser, 1980). The application of such "normative" tests to the mentally retarded has to be questioned, bearing in mind the theoretical and practical objections outlined briefly above, even though intelligence tests were originally developed for diagnostic and prognostic assessment of retarded children and of their school careers (Binet and Simon, 1902; 1905).

In the Federal Republic of Germany, a systematic attempt has been made, with the development of the Test Battery for the Mentally Retarded (TBGB) (Bondy et al., 1971), to retain the advantages of a standardized psychometric test procedure and at the same time to avoid the drawbacks of normative intelligence tests, standardized for the whole child population. The TBGB does not generate a single over-all score corresponding to a general intelligence factor, but instead concentrates on building a profile derived from sub-tests of relatively specific abilities, including non-verbal intelligence, passive vocabulary, fine motor functioning, gross motor coordination, attention, motivation and social maturity.

If I mention some of the limitations of the TBGB, this is in no sense intended as criticism of a pioneer achievement in this field of study, but simply because it is important to look dispassionately at the pros and cons of all the available methods. In four sub-tests of the battery which we used in our own study of a sample of 290 mentally retarded children in Mannheim, we found that the Columbia Mental Maturity Scale gave no score in 25%, the Peabody Picture Vocabulary Test in 20% and the "dotting" test of fine motor function in 25% of cases (Liepmann, 1979). Children with clinical evidence of brain damage were the most likely to be classed as "untestable" on these sub-tests. If, as the authors of the TBGB have proposed (Bondy et al., 1971, p. 31), the "untestable" children should be excluded from statistical analyses, this means that a large proportion of all those handicapped children for whose assessment the test-battery was originally intended must in effect be left out of the reckoning. Incidentally, differentiation between children who cannot perform the tests because of severely subnormal intelligence and those who cannot be tested because they are too uncooperative is by no means easy. For statistical analysis these data should be divided into "censored data" (i.e., variables where it is known only that they lie below a certain level of quantification) on the one hand, and true "missing values" on the other.

Apart from the problem of "untestable" children, the test-battery does not appear to discriminate clearly between mentally retarded and educationally backward children, especially in the main sub-test of intelligence, the Columbia Mental Maturity Scale: a point already noted by two of its authors (Lüer and Steinhagen, 1972).

In summary, one may say that with the TBGB an attempt was made to provide a measure of relatively specific abilities of mentally retarded children based on psychometric tests; to generate, rather than a single over-all score, a profile giving more information about each child and, finally, to afford a possibility of comparing individual test-scores within the population of mentally retarded children. However, the authors of the TBGB were not able to develop an instrument which conformed to the requirements of classic test theory and at the same time provided an effective way of measuring the handicaps and abilities of the more severely handicapped children.

Learning tests

In recent years the use of learning tests has been increasingly advocated as an alternative or supplement to the more conventional type of psychometric test procedure. By learning — as opposed to intelligence — tests is understood a form of procedure in which the individual child's levels of achievement in various test situations are first established, then systematic teaching methods are applied and subsequently the levels of achievement are retested to ascertain how much progress has occurred in the interval.

Well-known techniques of this kind have been described by Guthke (1969; 1974) and Budoff (1973). The latter employed for the purpose non-verbal tests such as Raven's Progressive Matrices. Sets of teaching programmes are now available, including 'DISTAR' (Englemann and Bruner, 1969; Engelmann and Carnine, 1970) and the Learning Potential Assessment Device (LPAD) (Feuerstein, 1972; Haywood et al., 1975). These techniques permit direct comparison of the child's performance at different points in time, rather than trying to establish his relative standing on a normative scale. As in certain other kinds of clinical procedure (e.g., in neuropsychological assessment), application of the method involves a form of experimental intervention, aimed at enhancing the individual's capacities (Haywood, 1975). There are now a number of such techniques available, but the majority have been developed for use with normally gifted children (Kleber, 1979).

Learning tests have an important predictive function in the field of special education (Mittler, 1973; Clarke and Clarke, 1973). They have been claimed to differentiate those children who after leaving school will be able to cope without further special help and training, and who therefore are more correctly classed as "pseudo-retarded" rather than as mentally retarded in the strict sense (Budoff, 1973). Moreover, it seems possible to distinguish, at each level of severity of handicap, between groups of children with different types of learning response.

A number of theoretical issues have still to be resolved; for example, the question as to how far patterns of learning are specific for different abilities, or to what extent formal test procedures can be replaced by "criterion" tasks which are not standardized. In general, it seems clear that the learning-test approach constitutes an important advance but that it still focuses on the assessment of children's achievements in situations that are basically artificial.

Direct observation

In contrast, direct observation techniques are designed to permit assessment of the child's behaviour and achievement in his normal daily routine. Direct observation of individuals in their natural habitat was first introduced as a research technique in animal ethology and subsequently extended to the study of young children. Today it plays an important role in behaviour therapy, especially in connection with the application of behavioural techniques to mentally retarded children (Redlin, 1974). Such methods may also be employed to check the validity of survey instruments (Rutter and Graham, 1968; Graham and Rutter, 1968; Weisber and Russel, 1971) and, more generally, when other kinds of external criterion are lacking. Not infrequently, the use of direct observation techniques forms part of a complex research design. Thus, classroom observation of the participation of pupils in discussions formed part of an experimental study of behaviour modification in retarded and behaviour-disordered children (Hall and Broden, 1977).

Observational techniques can be classificed according to the relationship involved between the research worker and his subject; for example, participatory v. non-participatory, systematic v. unsystematic, or observations in the field v. observations in the experimental laboratory (Alemann, 1977). In participatory observation, the researcher himself forms an integral part of the situation or field he observes, whereas in non-participatory observation he remains outside the situation as a detached onlooker. Systematic observation is characterized by three stages (Bayer, 1974):

(1) Definition of the behaviour to be observed, in terms of type of behavioural items (verbal or non-verbal, etc.), situation in which the behaviour is to be observed, frequency and time-intervals of observation.
(2) Carrying out the observation and recording the observed items of behaviour in terms of description, classification and rating on scales, if appropriate.
(3) Analysis of the recorded data.

As in the coding of survey data, a system of classification must be available which is simple enough to be reliably applied but comprehensive enough to permit every item of behaviour to be categorized. As a rule, systematic protocols are used in conjunction with video- or sound tape recordings.

These three main stages of systematic observation are not easy to carry out completely and without error. The most important sources of error are the following:

(1) Unrepresentative selection of behavioural items, time-periods and situational contexts.
(2) Undue concentration on very small units of behaviour which are of low predictive power as regards the patterns of behaviour of the individual in real-life situations. Here it should be noted that ". . . concern with finer and finer units of behaviour does not necessarily lead to greater reliability" (Rutter and Graham, 1968, p. 574).
(3) Selective processes operating in the perception and remembering of observed behaviour.
(4) Modification of the patterns of behaviour due to the presence of the observer, which must raise doubts as to how far the "real" behaviour of individuals can ever be directly observed.

The fact that methods of direct observation, which undoubtedly offer important theoretical advantages for mental retardation research, have not been used more widely or on a larger scale than hitherto, must be attributed to their cost in time and manpower, as well as to the problems of method listed above. It appears probable that their most valuable function will continue to be as a form of cross-check and validation of less intensive methods of assessment, and in this context they may be seen as providing a valuable accompaniment to large-scale studies based on psychometric tests, informant interviews or other relatively extensive techniques.

Informant interviews

A number of questionnaires and interview schedules have been constructed for use with parents, teachers or other key informants and some of these form the basis of scales for rating "social maturity", "social adaptation" or related variables, making use of normative models and standardized calibration in the same way as intelligence tests. Among the best-known such instruments are the Progress Assessment Charts (Gunzburg, 1963; 1966), the Vineland Social Maturity Scale (Doll, 1953; 1964), the A.A.M.D. Adaptive Behaviour Scale (Nihira et al., 1969; 1974) and the Balthasar Scales of Adaptive Behaviour (Balthasar, 1971).

With instruments of this kind, we have moved a step away from the experimental paradigm of the psychometric test. Judgments concerning the specific abilities and skills of a mentally retarded individual are made by one or more key informants, or by a research interviewer, without the individual himself being submitted to a test situation. For the criterion of general intelligence, another such as capacity for self-care is substituted, which is thought to have more immediate practical relevance.

The questioning procedure used with such scales is prescribed by a structured schedule, so that question and answer conform basically to a stimulus-response model and the possible responses are pre-coded. In practice, however, the use of single questions as standard stimuli may give rise to serious difficulties; indeed it can wreck an investigation if the questions are too formally worded and bear little relation to the everyday speech and vocabulary of the informants (Atteslander and Kneubühler, 1975).

All methods of assessment based on a normative, standardized approach make the assumption that the characteristics in question are continuously distributed in the target population. This is a questionable assumption in respect of many forms of handicap. Too little is known as yet about the distribution of various forms of developmental lag and behavioural abnormality among both mentally retarded and normal children. There is therefore an open question as to how far scaling techniques and standardization are appropriate and how far division into categories is more suitable, bearing in mind that these two alternatives are not mutually exclusive (Cooper and Liepmann, 1980).

Some of these problems can be overcome by the use of a more flexible "semi-structured" type of interview technique, in which the findings depend to a large extent on the clinical experience and judgment of the individual investigator. With the help of such semi-structured interviews — of which the Children's Handicaps, Behaviour and Skills Schedule (HBS) of Wing and Gould (1978) may be taken as an example — it is possible to gain information on the adaptive behaviour, individual abilities and skills of the child, as well as on any behavioural disorders. Similar techniques can be used to assess social and family characteristics of kinds known to influence the severity of handicap and the behaviour of children (Rutter, Graham and Yule, 1970; Rutter and Quinton, 1978).

Like the TBGB and the various social maturity measures I have mentioned, the HBS-Schedule is thus designed to provide information of immediate practical relevance for prognosis and management of the child. It has, however, the additional advantage of flexibility, since the questioning can be modified by means of alternative formulations and probe-questions, to meet the requirements of each interview situation and each type of informant. The technique assumes that the interviewer is versed in the problems of mentally retarded children and has undergone an intensive initial training in the use of the instrument. It has been shown that, given these conditions, a high standard of reliability can be achieved, as measured by inter-rater agreement (Wing and Gould, 1978; Ort and Liepmann, 1980).

The basis of our reliability study in Mannheim comprised 15 interviews with mothers of mentally retarded children attending a special school in a small town nearby. The interview was carried out in each instance in the child's home with the mother acting as primary informant. Two research workers took turns in acting as interviewer and observer and made their scores independently of one another.

In view of the small sample size, the results of this study can be interpreted only as preliminary trends; they are nonetheless encouraging as regards the level of the inter-rater agreement attained. According to the operational criteria used, agreement was good in well over 90% of all items. The schedule appeared to be of great value for mental retardation research (for a detailed discussion, see Ort and Liepmann, 1980).

Much more difficult is the assessment of validity of information provided by key persons — in this instance by the mothers — about the handicaps and behaviour of children (Brown and Rutter, 1966; Rutter *et al.*, 1970). As a first approach to this problem, we have compared the responses of the mothers on questioning with those given by the children's class-teachers in reply to the same schedule. Direct comparison between mothers' and teachers' judgments was deemed possible in respect of 65% of all items contained in the schedule; the remaining 35% concern aspects which, in our opinion, cannot be observed reliably and consistently both at home and at school. For the 83 items included in the analysis, the general level of agreement between mothers and teachers proved relatively low. Using the same operational criteria as in the earlier part of the study, we found good reliability for 44 items (53·0%) and acceptable reliability for altogether 65 items (78·3%).

The criteria here applied were fairly stringent — involving perfect agreement on 9- or 10-point scales. However, when the ratings based respectively on mothers' and teachers' information were compared by means of rank correlation, the values obtained were also relatively low. The level of agreement was not satisfactory for any sub-group of items, though on average rather better for the "developmental" items than for those relating to deviant behaviour.

While a high standard of agreement between mothers and teachers would not in itself prove the correctness of information obtained from either, a finding of low agreement between these two groups of informants must throw some doubt on the validity of the method.

It is not yet clear whether our findings are in general worse in this respect than those reported by Wing and Gould (1978), since different methods of estimating inter-rater agreement have been applied in the different studies. Most workers in this field of research have reported rather poor agreement between parents and teachers in their ratings of children's behaviour (Mitchell and Shepherd, 1966; Rutter et al., 1970), so that in the general context the Mannheim findings are not notably discordant. It seems probable that more refined techniques, including direct observation of groups of children or special training of selected teachers in the research technique, will be necessary for further studies of validity.

In passing it may be mentioned that the problem of validity — here illustrated by low agreement between different informants — cannot be a result of the flexibility of the technique, because it presents with equal force when highly structured questionnaires, or even psychometric tests, are used (Friedrichs, 1973; Holm, 1976; Alemann, 1977; Halpern, 1977). A large part of the variance is presumably due, therefore, not to informer-bias or interviewer-error, but to the fact that the child's behaviour is in large measure situationally determined and, for example, different at home and at school. This point is obviously of direct relevance to the psychometric-normative approach, which assumes that the relevant psychological characteristics are independent of the test-situation.

The problems of construction of scales are basically similar for semi-structured and fully-structured schedules: a hierarchy of levels of performance or degrees of severity must first be established for each individual item, using as far as possible developmental criteria (e.g. by comparison with norms derived from an adequate age-distribution), and the relationships between the items then explored by means of factor-analytic or related statistical techniques. Here, one is at once confronted by a general problem of this type of multivariate analysis; namely, that the identified groupings and patterns may prove difficult to interpret in terms useful for diagnosis, prognosis and other kinds of practical application.

Conclusion

This brief review of some problems of method and interpretation posed by different assessment techniques serves to emphasize the importance for clinical investigation of using a combination of such techniques: psychometric tests, informant interviews and direct observation of the child in his normal environment. Only in this way can a rational basis for therapeutic and remedial programmes be provided.

In extensive surveys, such as the kind of epidemiological research we are undertaking, only a limited number of methods of assessment can be applied to the whole sample. From the experience so far gained, we consider that both psychometric tests and informant interviews should be carried out whenever possible. A battery of psychometric tests is required, which has been constructed and standardized with the problems of the mentally retarded in mind and which yields a profile of abilities, rather than an overall score. Interviews should be carried out with key informants; they should be based on "guided" or semi-structured interviews and should be administered by specially-trained interviewers.

To some extent, opinions and attitudes on these questions tend to differ with the professional group concerned. Psychologists have tended to concentrate on the theoretical aspects of measurement and to be less concerned with the practical consequences for the child and his family. Criticisms of conventional psychometric tests has come largely from persons concerned with the practical problems of education, training and care — remedial teachers, residential staff, etc. The search for reliable and valid assessment techniques may be anticipated to lead to a closer cooperation between these various professional groups and ultimately to a closer integration of theory and practice in the mental retardation field.

Acknowledgement

The research project on mentally retarded children in Mannheim, referred to in this chapter, is supported financially by the German Research Association (Deutsche Forschungsgemeinschaft) and forms part of Special Research Programme (Sonderforschungsbereich) 116, Psychiatric Epidemiology, of the University of Heidelberg.

References

Alemann, H.v. (1977). Der Forschungsprozess. Eine Einführung in die Praxis der empirischen Sozialforschung. Teubner Studienskripten: Stuttgart.

Atteslander, P. and Kneubenbühler, H.U. (1975). Verzerrungen im Interview — zu einer Fehlertheorie der Befragung. Studien zur Sozialwissenschaft. Westdeutscher Verlag: Opladen.

Balthasar, E.E. (1971). The assessment of adaptive behaviour. In: Primrose D.A.A. (ed.): Proceedings of the second Congress of the International Association for the Scientific Study of Mental Deficiency, pp. 566–570. Polish Medical Publishers: Warsaw.

Bayer, G. (1974). Verhaltensdiagnose und Verhaltensbeobachtung. In: Kraiker, Ch. (ed.): Handbuch der Verhaltenstherapie. Kindler Verlag: München.

Binet, A. and Simon, Th. (1905). Sur la nécessité d'établir un diagnostic scientifique des états inférieurs de l'intelligence. Année Psychol. 11, 163–190.

Binet, A and Simon, Th. (1908). Le développement de l'intelligence chez les enfants. Année Psychol. 14, 1–94.

Bondy, C., Cohen, R., Eggert, D. and Lüer, G. (1971). Testbatterie für geistig behinderte Kinder (TBGB). (Hrsg. Ingenkamp K.). Beltz: Weinheim.

Brown, G.W. and Rutter, M.L. (1966). The measurement of family activities and relationships. A methodological study. Hum. Rel. 19, 241–263.

Budoff, M. (1973). Learning potential and institutional discharge status among young adult school-age-defined educable mentally retarded. Progress Report. US Dept. of Health, Education and Welfare: Washington.

Burgemeister, B.B., Blum, L.H. and Lorge, J. (1954). The Columbia Mental Maturity Scale, Manual. World Books: Yonkers on Hudson, New York.

Clarke, A.D. & Clarke, A.M. (1973): Assessment and prediction. In: Mittler, P.J. (ed.): Assessment for Learning in the Mentally Handicapped, pp. 23–47. Churchill Livingstone: Edinburgh & London.

Cooper, B. and Liepmann, M.C. (1980). Epidemiologie psychischer Störungen. In: Baumann, U., Barbalk, H. und Seidenstücker, G. (Hrsg.): Klinische Psychologie. Trends in Forschung und Praxis. Huber-Verlag: Berlin.

Cooper, B., Liepmann, M.C., Marker, K. and Schieber, P.M. (1979). Definition of severe mental retardation in school-age children; Findings of an epidemiological study. Soc. Psych. 14, 197–205.

Dietrich, R. (1973). Psychodiagnostik: Grundlagen und Probleme. Reinhardt-Verlag: München.

Doll, E.A. (1935). The Vineland Social Maturity Scale. Train. sch. Bull 32, 1–7; 25–32; 48–55; 68–74.

Doll, E.A. (1953). The measurement of social competence. A manual for the Vineland Social Maturity Scale. Educational Publishers: Minneapolis.

Engelmann, S. and Bruner, E.C. (1969). DISTAR Reading: An instructional system. Science Research Associates: Chicago.

Engelmann, S. and Carnine, D. (1970). Arithmetic: An instructional system. Science Research Associates: Chicago.

Feuerstein, R. (1972). Cognitive assessment of the socioculturally deprived child and adolescent. In: Cronbach, L.J. and Drenth, P. (eds): Mental Tests and Cultural Adaptation. Monton: The Hague.

Friedrichs, J. (1973). Methoden empirischer Sozialforschung. Rowohlt Taschenbuch Verlag: Reinbek bei Hamburg.

128   M.C. Liepmann

Gasser, Th. (1980). Personal communication.

Graham, P. and Rutter, M. (1968). The reliability and validity of the psychiatric assessment of the child: II. Interview with the parent. *Br. J. Psychiatry* **114**, 581–592.

Gunzburg, H.C. (1963). *Progress assessment charts*. N.A.M.H.: London.

Gunzburg, H.C. (1966). *The primary assessment of social development*. SEFA (Publications) Ltd: Birmingham.

Guthke, J. (1969). Lernfähigkeit und Leistungsdiagnostik. *Probleme und Ergebnisse der Psychologie* **27**, 25–48.

Guthke, J. (1974). Zur Diagnostik der intellektuellen Lernfähigkeit. Berlin VEB Verlag der Wissenschaften: Berlin. 2. Auflage.

Hall, R. and Broden, M. (1977). Helping teachers and parents to modify behaviour of their retarded and behaviour-disordered children. In: Mittler, P. (ed.): *Research to Practice in Mental Retardation*, Vol. 2, Education and Training. University Park Press: Baltimore.

Halpern, A.S. (1977). Testing social and prevocational awareness of retarded adolescents and adults. In: Mittler, P.J. (ed.): *Research to Practice in Mental Retardation*, Vol. 2, Education and Training. University Park Press: Baltimore.

Haywood, H.C., Filler, J.W., Shifman, M.A. and Chatelanat, G. (1975). Behavioral assessment in mental retardation. In: McReynolds, P. (ed.): *Advances in Psychological Assessment*, Vol. 3. Jossey-Bass: San Francisco.

Haywood, H.D. (1977). Alternatives to normative assessment. In: Mittler, P.J. (ed.): *Research to Practice in Mental Retardation*, Vol. 2, Education and Training. University Part Press: Baltimore.

Heber, R. (1959). A manual on terminology and classification in mental retardation. *Am. J. Ment. Defic.*, Monograph Suppl., No. 2.

Holm, K. (1976). Die Gültigkeit sozialwissenschaftlichen Messens. In: Holm, K. (ed.): *Die Befragung*, Vol. 4, pp. 123–133. Franke Verlag: München.

Kleber, E.W. (1979). Tests in der Schule. Verlag Ernst Reinhard: München, Basel.

Liepmann, M.C. (1979). *Geistig behinderte Kinder und Jugendliche. Eine epidemiologische, klinische und sozialpsychologische Studie in Mannheim*. Verlag Hans Huber: Bern, Stuttgart, Wien.

Lüer, G. and Steinhagen, K. (1972). Probleme der Differenzierung im Subtest CMM der "Testbatterie für geistig behinderte Kinder (TBGB)". In: Eggert, D. (ed.): *Zur Diagnose der Minderbegabung*, pp. 147–151. Beltz: Weinheim.

McClelland, D.C. (1967). Die Ermutigung zur hervorragenden Leistung. In: McLelland, D.C. (ed): *Motivation und Kultur*, pp. 70–91. Hans Huber: Bern.

McClelland, D.C. (1973). Testing for competence rather than for intelligence. *Am. Psychol.* **28**, 1–4.

Mitchell, S. and Shepherd, M. (1966). A comparative study of children's behaviour at home and at school. *Br. J. Educ. Psychol.* **36**, 248–254.

Mittler, P.J. (1973). Purposes and principles of assessment. In: Mittler, P.J. (ed): *Assessment for Learning in the Mentally Handicapped*, pp. 1–21. Churchill Livingstone: Edinburgh and London.

Nihira, K. (1975). Factorial dimensions of adaptive behavior in adult retardates. *Am. J. ment. Defic.* **73**, 868–878.

Nihira, K., Foster, R., Shellhaas, M. and Leland, H. (1974). *AAMD — adaptive behavior scale for children and adults*, 1974 revision. American Association on Mental Deficiency: Washington, D.C.

Ort, M. and Liepmann, M.C. (1980). The schedule of children's handicaps, behaviour and skills: Reliability and discrimination. In: Mittler P.J. (ed.):

Frontiers of Knowledge in Mental Retardation. Proceedings of the 5th Congress of the IASSMD. University Park Press: Baltimore. (In press).

Raven, J.C. (1941). Standardization of progressive matrices (1938). *Br. J. Med. Psychol.* **19**, 137–150.

Raven, J.C. (1956). *The Standard Progressive Matrices — A non-verbal test of a person's present capacity for intellectual activity*. H.K. Lewis: London.

Raven, J.C. (1956). *Guide to Using the Progressive Matrices (1938)*. H.K. Lewis: London.

Raven, J.C. (1958). *Guide to Using the Coloured Progressive Matrices (1947), Sets A, Ab, B*. H.K. Lewis: London.

Redlin, W. (1974). Praktische und theoretische Probleme der Verhaltenstherapie bei geistig behinderten Kindern. In: Kraiker, Ch. (ed): *Handbuch der Verhaltenstherapie*, pp. 487–513. Kinder Verlag: München.

Rutter, M. and Graham, P. (1968). The reliability and validity of the psychiatric assessment of the child: I. Interview with the child. *Br. J. Psychiatry* **114**, 563–579.

Rutter, M., Tizard, J. and Whitmore, K. (1970). *Education, Health and Behaviour*. Longmans: London.

Rutter, M., Graham, P. and Yule, W. (1969). *Neurological disorders in childhood: A study in a small community*. Heinemann: London.

Rutter, M. and Quinton, D. (1977). Psychiatric disorders — ecological factors and concepts of causation. In: McGurk, H. (ed.): *Ecological Factors in Human Development*. Elsevier: Amsterdam.

Terman, L.M. and Merill, M.A. (1960). *Stanford-Binet Intelligence Scale*, Manual for the third revision form L–M. Houghton & Mefflin: Boston.

Wechsler, D. (1949). *Wechsler Intelligence Scale for Children (WISC)*. Manual. Psychological Corporation: New York.

Wechsler, D. (1955). *Wechsler Adult Intelligence Scale (WAIS)*. Psychological Corporation: New York.

Wechsler, D. (1964). Die Messung der Intelligenz Erwachsener. Textband zum Hamburg-Wechsler-Intelligenztest für Erwachsene (HAWIE). 3. Aufl. Huber: Bern.

Weisber, P. and Russel, J. (1971). Proximity and interactional behaviour of young children to their "security blanket". *Child Dev.* **42**, 1575–1579.

Wing, L. and Gould, J. (1978). *Schedule of Children's Handicaps, Behaviour, and Skills* (2nd edn). Medical Research Council: London. (Unpublished).

Wolfensberger, W. (1968). Counselling parents of the retarded. In: Baumeister, A. (ed.): *Mental Retardation: appraisal, rehabilitation, and education*, p. 229. University of London Press: London.

Wright, H.F. (1960). Observational child study. In: Mussen, P.H. (ed.): *Handbook of Research Methods in Child Development*. Wiley: New York.

Part 4
Patterns and Profiles of Handicap in the Mentally Retarded

9 A schedule for deriving profiles of handicaps in mentally retarded children

LORNA WING

MRC Social Psychiatry Unit, Institute of Psychiatry, London, UK

Background to development of the schedule

When planning services for any group of chronically handicapped people, there are three aspects to be considered, which are in hierarchical relationship to each other. The first, and most fundamental, is the analysis of the nature of the handicaps in those for whom the services are intended, and the estimation of the prevalence of such handicaps among the total population of the area. The second is the prescription of methods of management, education and, if possible, treatment which are likely to be most effective in coping with the handicaps. The third is the organization of the services, so that the most appropriate methods of management, education and treatment are made available to all those requiring them.

Planning for the mentally retarded is particularly difficult, because the term covers a wide range of conditions that vary in aetiology, types of disability and patterns of overt behaviour. All they have in common is impairment of intellectual development and failure to acquire the skills necessary for living and working independently in adult life. To group people as mentally retarded is convenient for administrative purposes, but tends to obscure the great variety of their needs.

An epidemiological study of mentally retarded children (Wing and Gould, 1979) has been carried out in an area of south-east London, corresponding to the former Borough of Camberwell, with the ultimate aim of providing information for service planning, but was designed primarily to examine the first of the three aspects listed above — that is, the nature of the handicaps to be found among those diagnosed as mentally retarded. The word "handicap" is used here to mean the basic impairments of function due to biological causes, together with the effects these have on overt behaviour. As pointed out by J.K. Wing (1972) environmental factors such as family poverty, lack of education, and a grossly understimulating environment can also exacerbate the severity of handicap. However, among the severely mentally retarded, it is likely that the biological impairments have the most influence on the clinical picture.

The Camberwell study was concerned with all children who functioned as severely retarded, whatever the cause. For example, those with physical handicaps or sensory impairments, and those with the behaviour patterns found in early childhood psychosis, including autism, were investigated, as well as children with uncomplicated mental retardation. For this reason, it was necessary to find methods of analysing the handicaps that covered a wide range of problems.

A number of instruments are available for assessing impairments and skills and for recording overt behaviour. There are a variety of standardized psychological tests, as described in this volume by Gould (see Chapter 6) which require the co-operation of the subject. In the study of Camberwell children, it was decided to use such tests to examine the levels of visuo-spatial and language skills (Gould, 1976), but these methods did not reveal how the child actually functioned in everyday life, nor did they cover abnormalities of behaviour.

Practical and social skills are recorded on the Vineland Social Maturity scale (Doll, 1965) and the Gunzberg Progress Assessment Chart (Gunzberg, 1966), both of which are completed by interviewing an informant. Behaviour problems are included in the Wessex Social and Physical Incapacity Scale (Kushlick, Blunden and Cox, 1973). None of these was considered sufficiently detailed for the purposes of the Camberwell research, because they did not cover certain aspects of development and types of abnormal behaviour that were of relevance to the population studied.

A new instrument, the MRC Handicaps, Behaviour and Skills (HBS) Schedule was constructed. This consists of two types of item. The first deals with aspects of child development as revealed in everyday performance in areas such as mobility, self care, language, sociability, visuo-spatial skills and educational, artistic and domestic tasks; the second with abnormalities of behaviour or deviations from normal development. Much of the contents of the schedule covers the same ground as that in other scales for rating the mentally retarded. Its advantage is that it also enables information to be recorded on certain developmental and behavioural variables not included in such a comprehensive and detailed form in any other instrument in use in the field. These variables are: comprehension and use of non-verbal as well as verbal communication, social uses of language, imitation, imaginative activities and social play, echolalia, reversal of pronouns, repetitive speech, abnormal response to stimuli, stereotyped movements, repetitive routines, special fears, poor eye contact and abnormal quality of social interaction. The sections on difficult, disruptive behaviour include more types of problems than the Wessex scale. In addition such problems are considered under two headings — those that occur with awareness of their social consequences, and those that occur without such awareness. This differentiation was found to be important in relation to the individual's pattern of impairments of function.

Structure of the schedule

The HBS schedule is a semi-structured interview designed to elicit clinical information systematically, for use in assessment and diagnosis. It is not a psychometric instrument, nor a standardized questionnaire or check list, though numerical ratings are given. The aim of the interview is to elicit enough information for the interviewer to make the appropriate rating for each variable. In order to do this the informant is asked, by the use of standard introductory questions, to talk about the child's behaviour in specific situations. The interviewer structures the conversation by guiding the informant to give details relevant to the variable being rated, and then moving on to the next topic, but free descriptions and illustrative ancedotes are encouraged as aids to correct rating.

Instructions for the interviewer are incorporated in the schedule, but these are not detailed enough to allow for its general use. As with the Psychiatric State Examination (PSE) designed for work with adult psychiatric patients (Wing, Cooper and Sartorius, 1974), the HBS schedule is suitable for use only by those who are trained to administer it. It is an advantage to have had previous experience with mentally retarded, psychotic, or young normal children.

There have been two editions of the schedule. The first was described in Wing and Gould (1978). The second is constructed on the same principles as the first, but is slightly shortened and modified so that it can be applied to adolescents, and to the mildly as well as the severely retarded.

There are 31 sections, 17 covering developmental skills and 14 covering abnormalities of behaviour (see Table 1). The second edition also has two appendices, one dealing with problems relating to sexual behaviour and the other to additional psychiatric conditions. Each section contains one or more sub-sections. For example the section on "mobility" has three sub-sections, covering walking on level surfaces, walking up and down stairs and maturity of gait. That on "abnormal responses to visual stimuli" has four; namely, fascination with shiny objects, interest in watching things spinning, twisting hands near eyes and studying angles and corners.

Each sub-section is made up of a series of items. Those for developmen-

Table 1   MRC HBS Schedule. List of sections

1	Mobility
2	Skilled movements
3	Feeding
4	Washing
5	Dressing
6	Continence
7	Comprehension of speech
8	Ability to use speech
* 9	Abnormalities of speech
10	Comprehension of non-verbal communication
11	Ability to use non-verbal communication
*12	Interest in communication (verbal and non-verbal)
13	Education achievements
14	Interest in entertainment
15	Imaginative activities
*16	Abnormal imaginative activities
*17	Eye contact
*18	Social responsiveness
19	Social play
*20	Quality of social interaction
*21	Abnormal response to sounds
*22	Abnormal response to visual stimuli
*23	Abnormal peripheral stimulation
*24	Abnormal bodily movements
*25	Routines and resistance to change
*26	Behaviour problems involving limited or no social awareness
*27	Behaviour problems with social awareness
28	Practical skills
29	Initiative and perseverance
30	Level of independence
*31	Sleeping problems

Appendix
*A1	Psychiatric problems
*A2	Sexual problems

---

* These items concern abnormalities of behaviour, or deviations from normal development.

The unmarked items concern the normal sequence of development.

tal skills are arranged in a sequence following the steps of normal development. The approximate average ages at which normal children attain each of the steps are noted on the schedule. (These age norms are derived from standard works on child development, such as those of Egan, Illingworth and MacKeith (1969) and Sheridan (1977).) Each item is numbered so that the higher the number, the higher the developmental level. Thus, for each sub-section, the child can be given a numerical rating that represents the level he has reached at the time of the interview.

Items concerning abnormalities of behaviour are arranged according to the level of severity, and numbered in sequence. A low rating means that the child has the abnormality in severe form, a high rating means that the abnormality is absent. On the schedule it is suggested that behaviour over the previous month should be rated, but the time-period can be varied, depending on the purpose for which the schedule is used.

Codes for "not known" and "not applicable" are specified. The ratings for each of the sub-sections can be entered onto a coding sheet which is suitable for punching onto an 80-column punch card. The schedule requires two such cards and the two appendices can be punched onto a third.

It is possible to extract from the HBS schedule the information required to complete the Vineland Social Maturity Scale.

Reliability

For the first edition of the schedule, a study of reliability was carried out (Wing and Gould, 1978). Very high levels of agreement on the scores for each sub-section were obtained between two trained interviewers rating the same interviews. Lower levels of agreement were found between parents and professional workers describing the same child, but in different environments (for example, home and school). When section scores were derived from sub-section ratings and collapsed into 3-point scales, acceptable levels of agreement were obtained. These were better for the items concerned with developmental skills than for those concerned with behavioural abnormalities.

The disagreements between informants were partly due to variations in the children's behaviour in different situations. This applied particularly to behavioural abnormalities, since these occur intermittently and can, to some extent, be exacerbated or diminished by environmental factors. Another reason for disagreement was that informants differed in the detail and accuracy of their observations and in their ability to describe what they had seen.

In intensive studies of comparatively small groups of children, discrepancies between informants can sometimes be explained or resolved by further discussion and by direct observation of the child. This technique was used by Wing, Gould, Yeates and Brierley (1977) and by Wing and Gould (1979).

In clinical work, and also in some research studies, the contrasts between a child's behaviour and achievements in one environment as compared with another, which may be brought to light by the schedule, are of particular interest. They may indicate the type of environment and method of management that suit the child best, or the circumstances that produce problems.

The reliability of the second edition of the HBS schedule in German translation is currently being studied by Ort and Liepmann in Mannheim (see this volume, chapters 8 and 11).

Uses of the schedule

The schedule has been used for a number of different purposes. The present author and colleagues have found it helpful in clinical practice for individual assessment, for diagnosis, and for making recommendations for placement in educational or other services.

In epidemiological research it has been used to identify children with early childhood autism (Wing et al., 1976) and other forms of early childhood psychosis (Wing and Gould, 1979). Individual sections or groups of sections have been selected for analysis in various studies, such as an investigation of symbolic play in retarded and autistic children (Wing et al., 1977) and of language and communication in severe mental retardation (Gould, 1976).

From the point of view of service planning, the most important application of the schedule is for sub-grouping severely retarded children. It is, of course, possible to sub-classify the mentally retarded on a variety of different parameters. Medical aetiology and pathology, for example, are important in the search for methods of prevention and cure, but are not related closely enough to patterns of skills and overt behaviour to be useful in prescribing methods of management and education. Level of intelligence, perhaps the most widely used basis for sub-classification gives some information relevant to performance in real life, but, on its own, is insufficient for planning purposes.

The results of the study in Camberwell suggested that the various aspects of development could be impaired to differing degrees, and that profiles of level of performance in different functions could be constructed from HBS schedule ratings. Children could be sub-grouped according to the patterns of their profiles.

In theory, any of the variables examined in the schedule could have been used in the classification scheme, but, in the Camberwell study (Wing, 1981), five aspects of development were chosen, because of their special relevance to competence in daily living. These were mobility, executive motor skills, visuo-spatial skills, comprehension and use of speech, and quality of social interaction and communication. This last is the interest in the ability to take part in two-way social interaction, including understanding and using appropriate non-verbal behaviour such as facial expression, eye contact, bodily posture, and gesture.

The pattern of the profile appeared to be more important in predicting behaviour than the overall mental age or IQ. Wing and Gould (1979) found that the quality of social interaction (one of the variables the schedule was specially designed to examine), was of major importance in relation to behaviour and to educational, management and service needs. Those who were impaired in this area were repetitive and stereotyped in their activities, and had few or no imaginative pursuits. They were the most difficult group to manage, as they were not amenable to the usual forms of social control. Some were restless, destructive, aggressive or self-injuring. They needed a structured and organized environment and much supervision, in contrast to the sociable mentally retarded for whom a more relaxed regime was appropriate and who enjoyed social activities. The socially impaired had the behaviour described as occurring in early childhood psychosis, and some were classically autistic (Wing and Gould, 1979).

From the prevalence rates found in the Camberwell study, it is possible to calculate the numbers of mobile socially impaired children one could expect to find in a notional population of 250,000 people (all ages) with the same demographic and social characteristics as an inner working-class suburb of south-east London. There would be approximately 95 such children who were also severely mentally retarded, 21 who were mildly retarded and 6 in the normal range of intelligence. A similar study in Salford, a city in north-west England, gave a prevalence which was half that of Camberwell. The reasons for the differences need to be investigated, but the point to emphasize is that, in both areas, mobile socially impaired children formed a substantial minority of all those who were severely retarded.

In order to cope with children of this kind, a high staff ratio and a sufficient number of workers who are trained and experienced in understanding the handicaps and managing difficult behaviour are necessary. Units should also have adequate space, indoors and out, and enough rooms so that children can be separated from the group when they are severely disruptive in behaviour. It can be argued that specialized facilities are needed, and there is no doubt that some schools and other

140   L. Wing

units for autistic and similar children have developed a high level of expertise. Economic considerations make it unlikely that these can be provided for all, or even most such children. The educational, medical and social services for other kinds of handicaps, especially for the mentally retarded, now deal with the majority and are likely to continue to do so. The provision of extra staff, appropriate staff training, supervision from experienced professionals and concerned parents, and improvement of existing premises and equipment would make a difficult task somewhat easier. Parents of young handicapped children can be greatly helped by advice on management and teaching. Howlin *et al.* (1973) described a home-based programme for autistic children which could be adapted for use with other socially impaired children.

Within the two groups, the sociable and the socially impaired, further subdivisions could be made depending on levels of development in the other 4 variables — mobility, executive motor skills, visuo-spatial skills and speech. In general, among the sociable children the most amenable and easiest to manage were those with fairly even profiles, without marked peaks or troughs of skills.

The compilation of individual profiles from the HBS schedule, whether using the variables mentioned above, or other combinations of functions, is relevant to the question of reliability. Further studies are needed to compare the patterns of impairments derived from informants from different environments. Preliminary results from Camberwell, using the first edition of the schedule, suggest that profiles for the same individuals obtained from different informants tend to be similar in shape even if the absolute levels of the functions differ.

The HBS schedule is not a substitute for other methods of assessing mentally retarded people. It is best used in conjunction with, for example, appropriate psychological tests. Its main advantage is the scope and detail of the examination of language, social and practical skills and of abnormalities of behaviour. Its main use is in small scale intensive studies, in which the details of individual differences are of special interest.

References

Doll, E.A. (1965). *The Vineland Scale of Social Maturity: Condensed Manual of Directions.* American Guidance Service: Minnesota.
Egan, D., Illingworth, R.S. and MacKeith, R.C. (1969). *Developmental Screening 0–5 years. Clinics in Developmental Medicine No. 30,* Spastics International Medical Publications, Heinemann: London.
Gould, J. (1976). Language impairments in severely retarded children: an epidemiological study. *J. ment. Defic. Res.* **20**, 129–146.
Gunzberg, H.C. (1966). *The Primary Progress Assessment Chart of Social Development.* SEFA Publications: Birmingham.

Howlin, P., Marchant, R., Rutter, M., Berger, M., Hersov, L. and Yule, W. (1973). A home-based approach to the treatment of autistic children. *J. Autism Child. Schizo.* **4**, 308–336.

Kushlick, A., Blunden, R. and Cox, G. (1973). A method of rating behaviour characteristics for use in large scale surveys of mental handicap. *Psychol. Med.* **3**, 466–478.

Sheridan, M.D. (1973). *Children's Developmental Progress*. National Federation for Educational Research: Windsor.

Wing, J.K. (1972). Principles of evaluation. In: Wing, J.K. and Hailey, A. (eds): *Evaluating a Community Psychiatric Service*. Oxford University Press: London.

Wing, J.K., Cooper, J.E. and Sartorius, N. (1974). *Description and Classification of Psychiatric Symptoms: An instruction manual for the PSE and Catego Systems*. Cambridge University Press: London.

Wing. L. (1981). Language, social and cognitive impairments in autism and severe mental retardation. *J. Autism Dev. Disorders*. (In press).

Wing, L. and Gould, J. (1978). Systematic recording of behaviours and skills of retarded and psychotic children. *J. Autism Child. Schizo.* **8**, 79–97.

Wing, L. and Gould, J. (1979). Severe impairments of social interaction and associated abnormalities in children: epidemiology and classification. *J. Autism Child. Schizo.* **9**, 11–29.

Wing, L., Gould, J., Yeates, S.R. and Brierley, L.M. (1977). Symbolic play in severely mentally retarded and in autistic children. *J. Child Psychol. Psychiatry* **18**, 167–178.

Wing, L., Yeates, S.R., Brierley, L.M. and Gould, J. (1976). The prevalence of early childhood autism: a comparison of administrative and epidemiological studies. *Psychol. Med.* **6**, 89–100.

10 Handicaps, skills and behaviour of mentally retarded children: an epidemiological research method

A.H. BERNSEN

Paediatric Department, Municipal Hospital, Aarhus, Denmark

Introduction

Once the tendency to regard severe mental retardation as a static and insensible condition was overcome (at least by some professionals), it became obvious that the medical and psychological examination of a handicapped child should not be aimed solely at making a diagnosis. Of equal importance is the assessment of specific abilities and disabilities relevant to the functional capacities of the child in everyday life (Mittler, 1974; Haywood, 1977).

The numerous tests of formal intelligence — mostly standardized on normal populations — are of limited value in such an assessment and, moreover, the child must be amenable and cooperative in the test situation, conditions hard to secure with severely retarded children. In order to overcome such disadvantages, observational methods have been reconsidered and improved so that observations on behaviour are collected and recorded in a more systematic way (Kushlick et al., 1973; Wing and Gould, 1978). The observations may be made directly or may be reported at interview by an informant who knows the child well. Naturally, a combination of these two approaches will often be very fruitful.

Present study

An interview technique of this kind has been applied in an epidemiological survey of severely retarded children in Aarhus, Denmark and some of the findings will be presented here.

Material and methods

The sample comprises 148 children and young adults whose ages ranged between 3 years 8 months and 22 years 4 months at the time of the interview, with a mean age of 13 years 6 months. Parents — usually the mothers — and professionals (teachers, nurses or other care staff) in day-care or residential-care institutions were interviewed using the semi-structured Children's Handicaps, Behaviour and Skills (HBS) Schedule. This instrument, developed by the child psychiatrist Lorna Wing for the British Medical Research Council, has the advantage that it is specifically designed for use with retarded or psychotic children, each item containing questions which discriminate between very low levels of performance.

In this presentation a detailed description of the design of the HBS Schedule, its administration, the scoring procedures and the interpretations of the scores are omitted as this has been published elsewhere (Wing, 1980; Wing and Gould, 1978; Bernsen, 1980). It need only be mentioned that a varying number of items — from 3 to 11 — are grouped together in sections and subsections in hierarchical order following the sequence of development or degrees of severity of behaviour problems. There are 42 sections concerning developmental skills and 21 covering abnormalities of behaviour.*

In the Aarhus survey, parents were interviewed in their own homes by the author, while the interviews with professionals were carried out during their working hours by a social worker. Whenever possible, the child was also present so that a certain amount of direct observation could be taken into consideration. This procedure means that there were always two independent observations on each child.

Experiences and findings

An analysis of the findings with respect to reliability of the HBS Schedule has been reported (Bernsen, 1980). Here it need only be stated, that fairly good agreement was found between the two informants concerned with each individual child. Acceptable concordance was also revealed when the Danish results were compared with those from a similar survey in Camberwell, London (Wing and Gould, 1978). Here, attention will be focused on the interview technique and on what can be deduced from this method about the handicaps of individual children or groups of children.

In all forms of survey research, the initial approach to those persons who make up the sample is of crucial importance in securing their co-operation. Once the necessary assistance from the professionals in the mental retardation service had been secured, parents were informed

*In the first edition; the revised addition has 31 sections in all (see Chapter 9 this volume, by Lorna Wing).

about the survey by letter and asked to agree to the inclusion of their children in the study. As soon as permission was granted, the social worker carried out her interview. If the child was in residential care, the staff was asked about family contacts and whether an approach to the family would be appropriate. Most responses were positive, even if the family contacts had been sporadic for years. There were nine children with no family contacts at all. No attempt was made to approach these families, as it seemed probable that they had tried to forget their retarded children. In three instances an approach was considered inappropriate for various reasons. A further three families did not respond to letters and could not be contacted by telephone calls or home visits. Separate interviews could, however, be obtained in all these cases with two different members of the staff. Direct refusal to participate in the interviews occurred in nine families, but only four of these (with children living at home) had objections to the child being included in the survey.

Among the 171 children identified in an initial prevalence survey in the area, 14 had died before the interview study was started and two moved out of the country. This leaves 155 children and families as potential candidates for the interview study. With only four definite refusals, the response rate reached 97·4%, which is very satisfactory in this kind of survey. Cox et al. (1977) have reported a response rate of 94·1% on the Isle of Wight and 92% in an inner London borough, while Wing et al. (1977) found a much lower response rate of 82·1% in a population study on the reliability of the PSE Schedule. Three of the children living at home did not attend any day-care institution so that only the parent interview could be obtained.

The interviews

The appointments for interview with the parents were arranged whenever possible by telephone calls, but in a few instances by an introductory home visit a few days beforehand. Parents were asked when an interview would be most convenient to them, and the interviewer accepted evening visits.

It soon became clear that the term mentally retarded should not be mentioned at interview, the word handicapped being much more acceptable to parents. Later in the interview one could adopt the term or euphemism for mentally retarded preferred by the parents. It took anything from one to 2½ hours to complete the HBS Schedule, the time needed to interview the professionals being shorter as a rule than that required for the parents. The wide variation was due to a number of factors: the extent and complexity of the children's handicaps varied greatly, as did the ability of the informants to give adequate descriptions; moreover, the interviews offered a rare opportunity for the parents to talk at length about the problems of their handicapped children. In general, the duration was found to be acceptable both to the interviewer and to the informants. The problems of bias due to leading questions was overcome by a series of introductory questions in the HBS Schedule, but sometimes paraphrasing was necessary to make sure that the informant understood the meaning. Examples given in the schedule or selected as the interviewer became more experienced proved very useful. It also occurred that some items had to be re-rated as the interview proceeded and new evidence was brought to light.

For each child, a handicaps-profile can be constructed by adding the item-scores for each section and expressing this sub-total as a percentage of the total possible score in the section. These percentages or indices constitute the "landmarks" in the profile. The areas of functioning covered are: self-help, social development, communication, visuo-motor skills, activities and behaviour problems. It must be noticed that, due to built-in characteristics of the HBS Schedule, an index of 1·0 does not correspond to fully normal development in non-handicapped children.

In order to restrict the number of illustrations but still convey as much information as possible, it has been necessary to superimpose profiles from two or three children in each of the accompanying Figs 1, 2 und 3. Figure 1 shows two typical profiles of children with cerebral palsy, while Figures 2 and 3 illustrate three profiles of children with Down's syndrome and children with psychotic disorders respectively.

These profiles give a broad impression, first of the overall level of functioning of each child; secondly of the heterogeneity in levels of performance in different areas of functioning, and finally of the similarity of profiles for children from different diagnostic categories.

By demonstration of the child's handicaps profile to the parents and teachers it proved possible to help them understand whether the child's level of performance came close to his potential ability, or whether some functions were lagging behind. In the latter instance, the natural consequence would be to strengthen the efforts of training. Moreover, to emphasize the areas where the child is functioning relatively well may have a positive psychological effect on the parents' perception of his capacities, whose value should not be underestimated. In the past, parents have usually been questioned in such a way that they must report what the child is unable to do or must report only his deviant behaviours.

Though impossible to demonstrate here, as data are not yet available, it may be anticipated that the HBS Schedule or selected sections from it will also be very useful in follow-up examinations of individual children, for instance in order to evaluate the efficiency of remedial training programmes.

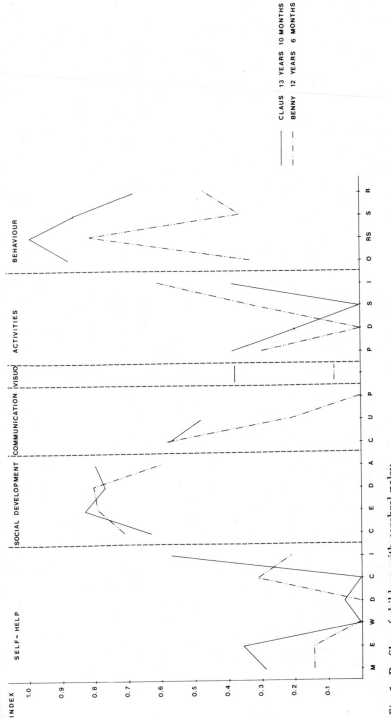

Fig. 1. Profiles of children with cerebral palsy.
Self-help: M, Mobility; E, Eating; W, Washing; D, Dressing; C, Continence; I, General independence.
Social development: C, Contact; E, Emotional; D, Destructive; A, Aggressive.
Communication: C, Language comprehension; U, Use of language; P, Pronunciation.
Activities: P, Play; D, Domestic, practical skills; S, School skills; I, Interests.
Behaviour: O, Oral (dribbling, etc.); RS, Reaction to sensory stimuli; S, Stereotypies; R, Routines.

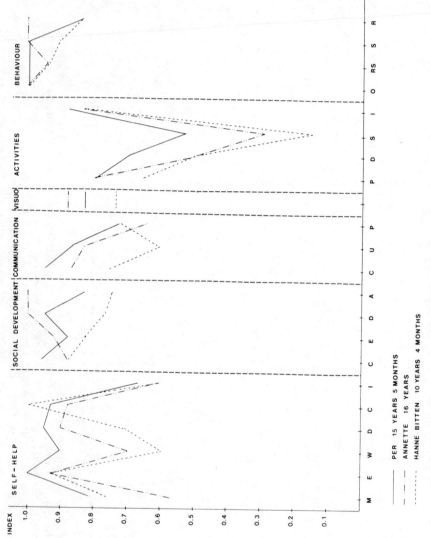

Fig. 2. Profiles of children with Down's syndrome. Key as in Fig. 1.

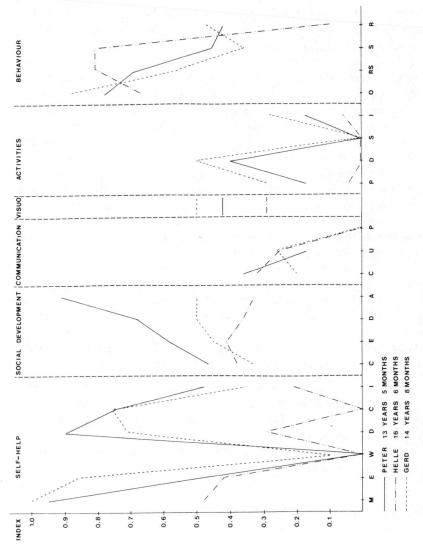

Fig. 3. Profiles of children with psychotic traits. Key as in Fig. 1.

It is well-known among professionals working with the mentally retarded that a specific behaviour may be more prevalent in certain environments than in others. This situation-specificity of behaviour may be disclosed by comparing profiles obtained in different setting.

From these examples of the potential usefulness of the HBS Schedule, we now turn to consider a problem where the schedule has already proved to be a useful instrument, namely, in the sub-classification of groups of severely retarded children.

While it is relatively simple to decide which children in a group should be classified as ambulant or non-ambulant, allocation to groups according to language ability or social responsiveness is much more complicated, since the assessment of these faculties is far more complex and difficult. By means of the ratings in the HBS Schedule and computerized analysis of the results, sub-groupings according to these more complex variables have proved possible. On the basis of clinical experience threshold values for minimal attainment were operationally defined to distinguish between major and minor handicaps in the above-mentioned areas.

In the analysis of social impairment, non-ambulant children have been excluded as their inability to walk unaided limits their possibilities of exhibiting abnormal behaviour.

Table 1 shows that out of the 106 mobile children 42% were characterized as socially impaired. As could be expected, social impairment was strongly associated with the more severe degrees of retardation ($\chi^2 = 29 \cdot 1$; d.f. $= 2;p$ <0·001), but there was no difference according to sex.

With respect to language abilities, the 148 children from the Aarhus study could be grouped as demonstrated in Fig. 4:

(1) Comprehension of speech means that the child can understand simple instructions one at a time, not dependent on context.
(2) Use of speech means that he can say 2–3 word phrases and use these meaningfully to make a request.
(3) Comprehension of gesture means the child's understanding of pointing, beckoning and exaggerated facial expression.

Table 1 Sociability according to level of retardation for 106 mobile children

	Profound	Severe	Moderate	Total
Socially impaired	21	13	10	44 (41·5%)
Sociable	3	22	37	62 (58·5%)
Total	24	35	47	106

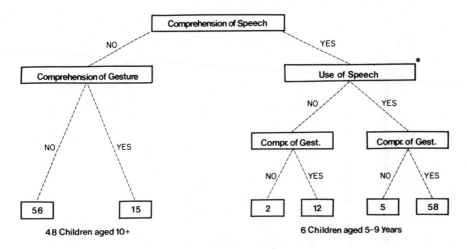

Fig. 4. Language abilities in 148 children. * One blind child could understand and use speech.

A major handicap concerning language abilities was found in 71 children (48%) and no fewer than 56 children could neither comprehend nor use speech or gesture. The majority of these children were more than ten years old when assessed. Among the 77 children with at least some language abilities there were 14 who were unable to use speech, whereas 58 children were capable of understanding speech as well as gesture and also of using speech according to the definition.

It is also possible from relevant sections in the HBS Schedule to derive a score on the Vineland Social Maturity Scale (Doll, 1965). The relationship between the Vineland scores thus obtained and the level of retardation assessed by psychological examination is demonstrated in Fig. 5.

Each level of retardation reveals a peak corresponding to the number of children whose Vineland scores fall within the interval marked on the abscissa. It can be seen that the distinction between the profoundly and severely retarded groups is more clear-cut than between the severely and moderately retarded groups on this scale of social competence. A few children in the moderately retarded group who obtained very low Vineland scores had severe psychotic behaviour disturbances which made psychological examination very difficult.

Final remarks

In adopting a dynamic concept of mental retardation, alternative

NO OF CHILDREN

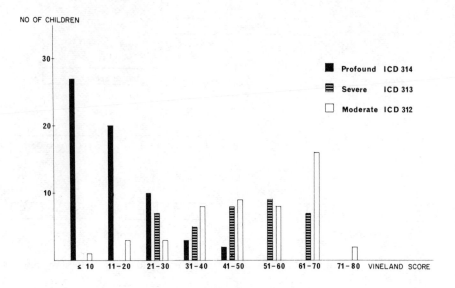

Fig. 5. Vineland score and level of retardation for 148 children.

methods of assessment have to be applied— methods that could promote constructive intervention.

Although many theoretical questions must be considered in connection with an assessment based on interviews (some of these are discussed by Liepmann in Chapter 8), experience so far has shown that the HBS Schedule is a very valuable research instrument.

It can amplify the knowledge about individual children and also to some extent about severely retarded adults. Profiles obtained from the schedule are illustrative to parents and professionals and form a good basis as guidelines for intervention. For research purposes, several subgroups of mentally retarded children can be defined to give the frequency of various abilities and characteristics. Additionally, the sub-grouping may provide a useful basis for further study of the inter-relationships between characteristics such as social responsiveness, symbolic play and language development.

The fact that good inter-rater reliability, and also fairly good agreement between different informants, were obtained in rating the handicaps of a defined sample of mentally retarded children indicates that the construction of the schedule and the instructions for its use are precise and clear enough to overcome major problems of interpretation. This conclusion is supported by the very similar distribution of handicap-profiles revealed by the use of this instrument in studies in two countries.

References

Bernsen, A.H. (1980). An interview technique in assessing retarded children: a comparative study of the reliability of the Children's Handicaps, Behaviour and Skills (HBS) Schedule. *J. ment. Defic. Res.* **24**, 167–179.

Cox, A., Rutter, M., Yule, B. and Quinton, D. (1977). Bias resulting from missing information: some epidemiological findings. *Br. J. Prev. Soc. Med.* **31**, 131–136.

Doll, E.A. (1965). *The Vineland Scale of Social Maturity: Condensed Manual of Directions.* American Guidance Service: Minnesota.

Haywood, H.C. (1977). Alternatives to normative assessment. In: Mittler, P. (ed.): *Research to Practice in Mental Retardation.* Vol. 2, *Education and Training,* pp. 11–18. University Park Press: Baltimore.

Kushlick, A., Blunden, R. and Cox, G. (1973). A method of rating behaviour characteristics for use in large scale surveys of mental handicap. *Psychol. Med.* **3**, 466–478.

Mittler, P.J. (1974). Assessment of handicapped children: some common factors. In: Mittler, P. (ed.): *The Psychological Assessment of Mental and Physical Handicaps,* pp. 343–373. Methuen: London.

Wing, J.K., Nixon, J.M., Mann, S.A. and Leff, J.P. (1977). Reliability of the PSE (9th edn) used in a population study. *Psychol. Med.* **7**, 505–516.

Wing, L. and Gould, J. (1978). Systematic recording of behaviours and skills of retarded and psychotic children. *J. Autism Child. Schizo.* **8**, 79–97.

11 Patterns of impairment in relation to psychometric test results

M. ORT

Department of Epidemiological Psychiatry, Central Institute of Mental Health, Mannheim, FRG

Introduction

A special problem in the field of epidemiological research on mental retardation is the definition of a case (Stein and Susser, 1971). The concept of mental retardation encompasses three main components: organic pathology, psychological impairment and social handicap. The organic component is related to impairment of the brain's structure or of its metabolism, to chromosomal abnormality, as in Down's Syndrome etc. The psychological impairment — predominantly expressed in intellectual deficit — means in general terms the limitation which is imposed on psychological functions by brain damage or other factors and by the individual's reaction to his limitation. The third component, the social handicap, is defined by the manner and degree in which organic and psychological factors affect the individual's performance of social roles.

These three components of mental retardation do not have a one-to-one relationship with each other: on the contrary, there are children with severe biological impairment (e.g. in cerebral palsy or occasionally in Down's Syndrome) who have little or no intellectual deficit. Conversely a large proportion of mentally retarded children (e.g. so-called "socio-culturally deprived" children) show no evidence of organic impairment. Last but not least, there are children with behaviour disorders who are socially handicapped, who live in institutions or attend special schools, but who have neither organic impairment nor severe psychological dysfunction as expressed, for example, in intelligence test scores.

During the years 1974–1977 as the first part of our investigation our research group carried out a prevalence survey of mentally retarded children, aged seven to 16, in Mannheim (Liepmann, 1979; Cooper *et al.*, 1979) in which the psychological, and to some extent the organic impairments also, were analysed.

In the second stage of the research programme we are undertaking more detailed studies of the children and their families, in order to examine the relationship of the three main components of mental retardation — organic, psychological and social — to one another.

In this chapter I shall refer only to results from a preliminary analysis of the second and third components, i.e. psychological dysfunction and social handicap. These components are operationalized by the widely-accepted definition of mental retardation by Heber (1959) for the AAMD, who integrated in it the three criteria "school achievement", "intelligence" and "adaptive behaviour". The AAMD-definition makes no mention of either the cause of mental retardation or its prognosis. This point emphasizes the outstanding importance of functional disability for the label "mentally retarded".

Aims and methods

Sample

In this stage of the research programme we are again investigating the whole population of mentally retarded children from seven to 16 years of age, whose parents are resident in Mannheim. The sample, based on a census day (30·09·78), contains in all 280 children, predominantly from a lower social class background. Findings are here reported for the first 84 children living at home (though not for those in institutions, whom we have not yet investigated in this phase of the research).

Method of investigation

Our method of data-gathering consists of five steps, as follows:

(1) First, we seek information about the retarded children from various official sources, the most important being the public health department in Mannheim;
(2) Next, we carry out a standard medical/neurological examination of the children, designed in particular to assess the probability of brain damage;
(3) Thirdly, we test the children with a number of psychometric tests from a German test battery for mentally retarded children (Bondy *et al.*, 1971). Although in the research literature there is a growing dissatisfaction with psychometric test results as the main basis for the assessment of mentally retarded children (cf. the contributions by Gould and Liepmann, Chapters 6 and 8 respectively), such tests are not being abandoned but rather are increasingly being applied in a more restricted way; for example as screening procedures to identify

groups of children with severe handicap or to estimate the probability that individual children are suffering from organic impairment (see e.g. Cooper *et al.*, 1979). As the next stage in our research programme we decided to test the hypothesis that IQ-data are useful in discriminating in an economic way between severely retarded and mildly retarded children.

(4) In a fourth step we use a German translation of the schedule for the assessment of children's handicaps, behaviour and skills, the HBS-Schedule, developed by Wing and Gould (1978), to interview the person or persons who are in closest contact with the child, normally his mother or both parents. We decided to use the HBS-Schedule for this purpose because it is particularly extensive and detailed as regards comprehension and use of both verbal and non-verbal communication and, in addition, if offers the possibility of making a profile analysis, which is of special importance for assessing the needs for care of mentally retarded children.

(5) Finally, we interview the same informants with a family interview schedule, specially constructed for this project, which is intended to assess the social problems and burdens of the family.

Aims of the preliminary analysis

This preliminary analysis of the data has been undertaken with three principal aims:

(1) To test once again the utility of psychometric test data, especially of IQ-scores, for an adequate assessment of mentally handicapped children, we correlated four psychometric measures with several variables of the HBS-Schedule, using Kendall's rank correlation coefficients.

(2) To assess an IQ of 50 as a "cut-off' score in discriminating between severe functional disability and relatively mild handicap. For this purpose, we divided our sample into two sub-groups (the one consisting of children with IQ 50 and above, the other with IQ below 50) and then looked for significant differences between the two groups in respect of their ratings on the HBS-Schedule.

(3) To examine the possibility of profile analysis. To reach this goal, we first divided the HBS-Schedule into several parts which we regarded as internally coherent and examined each of these parts by means of a factor analysis, to find out the most relevant items for each dimen-

158   M. Ort

sion*, The next step consisted in a cluster analysis of the relevant items of the different parts of the HBS-Schedule. This procedure served to identify sub-groups of children with characteristic patterns of disabilities, as a first step towards establishing the need for special education and care-provision.

Results

Correlation of HBS-ratings with psychometric test scores

The findings indicate that, for assessing the special needs of mentally retarded children, it is most useful to differentiate groups which are characterized by their behavioural and developmental profiles, rather than medical-diagnostic categories or groups defined by IQ-level: a point illustrated by the following correlational data. In Table 1 can be seen inter-correlations of IQ-score with three subtest-scores (standardized t-scores) of the test-battery.

As can be seen from Table 1, the intercorrelations between the psychometric measures are mostly high (correlations with one asterisk are significant at the 1% level, correlations with two asterisks are significant at the 0·1% level); this result is expected and well-known from the literature (e.g. Eggert, 1969).

In Table 2 can be seen the correlations of the four psychometric scores with various items of the HBS-Schedule. The psychometric measures have several significant correlations with the items of the HBS-Schedule (e.g. dressing, understanding of facial expression, use of symbolic gesture, use of scissors and three-dimensional modelling) but they lack satisfactory correlations with many other items of this instrument, which are of great importance for everyday life (e.g. mobility, bladder and bowel control during day, comprehension of speech, development of grammar, intelligibility, writing, understanding of numbers and of time and awareness of danger).

This indicates that psychometric scores (at least from the tests) are of very limited value as descriptive measures with practical relevance for the needs of individual mentally retarded children.

---

* As criteria for the termination of the extraction procedure, we defined the following in combination: Eigenvalue $\geq$ 1; factor loadings of at least 0·50; a cumulative variance-percentage of at least 70.

To get a simple structure of the factor matrix, we rotated this matrix by using the Varimax-criterion, the most common criterion for an orthogonal rotation (Harman, 1970).

Table 1   Inter-correlations of four psychometric scores

Psychometric variable	IQ	Columbia Mental Maturity Test (CMM)	Peabody Picture Vocabulary Test (PPVT)	Coloured Matrices (CM)
IQ	—			
Columbia Mental Maturity Test	0·44**	—		
Peabody Picture Vocabulary Test	0·39*	0·64**	—	
Coloured Matrices	0·31	0·56**	0·52**	—

* Significant at 1%-level; ** Significant at 0·1%-level.

IQ = 50 as cut-off score

Although the IQ, as we have demonstrated above, has only limited significance for assessment of the individual mentally retarded child, there still exists the possibility that IQ-data may be useful in discriminating between groups of severely retarded and mildly retarded children in an economic way. To test this hypothesis, we divided our sample into a group of children with IQ above 50 and a group with IQ below 50 and looked for differences between the handicaps-profiles of these two groups. Examination of the data revealed that median-differences for the "developmental" items all pointed in the same direction.

Figure 1 shows that — despite the fact that the two groups are of nearly the same chronological age — the children with an IQ of 50 and above show on all variables a substantially higher level of functioning. Analysis of the developmental items of the schedule in no instance revealed a higher median score for the group with IQ under 50.

In contrast, it is noteworthy that no significant differences were found between the two groups in respect of the behaviour abnormality items. The differences regarding the developmental sections justify using IQ 50 as a cut-off score for research purposes when it is sufficient to have significant median differences. For individual cases we can only regard such differences between the two IQ-groups as useful when there is little or no overlap. We therefore analysed the developmental age-ranges of the various sections and found that these ranges are in nearly all sections for both IQ-groups identical. As an example, Fig. 3 shows the ranges of both groups for the first four sections of the HBS-Schedule.

We must therefore conclude that, for individual assessment, treatment and care of mentally retarded children the IQ is only a very rough

Table 2 Correlations of four psychometric tests with various HBS-items

Rating of performance level (HBS-Schedule)	No. of item	IQ	Columbia MMT	Peabody PVT	Coloured Matrices
Walking	77	0·23	−0·25	−0·21	0·01
Maturity of gait	79	0·22	0·10	−0·00	0·38*
Manual dexterity	81	0·26	0·01	−0·20	0·18
Feeding	83	0·09	0·21	0·20	0·35*
Dressing	88	0·25	0·51**	0·38*	0·35*
Hair brushing	91	0·21	0·42*	0·29	0·19
Comprehension of speech	96	0·06	0·05	0·05	−0·00
Development of grammar	98	0·22	0·33	0·18	0·26
Understanding of gestures	107	0·21	0	0	0
Understanding of facial expression	108	0·36*	0·24	0·28	0·35*
Copying gestures	111	0·05	0·18	0·14	0·35*
Use of symbolic gesture	112	0·25	0·41*	0·37*	0·12
Willingness to communicate	114	0·17	0·17	0·06	0·06
Use of scissors	117	0·54**	0·12	0·06	0·06
Three dimensional modelling	118	0·41*	0·34*	0·36*	0·15
Painting	121	0·37*	0·10	0·09	0·07
Colouring inside lines	122	0·32	0·28	0·27	0·22
Reading	127	0·34*	0·24	−0·09	−0·07
Writing	128	0·24	0·18	−0·02	0·01
Arithmetic	129	0·20	0·28	−0·03	0·08
Level of social play	145	0·23	0·20	0·28	0·21
Quality of social interaction	147	0·11	0·26	0·18	0·11
Understanding of danger	197	0·13	0·10	0·17	−0·07
Score: Behaviour abnormalities	148 −188	−0·10	−0·08	0·04	0·04

* Significant at 1%-level; ** Significant at 0·1%-level.

indicator of the degree and severity of functional handicap. For a better and more adequate assessment, we decided to look for profiles of handicap that are directly relevant to the retarded child's situation.

Profile analysis

To reduce the number of variables, a factor analysis was first carried out. Thirty variables with high factor loadings were selected for the subse-

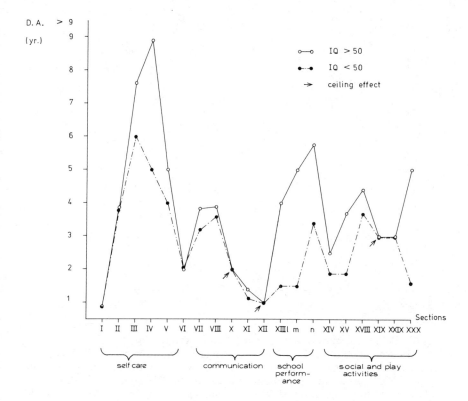

Fig. 1. Developmental ages (D.A., years) of the two IQ groups (medians).
   Self-care:
I, Mobility; II, Motor skills; III, Feeding; IV, Washing; V, Dressing; VI, Continence.
   Communication:
VII, Comprehension of speech; VIII, Use of speech; X, Comprehension of non-verbal communication; XI, Use of non-verbal communication; XII, Interest in communication.
   School performance:
XIIIl, Reading; XIIIm, Writing; XIIIn, Arithmetic.
   Social and play activities:
XIV, Interest in entertainment; XV, Imaginative activities; XVIII, Social respon-siveness; XIX, Social play; XXIX, Initiative and perseverance; XXX, Level of in-dependence.

quent cluster analysis. This cluster analysis gave five handicap-profiles; examples of these profiles are shown in Figs. 4 and 5.

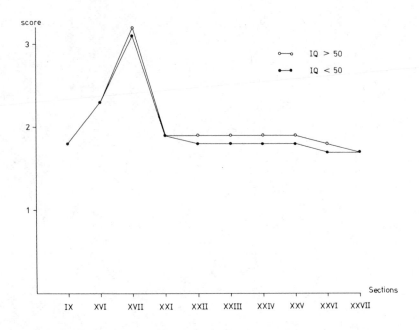

Fig. 2. Behaviour abnormalities of the two IQ groups (medians).
IX, Abnormalities of speech; XVI, Abnormal imaginative activities; XVII, Eye-contact; XXI, Abnormal response to sounds; XXII, Abnormal response to visual stimuli; XXIII, Abnormal peripheral stimulation; XXIV, Abnormal bodily movements; XXV, Routines and resistance to change; XXVI, Behaviour problems with limited or no social awareness; XXVII, Behaviour problems with social awareness.

The cluster whose handicaps-profile is shown in Fig. 4 comprised a relatively mildly retarded group of children. To help in interpreting the profiles we indicate the limits of severe handicap for each section of the HBS-Schedule by means of the shaded area. As a basis for the definition of these cut-off-points we used the criterion of *independence* — i.e. performance of the function without help — as it is expressed in each score. Comparing the shaded area with the profile of cluster 1 we can see that the children in that group have to be judged as severely retarded only in the sections regarding school achievement (i.e. reading, writing, arithmetic); the scores of all other sections are higher than the cut-off marks. This is consistent with the relatively high mean IQ of this group of children, namely 55 points.

The cluster in Fig. 5 demonstrates the profile of a group of non-mobile

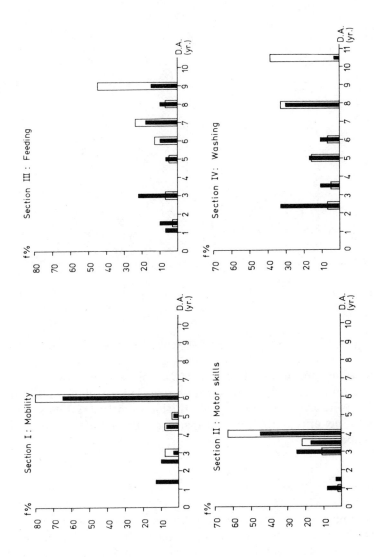

Fig. 3. Overlap of the two IQ groups (four examples; D.A. = developmental age; black = IQ <50; white = IQ <50) (cumulative %).

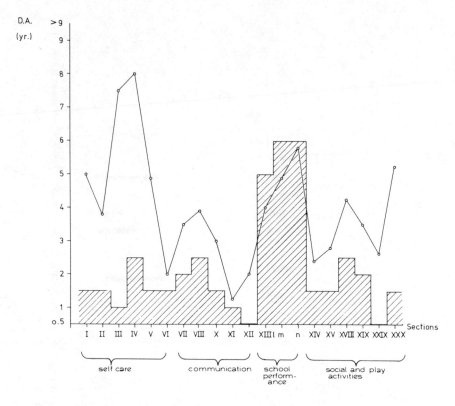

Fig. 4. Handicap profile; Cluster 1 (D.A. = developmental age). Key as in Fig. 1.

children who are profoundly handicapped in all sections of the HBS-Schedule. A more detailed data-inspection revealed that these children, all of whom were living at home, were unable to visit a special school because of the severity of their handicaps. The mean IQ of this group of children is about 42.

Conclusions

For research purposes and in assessing the needs of groups of mentally retarded children, it is possible to derive profiles of handicap by means of cluster analysis, which may then serve as a basis for decisions regarding care and education. However, the number of items in the schedule should not be reduced, except — if it is needed — in the evaluation phase; otherwise much important information on the individual child would be lost. In the assessment of individuals, it is necessary to complete the

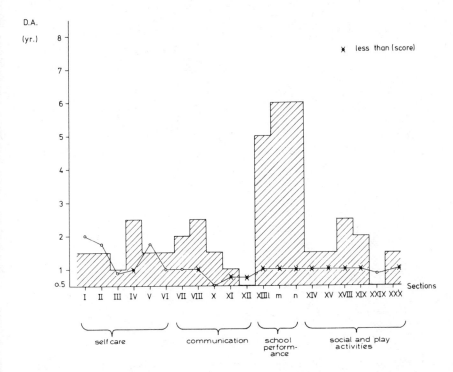

Fig. 5. Handicap profile; Cluster 5 (D.A. = developmental age). Key as in Fig. 1.

interview with the whole HBS-Schedule; such a procedure enables us to make decisions on the basis of detailed individual handicap profiles. As in the case of group profiles, here too the cut-off area can help with the interpretation and the planning of care and education. Two examples can be seen in Fig. 6.

Figure 6 shows the handicap profile of a girl of 11 suffering from severe mental retardation and early childhood autism; she has good motor development, but little comprehension or use of spoken or non-verbal language and very low scores in imaginative activities and social sections of the schedule. Also shown in this figure is the handicaps profile of a boy of 13 with no neurological deficits, who obtained normal scores in all areas other than school achievement. He appears to be typical of one form of so-called "subcultural" retardation.

As demonstrated above, the IQ is suitable as a basis for the assessment of mentally retarded children in such research, which has to do with the comparison of group-means or medians. In the field of care-related diagnosis the IQ can be regarded only as a rough indicator of the existence of mild or severe retardation, when the score 50 is used as cut-off. Appli-

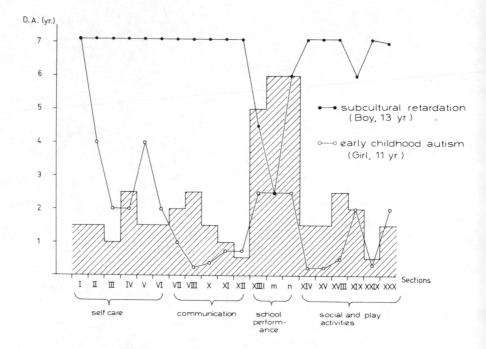

Fig. 6 Profiles of a girl with early childhood autism and a boy with "subcultural" retardation. Key as in Fig. 1.

cation of an interview schedule of this type should be seen as an essential adjunct to psychometric test procedure in the assessment of the mentally retarded child. The use of the HBS-Schedule is basically as economic as that of a psychometric test-battery, and just as important. However, much methodological research is still need to establish and compare the reliability, validity and discrimination of this and similar instruments.

Acknowledgments

The research project on mentally retarded children in Mannheim, referred to in this chapter, is supported financially by the German Research Association (Deutsche Forschungsgemeinschaft) and forms part of Special Research Programme (Sonderforschungsbereich) 116, Psychiatric Epidemiology, at the University of Heidelberg.

References

Cooper, B., Liepmann, M.C., Marker, K.R. and Schieber, P.M. (1979). Definition of severe mental retardation in school-age children: findings of an epidemiological study. *Soc. Psych.* **14**, 197–205.

Gould, J. (1976). Language development and non-verbal skills in severely mentally retarded children: an epidemiological study. *J. ment. Defic. Res.* **20**, 129–146.

Harman, H.H. (1970). *Modern Factor Analysis* (3rd edn). The University of Chicago Press: Chicago.

Heber, R. (1959). A manual on terminology and classification in mental retardation. *Am. J. Ment. Defic.* Monograph Suppl. No. 2.

Liepmann, M.C. (1979). *Geistig behinderte Kinder und Jugendliche.* Huber: Bern.

Liepmann, M.C. and Ort, M. (1980). Assessment of handicaps in mentally retarded children. In: Strömgren, E., Dupont, A. and Nielsen, J.A. (eds.): *Epidemiological Research as Basis for the Organization of Extramural Psychiatry. Acta Psychiatr. Scand.*, Suppl. 285, Vol. 62.

Ort, M. and Liepmann, M.C. (1981). The schedule of children's handicaps, behaviour and skills: reliability and discrimination. In: Mittler, P. (ed.): *Frontiers of Knowledge in Mental Retardation.* Proceedings of the 5th Congress of IASSMD, University Park Press: Baltimore. (In press).

Stein, Z.A. and Susser, M.W. (1971). Changes over time in the incidence and prevalence of mental retardation. In: Hellmuth, J. (ed.): *Exceptional Infant,* Vol. 2.: Studies in Abnormalities. Brunner/Mazel: New York.

Wing, L. (1973). *The Handicaps, Behaviour and Skills (HBS) Structured Interview Schedule for Use with Mentally Retarded Children.* Medical Research Council of Great Britain: London.

Wing, L. and Gould, J. (1978a). *Schedule of Children's Handicaps, Behaviour and Skills.* Medical Research Council: 2nd edn. London.

Wing, L. and Gould, J. (1978b). Systematic recording of behaviour and skills of retarded and psychotic children. *J. Autism Child. Schizo.* **8** (1), 79–97.

Part 5
Assessing the Family Situation

12 Family, environmental and developmental variables in mental retardation: a multi-dimensional approach

D. EGGERT

Faculty of Education, University of Hannover, Hannover, FRG

Although in the Federal Republic of Germany (FRG) there is now a wide range of institutions and programmes for the education of the mentally retarded child, basic research in the developmental and social psychology of the mentally retarded is definitely lagging behind. There is a lack of any *satisfactory* theory of development and of developmental tests (and also test-application strategies) particularly in the field of diagnosis and treatment of mental retardation. Scientific attention has largely concentrated either on psychodiagnostic research (Eggert, 1972) or on techniques of behaviour therapy and similar training programmes (Kane and Kane, 1976). Even multi-dimensional test batteries or behaviour rating or observational scales are mainly used for classification purposes and not for a proper linking of test-strategies and intervention procedures within the range of educational objectives.

Psychological and educational research is undertaken as a rule in different university departments, and there is a very unfortunate division between educational practice and scientific research work, which presents difficulties in the application of research findings to educational practice. The theoretical concepts of the two groups also differ, so that research strategies are not interdisciplinary, but rather tend to cover a wide range from bio-medical models (Keupp, 1976) to an interaction model of deviant behaviour and its therapy (cf. Chapter 7 by Kornmann).

The work of the present author has been devoted to the field of mental retardation since 1965. The publication of the "Testbatterie für geistig behinderte Kinder — TBGB (test battery for mentally retarded children)" in 1969 marks a point of change in the psychodiagnostic strategy from selective diagnosis to a multi-dimensional and multi-functional approach (Bondy *et al.*, 1969). Up to that time, only intelligence tests were administered and only about 50% of all mentally retarded children had been tested. To assess the mental abilities of mentally retarded children properly, a total of 100 different tests were tried out on more than 350 subjects (for a detailed description, see Eggert, 1972) and, of these, the following were selected:

(1) German version of the Columbia Mental Maturity Scale;
(2) an extended version of Raven's Coloured Matrices Test;
(3) an abbreviated version of the Peabody Picture Vocabulary Test;
(4) a test of ability to follow directions;
(5) the "dotting" test of fine motor function, and
(6) a German version of the Lincoln Oseretzky Motor Development Scale.

A German version of the Vineland Social Maturity Scale was added, but was not included in the battery profile.

The TBGB as a test-battery profile should point to possible ways of therapeutic and educational intervention for different aetiological and functional sub-groups of mentally retarded children. It could be shown that the six tests of the TBGB (plus the additional short version of the Vineland Social Maturity Scale) had a significant value in discriminating not only between different sub-groups of mentally retarded children, but also within these groups. Different treatment strategies (e.g. different forms of institutional and educational care) could also be applied within the range of "indirect" trait-orientated tests of intelligence, memory, motor ability and verbal fluency.

These tests were selected after several item- and factor analyses and seemed to represent quite adequately the factorial structure of different abilities of mentally retarded children. In 1965–1968, the test battery was standardized on a sample of 1200 children from all parts of the FRG. Later on subsequent standardization samples were added, including non-retarded children in the age range from 2 to 6 years and children with learning disabilities as contrast groups.

These tests represented the technology and the theoretical framework of traditional trait-orientated psychometry. The selected tests were validated against a criterion of mental retardation, which has been mentioned earlier in this paper. An explicit theory of individual development as the development of the individual personality in a social context had not been included; Piaget's theory had not then the influence it has nowadays.

The following studies, which summarize the results of several research projects carried out in the Institute of Education of the University of Hannover, from 1969 to 1978, will present some aspects of an extended use of psychometric tests covering not only the study of individual potentials but, in addition, the study of relationships of individual and social-familial variables to mental retardation. The studies are described in detail in Eggert, Altemöller and Schomburg (1980).

Before summarizing the findings of these studies, a preliminary remark on the definition and classification of mentally retarded children in the FRG is necessary, since they differ in certain respects from those used in other countries. Mental retardation is defined as a subnormal functioning of intelligence, social competence and motor abilities, combined with a need for lifelong supportive care, and corresponds to the IQ-range below 55/60, according to Bach's (1974) definition. Children with IQs above 60/70 are classified as learning disabled (Lernbehinderte).

That even rather traditional psychometric tests, constructed on the basis of trait theory, can be useful in this connection, was demonstrated by the results of two projects: (1) a follow-up study, carried out up to 1977, of the children first tested in 1969; (2) a multivariate analysis of test and interview data gathered in 1972.

A follow-up study on mentally retarded children in Lower Saxony

In 1969, a total of 58 children (ages 6 to 13) was tested with the TBGB. All children attended day care centres run by the association "Lebenshilfe" (literally, "life-help" for mentally retarded children) and were shortly to attend a newly established school for mentally retarded children in a small town Neustadt am Rübenberge near the state capital Hannover. All the children had been ascertained as mentally retarded on the basis of medical examinations. Two children who obtained extremely high test scores on the TBGB were subsequently sent to a primary school and later to a comprehensive school. Ten were classified as learning disabled (ESN) and sent to a special school for this group, where only two did not succeed.

Fifty-five of the children could be re-tested in 1972 and 50 (now aged 15–21 years) in 1977. By that time 25 were attending a sheltered work-shop, six were still in a school for the mentally retarded and six in a special school for the learning disabled; two were in comprehensive schools and five were in gainful employment.

Figure 1 shows a steady increase of mean test scores for the sample over this eight-year period, all differences being statistically significant. The product-moment correlations between the three successive scores on individual tests are high (minimum + 0·24 and maximum + 0·68), show-ing a remarkable stability of traits and a high prognostic validity of the TBGB (frequency distributions were fairly normal).

For a majority of the children, the test scores tended to increase with time, the proportion showing a decline ranging from 6% (memory) to a maximum of 22% (motor scale). Adolescents who had left school showed a marked decline in test scores after leaving school and attending a

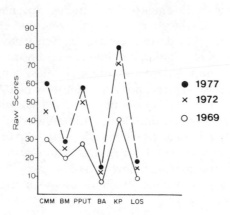

Fig. 1.   Mean raw scores in the TBGB subtests from 1969 to 1977.

sheltered workshop or a job. These findings suggest the conclusion that educational programmes for mentally retarded adolescents, including and indeed focusing on programmes of psychomotor abilities, should be continued after they leave school and while they are attending sheltered workshops.

Multivariate analysis of test scores and interview data

In a second study, funded by the Federal Ministry of Youth, Family and Health and undertaken in 1972, the parents of the mentally retarded children were interviewed in their homes, and information was collected on a wide range of familial and social variables. The interviews were carried out by special-school teachers, who also tested the mentally retarded children (a total of 335 children in the age range 7 to 12 years), using the TBGB. The interviews with the parents covered aspects of the socio-economic situation of the family, attitudes of members of the family and of neighbours towards mental retardation, as well as data on the developmental biography of the child, his medical and educational background, his play activities and his life-career. The interviews were completed in two to four sessions with the parents. All children were tested at home. The sample included only children living with their families in Lower Saxony (60·7% males, 39·3% females).

Statistical analysis of the interview and test data were carried out on three levels:

(1) descriptive analysis (absolute and relative frequency tables);

Table 1 Test battery for mentally retarded children: changes in sub-test scores, 1969–1977 ($n = 50$)

	CMM Columbia Mental Maturity Scale 97 items + 3			DM + CM Coloured and Progressive Matrices 60 items			PPVT Peabody Picture Vocabulary Test 70 items			BA Following Instructions Test			KP Dotting Test			LOS Lincoln Oseretzky Scale of Motor Developments 36 items		
	1969	1972	1977	1969	1972	1977	1979	1972	1977	1969	1972	1977	1969	1972	1977	1969	1972	1977
X	29·4	45·0	59·8	19·3	24·3	27·6	27·9	50·3	57·8	7·4	12·0	14·2	41·7	71·2	80·2	9·0	13·9	17·1
S	18·1	17·6	17·3	7·1	7·3	7·9	13·5	10·5	11·5	4·3	4·9	4·2	22·3	24·3	30·7	6·7	9·4	9·2
X Diff.	15·6	–	14·8	5·0	–	3·3	22·4	–	7·5	4·6	–	2·2	29·5	–	9·0	4·9	–	3·2
X Ges.Diff.	–	30·4	–	–	8·3	–	–	29·9	–	–	6·8	–	–	38·5	–	–	8·1	–
t 1972/77	–	7·1	–	–	3·9	–	–	6·7	–	–	4·0	–	–	2·9	–	–	3·7	–
p	–	<0·01	–	–	<0·01	–	–	<0·01	–	–	<0·01	–	–	<0·1	–	–	<0·01	–

Table 2   Correlations between TBGB sub-test scores, 1969, 1972 and 1977

		69/72 (n = 55)	72/77 (n = 50)	69/77 (n = 50)
Columbia Mental Maturity Scale	(CMM)	0·65	0·64	0·56
Progressive Matrices	(BM + CM)	0·68	0·70	0·50
Peabody Picture Vocabulary Test	(PPVT)	0·74	0·73	0·62
Following instructions Test	(BA)	0·77	0·62	0·68
Dotting Test	(KP)	0·55	0·69	0·24
Oseretzky Scale	(LOS)	0·75	0·79	0·63

(2) correlational analysis;
(3) multivariate analysis (including factor analysis, multiple regression analysis and multiple discriminant analysis).

Those children who were attending schools for the mentally retarded scored higher on all tests than children in day-care centres or children receiving no education (many of whom, however, were untestable); 30·4% of the children were attending a school for mentally retarded children and 57·8% a day-care centre run by "Lebenshilfe"; 3·3% were not attending any school or centre.

An analysis of the test data showed a normal distribution of the test scores and statistically different battery profiles for brain-damaged children and children with Down's syndrome. The battery profiles showed a general decline in motor test scores, particularly for children with Down's syndrome. The test scores tended to be lower according to the number of associated handicaps that were identified, and their specific nature (the commonest being speech and motor deficits).

Play activities showed a significant association with test scores: 69·2% of the children played by themselves, 34·4% with partners and 41·1% in groups. Children with Down's syndrome were able to join in group play more frequently than brain-damaged children (54·2% compared to 34·1%).

The children were allocated to social class categories according to the occupations of their fathers. In Table 4, the resulting distribution is compared with those found for educationally subnormal children and for pupils of a "Hauptschule" (lowest level of secondary school) by Klein (1973).

In each instance there is a highly significant difference between the

Table 3   Percentage of associated handicaps (*n* = 335)

Speech disorders	69·0%
Visual impairment	32·4%
Behavioural disorders	23·0%
Epileptic fits	21·0%
Motor handicaps	23·5%
Hearing handicaps	6·7%
MR and 1 ass. handicap	38·0%
2 ass. handicap	29·0%
3 ass. handicap	19·5%
4 ass. handicap	6·0%

groups: the upper and middle social classes are more strongly, and the lower social classes less strongly, represented among the mentally retarded children when compared with the educationally subnormal children, whereas the reverse is the case when they are compared with the "normal" children. However, the pattern appears to be changing: a later study showed that between 1965 and 1979 there was a marked increase in the numbers of children from lower social levels classified as mentally retarded (Eggert, Meywirth and Titze, 1981).

Only 29·8% of the mothers were going out to work daily (most of these mornings only) — a finding comparable with that of Bläsig and Schomburg (1968), who found that only 17·7% of mothers of children with severe cerebral palsy went out to work daily. There were differences in our sample between the social status groups: the higher the social status, the higher the percentage of working mothers. 91·7% of the children had siblings, 8·3% of the families had only one child. The mentally retarded child was the eldest child in the family in 25·2% and the youngest in 30·3%; 87·4% had no handicapped siblings, 10·7% had one, 1·5% had two and 0·4% had four.

80·6% of the children lived in houses or large apartments and only 19·4% in small family homes. No fewer than 46·2% of the families were classed as own-occupiers, a finding which indicates a tendency for these families to provide a stable, secure home background for their children.

Attitudes towards the mentally retarded children were classified as "positive", "neutral" or "negative" and assessed in respect of brothers and sisters, other relatives, neighbours and other children (both peers and strangers). The highest positive values were found for relatives, siblings and neighbours in that order; adults showed more positive reactions than child peers. These findings are similar to those reported by von Bracken (1976). Correlation of the attitude measurements with social data showed the influence of the following factors:

178   D. Eggert

Table 4   Social class distributions of mentally retarded, ESN and "normal" children

Occup. status of father	Mentally retarded children	Educationally subnormal * children	"Normal" children * (non-selective secondary schools
	%	%	%
I Unskilled	36·6	55·6	28·0
II Skilled manual	25·7	29·8	34·4
III Clerical	19·8	10·0	27·5
IV Managerial; self-employed	13·6	3·8	8·0
V Professional	4·3	0·8	2·1
Total	100·0	100·0	100·0
No. of children	335	2522	2455

* Klein, 1973.

MR: Educationally subnormal $\chi^2 = 181·5$; d.f.4; $p <0·001$.
MR: "Normal" $\chi^2 = 42·76$; d.f.4; $p <0·001$

(1) Where the social status of the father is relatively high, attitudes toward the child tend to be more positive;
(2) Mentally retarded girls are more readily accepted than boys;
(3) If non-retarded brothers and sisters are much older than their mentally retarded sibling, they are more likely to show positive attitudes;
(4) Where there is more than one mentally retarded child in a family the neighbours tend to show negative attitudes;
(5) If the mother shows the child much attention (and if the burden on the mother seems high), the attitudes of the neighbours towards the child tend to be more positive.

Informations on medical and causal factors obtained from the parents cannot be accepted as highly reliable. It was, however, possible from the data to distinguish three main groups of children:

(1) Down's syndrome (19·0%);
(2) brain-damaged children (41·4%);
(3) those with no known aetiology (39·6%).

Complications during pregnancy and birth were reported more frequently by mothers of brain-damaged children. The parents of these children were relatively satisfied with medical services and appeared to be getting more counselling and help than those in the other two groups. Parents of children with Down's syndrome tended to express a kind of resignation with regard to medical help, which they did not find as easily accessible as parents of brain-damaged children, and in particular as parents of children with motor or multiple handicaps. Physiotherapy, for example, was more frequently given to brain-damaged children than to those with Down's syndrome.

Significant correlations were found between the age of the mother and the father of the child and the aetiology. Briefly, parents of children with Down's syndrome were found to be relatively old (most mothers were over 35 at the date of birth), whereas significantly more mothers of younger age were found among the brain-damaged groups (62·2% in the age-group 20–29 years).

After these descriptive and correlational data analyses, multivariate analyses of test and interview data were carried out. At first only the test data were factorized (principal components method, Varimax rotation, Scree-test). In agreement with the findings of earlier studies, two significant factors were identified: a factor of cognitive abilities (60%) and a psychomotor factor (40%). The next step was a factor analysis of the interview data, in which five factors were identified: (1) interaction and communication; (2) medical treatment and special symptoms; (3) internal structure of the family; (4) sensorimotor and psychological development of the child, and (5) socio-economic status of the family.

In a further factor analysis, in which both test and interview data were included, these five factors could again be identified. When factor scores were computed, sensorimotor development and socio-economic status of the family were found to be significantly correlated with cognitive and motor abilities (Table 5).

Medical treatment was not correlated with test results in general, but the motor test scores were inversely correlated with the frequency of medical symptoms. Family social status was found to be related to severity of cognitive deficit, the children from a middle-class background being on the whole more severely handicapped in this respect. This finding could be explained by the relatively higher frequency of Down's syndrome in the higher social-class groups. Children with Down's syndrome showed relatively severe deficits in test abilities; they tended to come from families with comparatively high social status, to show fewer medical complications than the other groups and to be rated as relatively co-operative and socially well integrated.

Multiple correlations between test-dimension as criterion variables and interview factors as predictors showed relatively high multiple correlation (Beta-) coefficients ($R = 0.59, p < 0.01$). The highest correlations were found with sensorimotor and psychological development, demonstrating the extreme importance of sensorimotor development for individual prognosis of the mentally retarded child

Factor profiles of different aetiological groups were computed and

Table 5 Intercorrelations of test and interview factors ($n = 330$)

		TA	TK	TM	FI	FÄ	FF	FP
General ability (intelligence)	TA							
Cognitive level	TK	0·81 s.s.**						
Motor abilities	TM	0·50 s.s.**	−0·10					
Interaction	FI	0·07	0·09	0·01				
Medical aspects	FÄ	0·13 s.*	0·04	0·17 s.s.**	0·07			
Structure of family	FF	−0·11 s.*	−0·00	−0·18 s.s.**	−0·09	0·05		
Sensorimotor and psychol. development	FP	0·51 s.s.**	0·41 s.s.**	0·26 s.s.**	−0·01	0·02	−0·04	
Socio-economic level of family	FS	−0·22 s.s.**	−0·11 s.*	−0·23 s.s.**	−0·04	−0·02	−0·06	0·01

* Significant; ** Highly significant.

significant differences found between the different sub-groups (Fig. 2). By means of a series of multiple discriminant analyses it could be shown that the psychomotor test factor and the interview factor "sensorimotor and psychological development" constantly showed the highest Beta-coefficients for discrimination between the three diagnostic groups.

Discussion

The main findings of these studies can be summarized as follows: mental retardation represents from the psychological viewpoint a multiple handicap, in which cognitive impairments, speech disorders, motor impairments and disturbances of behaviour are associated with the social and psychological structure and situation of the affected families. Precisely those functions are impaired, which enable the normal child to adapt himself to his physical environment (motor functions) and to his social environment (verbal and behavioural responses). A mentally retarded child needs active help from his family and from medical, psychological and educational services in the community, in order to make this adaptation, beginning as early as possible and continuing as long as possible throughout his life-span.

The social situation of a mentally retarded child appears to be influenced by the following factors:

(1) The handicap itself and its influence on the child's life-course;

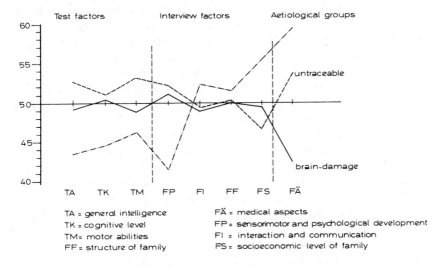

Fig. 2. Profiles of mean factor scores for three aetiological groups (Down's syndrome, "brain-damaged" and untraceable aetiology).

(2) The difficulties of the child's family, and also of the neighbourhood community, in coping with the phenomenon;
(3) The prevailing attitudes of society towards the mentally retarded, and
(4) The capability of the health care and educational systems to deal with mental retardation as a public problem.

The mentally retarded child is more dependent than other children upon the effectiveness of his family and his teachers as mediating agents, who intervene between him and the wider society and help to create possibilities for him to take part in social life in general.

These findings demonstrate that the application of methods of multivariate statistical analysis may be helpful in reducing empirical research data to meaningful dimensions and in drawing significant conclusions, even when they are based in part on data obtained from traditional, trait-oriented psychometric tests. The range of possible conclusions and implications could of course be greatly extended, if it were possible to apply more sophisticated psychometric techniques, and to relate the findings to a wider range of interview or observational data. However, in view of the enormous amount of practical and scientific information now available on individual mentally retarded children, and on mental retardation as a syndrome, the author considers that the psychological trait concept and the assumptions of classical test theory no longer provide an adequate framework for a systematic approach to planned intervention. Strategies of intervention should now be based *both* on traditional trait psychology and direct observational techniques *and* on consideration of the child's social environment in terms of his family situation, the state of the labour market and the values and expectations of society. In the author's experience, some practitioners, particularly in the sphere of school administration, have misused psychometric test data (either by administering a single sub-test from a test-battery, or by combining sub-test scores to give a meaningless IQ-equivalent) in order to classify and allocate children, without subsequently undertaking any therapeutic or educational intervention whatsoever.

The author also has some reservations about the validity of certain basic assumptions of classical test theory in the diagnosis of mental retardation (reference to the normal distribution, the assumption of a true score for a stable trait, and so on). These issues cannot be adequately discussed in the framework of the present chapter. It may, however, be mentioned in passing that a recent study by Bibl (1980) has shown that the concept of personal conpetence (Sundberg, Snowden and Reynolds, 1978; Carroll and Maxwell, 1979) together with procedures based on probabilistic test models (Rasch, 1971) may yield information of greater value from a developmental standpoint. Bibl applied competence scales for the diagnosis of severely retarded persons, using the scales of Uzgiris and Hunt (1975) and Piaget's developmental concepts. This general approach is in some respects similar to the task-analysis approach described by Wilkin in the present volume. The emphasis on dimensions of sensorimotor and social competence may lead to more satisfactory therapeutic and educational programmes and to a necessary unifying of theory, diagnostic practice and treatment.

Since, however, none of these models has been fully elaborated as yet, the author considers that any one of a number of provisional (proto-) theories may be fruitful, if it leads to the collection of data which assist in analysing the situation of the mentally retarded child as an individual in society, or the initiation of pragmatic measures helpful to the child, his parents, his teachers or the wider community.

As a final conclusion, the author believes that much more attention should be focused on retrospective analysis of the development of the individual mentally retarded child in a given life situation or social environment, and that the mode of functioning of educational services should be much more closely geared to such individual patterns of performance. There are "critical crossroads" in the life career of the child which can be identified and analysed by means of psychological assessment, and which may indicate the need for specific therapeutic or educational measures, directed either towards the child himself or towards his family. In the existing situation in the FRG, there tends to be too long an interval between medical diagnosis in early childhood and educational–psychological assessment during the school years, with no systematic monitoring of the child's development and life experiences during the intervening years.

References

Bach, H. (1974). Geistigbehinderte unter pädagogischem Aspekt. In: Deutscher Bildungsrat, Gutachten der Bildungskommission. Sonderpädagogik 3. Klett: Stuttgart.
Bibl, W. (1980). Diagnostische Möglichkeiten der kompetenzorientierten Verhaltensanalyse bei geistig schwerstbehinderten Menschen mit den Skalen von Uzgiris und Hunt. Unpublished thesis, University of Brunswick, FRG.
Bläsig, W. and Schomburg, E. (1968). Das zerebralparestische Kind. Thieme: Stuttgart.
Bondy, C., Cohen, R., Eggert, D. and Lüer, G. (1969). Die Testbatterie für geistig behinderte Kinder (TBGB) (Hrsg. K. Ingenkamp). Beltz: Weinheim.
Bracken, H. v. (1976). Vorurteile gegen behinderte Kinder, ihre Familien und Schulen. Marhold: Berlin.
Carroll, J.B. and Maxwell, S.E. (1979). Individual differences in cognitive abilities. Ann. Rev. Psychol. 30, 603–640.

Eggert, D. (ed.) (1972). *Zur Diagnose der Minderbegabung*. Ein Handbuch und Textbuch zur Testbatterie für geistig behinderte Kinder. Beltz: Weinheim.

Eggert, D., Meywirth, H. and Titze, I. (1981). Einige Daten zum Zusammenhang zwischen Behinderung und Sozialstatus. Z. Heilpädagogik (In press).

Eggert, D., Schomburg, E. and Altemöller, R. (eds.) (1980). *Familie, Umwelt und Persönlichkeit geistig Behinderter*. Huber: Bern, Stuttgart, Wien.

Kane, J.F. and Kane, G. (1976). *Geistig schwer Behinderte lernen lebenspraktische Fertigkeiten*. Huber: Bern.

Keupp, H. (1975). Der Widerspruch von Präventionsgedanken und "medizinischem Modell" in der Schulberatung. *Gruppendynamik* **6**, 415–436.

Klein, G. (1973). Die soziale Benachteiligung der Lernbehinderten. In: Heese, G. (ed.): *Aktuelle Probleme der Lernbehindertenpädagogik*. Marhold: Berlin.

Rasch, F. (1960). Probabilistic models for some intelligence and attainment tests. Danmarks Paedagogiske Institut: Copenhagen.

Sundberg, N.D., Snowden, S.R. and Reynolds, W.M. (1978). Towards assessment of personal competence and incompetence in life situations. *Ann. Rev. Psychol.* **29**, 179–221.

13 A task-oriented approach to the assessment of the distribution of the burden of care, levels of support and felt needs in the family

D. WILKIN

Research Section, Withington Hospital, Manchester, UK

The term "community care" contains a strong positive value component which makes it difficult to attempt a thorough critical appraisal of the actual practice, since to do so appears to question a state of affairs which is, by definition, desirable. It has been widely advocated as a more desirable and more cost effective alternative to institutional care for the physically disabled, mentally ill, mentally handicapped and other categories of chronically ill people. Advocacy of community care as a policy is, however, much easier than the actual implementation of an effective system of care. Richard Titmus (1961) once described it as; "that everlasting cottage garden trailer", implying that its superficial attractions can be used to conceal a state of affairs which is far from perfect. A careful appraisal of the existing system and its strengths and limitations is essential to the development of a pattern of care which fulfils the promise held out by the notion of community care. Failure to conduct such an appraisal is likely to result in inadequate care conveniently hidden from public scrutiny by a vague but attractive philosophy.

Although an analysis of the concept of community care might be seen as a fundamental pre-requisite to an appraisal of the system, it is frequently either ignored or only given scant attention. Care can be simply defined as meeting the physical, psychological and social needs of the individuals, although this leaves unanswered many questions concerning the definition of needs, the relative importance of different categories of need and the ways in which needs might best be met. At least as problematic is the definition of community in the context of the provision of care. Most care for mentally handicapped children is provided in a community context and the predominant mode of care is family care. However, it does not follow that family care can be equated with community care. Community implies a wider social grouping than the nuclear family, a sense of belonging, shared ideas and values and a way of life opposed to the bureaucracy of modern mass society (Plant, 1974). The authors of the Seebohm Report (1968) in the United Kingdom noted that; "the notion of community implies the existence of a network of reciprocal social relationships which, among other things, ensure mutual aid and give those that experience it a sense of well-being". Whether family care of most severely mentally handicapped children measures up to this standard is debatable. But what of family care itself? Our knowledge of role differentiation in the modern nuclear family suggests that reference to family care may obscure the important issue of who actually does the caring (Oakley, 1974). It is clear that care of most severely mentally handicapped children is undertaken *in* the family and *in* the community, but to what extent is this care *by* the family and *by* the community. The answers to these questions must be sought through an approach which is not limited by culturally determined expectations of family life and community involvement.

To the extent that British and American authors have addressed themselves to the problems of the handicapped child in the family, attention has frequently focused on the psychological and emotional impact on other family members (e.g. Kew, 1975; McMichael, 1971; McKeith, 1973). This in itself suggests an ordering of priorities in which the practical difficulties of providing day-to-day care are considered less important. The balance has been redressed to some extent in recent years through studies carried out by Hewett (1970), Bayley (1973), Jaehnig (1974) and Carr (1974) which have attempted to describe the day-to-day practical difficulties encountered by families and how these are coped with. Unfortunately, none of these studies has analysed the values and assumptions which underlie family care. Indeed one suspects that the authors find it difficult to stand aside from the norms of family life themselves. Their descriptions of the pattern of care in the family and the community are bound by culturally determined expectations of the roles of different individuals. Thus, Hewett reports that half of the fathers of cerebral palsied children were "highly participant" in the domestic routine, and Bayley that 40% of fathers contributed "much help". Similarly assessments of support contributed by relatives, neighbours and friends have resulted in the use of vague categories such as "frequent", "considerable" and "a good deal". Implicit in the use of such descriptions is an evaluation of what level of support *should* be provided by different categories of people which is based on social norms and values relevant to families with only non-handicapped children. There is, therefore, no means of establishing how these contributions related to the total burden of care or to the burden carried by mothers in the families studied. Similar criticisms can be applied to attempts to evaluate the provision of services, in that they tend to be assessed against their own criteria of appropriate

types of provision and acceptable levels, rather than against some measure of the extent and distribution of the burden carried by informal care
agents.

The purpose of this paper is to suggest an alternative approach to the
assessment of the distribution of the burden of care which, although it
requires further development, produces a very different and more reveal-
ing picture of family care in the community than those used in the studies
cited above. A major objective of a study of families caring for a severely
mentally handicapped child was to undertake a detailed description of
the process of community care (Wilkin, 1979).

Design and method

The fieldwork for the study of families was conducted in the Greater
Manchester area in the United Kingdom during 1974 and 1975. Samples
of severely mentally handicapped children were drawn equally from two
sources, firstly from the Salford Mental Handicap Register and secondly
from lists of children awaiting admission to long-term institutional care.
The reason for drawing samples from these two sources was that another
principal objective of the study was to examine the relationship between
patterns of care and support, and the decision to seek long-term care. The
findings concerning these issues are reported elsewhere (Wilkin, 1979).
For the purpose of this paper the two samples will be combined, since the
conclusions drawn concerning patterns of care apply equally to both
groups. The overall response rate for the two groups was 80%, which was
slightly lower than expected. Less than half of the non-responses were
due to refusals, the main reason for non-response being failure to contact
families whose child was on a waiting list because the family had moved
away from the area. Respondents were broadly representative of other
families in the research areas in terms of age of parents, numbers of
children, social class etc. The handicapped children in the group drawn
from the Mental Handicap Register represented a full range of handicaps
and behaviour problems, but the group awaiting admission to long term
care contained more profoundly handicapped and more behaviour disordered children.

A structured interview schedule was administered to the 120 mothers
of mentally handicapped children. All children sampled were members
of families in which the mother was present, and in all cases the mother
constituted a principal provider of care for the handicapped child. The
schedule contained five main sections; the child's handicaps, skills and
behaviour (derived from Wing, 1971), family circumstances, domestic
routine and patterns of care, felt needs for additional support and services
received.

This paper will focus on the section of the study concerned with the domestic routine and patterns of care. The schedule was devised following a detailed pilot study of seven families caring for severely mentally handicapped children, in which mothers and fathers were each interviewed twice. The pilot interviews revealed no substantial disagreements between mothers and fathers concerning accounts of their respective roles in the care of the handicapped children. The only difference was that fathers frequently referred the interviewers to their wives for information concerning physical child care and household tasks. It was felt, therefore, that little extra would be gained by interviewing fathers, since their accounts of the domestic routine and patterns of care corresponded closely to those provided by the mothers. The pilot interviews suggested 15 task areas which broadly encompassed day-to-day care in the family. These could be subdivided into three main areas: physical child care tasks (dressing, washing and bathing, changing nappies, toiletting, feeding, lifting and carrying); playing with or minding children during certain defined periods (after school, evenings, weekends, school holidays); household tasks (cleaning, cooking, washing dishes, washing clothes, shopping). In order to examine the domestic routine as a whole it was found to be necessary to include the care of non-handicapped children and household tasks, which were of course performed for other family members. For each defined task mothers were asked who usually performed the task, whether any other person (family member or others) ever helped and whether they would have liked more help with the task. Any individual usually performing a task (up to three could be recorded for each task) was defined as a participant, and any person helping (up to three for each task) was defined as a helper. In the pilot interviews,

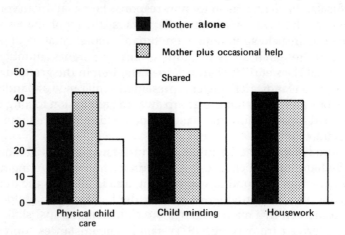

Fig. 1. Distribution of the burdens of child care and housework.

mothers spontaneously made a qualitative distinction between those who shared responsibility for a task and those who merely lent a helping hand.

For the main survey three interviewers including the author were used. Interviewer training consisted of briefing and debriefing sessions during pre-test interviews, including cross checking of questionnaires using tape recordings. High levels of inter-interviewer reliability were achieved on all parts of the schedule. Problems were minimised by the fact that most questions required respondent ratings rather than interviewer ratings. Thus, on patterns of care and domestic routine it was mothers' definitions of participants and helpers that were required. Random checks on tape recorded interviews were conducted throughout the fieldwork.

Results

I shall devote the remainder of this paper to a brief discussion of some of the findings obtained using this approach, since I think they illustrate the importance of a careful assessment of the distribution of the practical burdens of care as a means to describing the practice of community care.

In the vast majority of families it is the mother who is central to the continued care of the handicapped child in the community. The chart (Fig. 1) shows the degree of responsibility carried by mothers for a selected range of child care and household tasks. Physical child-care was clearly perceived as a maternal responsibility in most families, and although many mothers received help with tasks such as dressing and bathing the handicapped child, they retained responsibility and, for most tasks, more than a third of mothers received no help at all. The only exception to this pattern was with regard to lifting and carrying non-ambulant children, where the help of another family member was often essential. The mothers received relatively more help with minding children, although it should be remembered that shared care at weekends and evenings often meant only that someone else was present in the house. Household tasks are often ignored in attempts to assess the burden of caring for a handicapped child, but they frequently constitute a great difficulty for mothers, both because the child creates additional housework and because completion of household chores is made more difficult because of the presence of the handicapped child. As with physical child care, many mothers performed household tasks such as cleaning, cooking and washing clothes with little or no assistance from anybody. The fact that mothers reported receiving relatively little support with physical child care and household tasks should not be taken to imply that they regarded this as an unsatisfactory state of affairs. In general, they assessed themselves in terms of their ability to undertake the burden of these tasks, thus accepting the prevalent social definition of the obligations of the maternal role. Nevertheless, it might be argued that their expectations were inappropriate to the situation, since they are derived from socially acceptable standards for mothers of non-handicapped children.

It is apparent from what has already been said that a more appropriate term than community care or family care to describe the care of the handicapped child would be maternal care. However, although most mothers received relatively little support, it is important to look at the sources of what help they did receive and who might have done more to help. The most obvious potential source of support in most families was the fathers. 105 of the families studied had a father living with the family. Data were not collected on the reasons for the absence of that father among the 15 one-parent families. It is interesting to note, however, that a majority of one-parent families were found in the home group (i.e. those not seeking long-term institutional care of the handicapped child). This might suggest that the father's role in providing support is not as crucial in maintaining the handicapped child in the family as is sometimes supposed. Evidence in support of this interpretation is provided in Fig. 2.

The majority of the 105 fathers provided little support with most child

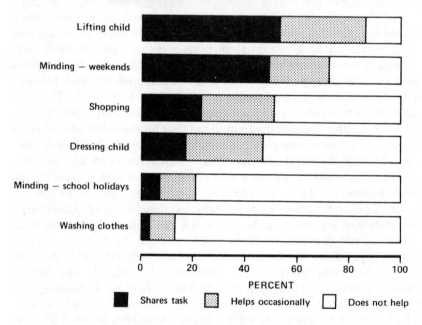

Fig. 2. Father's participation in selected tasks.

care and household tasks. Their pattern of involvement reflected traditional paternal role expectations. Thus they were not generally involved in physical child care but they did look after the children and play with them at certain times. Their participation in household tasks was usually limited to the "acceptable" tasks such as washing dishes and shopping. 92 (88%) fathers were in full-time employment and 13 (12%) were not working. Those not working were more likely to provide support with child care and housework. Of the 120 mothers 48 (40%) had some form of employment but only five mothers worked full-time outside the home. On the basis of their work commitments outside the home, one might have expected the fathers to have contributed somewhat less to the domestic routine than their wives. However, when a hypothetical "acceptable" level of participation across all child care and household tasks was calculated, only one third of fathers actually achieved this level. This "acceptable" level took account of fathers' absence at work during the day and required only that they "help" rather than "share" in the majority of tasks. The only other source of support in the family was from siblings of the handicapped child. In the event, they provided far less support than their fathers, and the support that was provided came particularly from teenage girls, suggesting that the sexual division of labour characteristic of the parents is being repeated in the following generation.

If other family members provided little support relative to the mother's contribution, then the amount of support provided by people outside the nuclear family was minute. The 588 individuals (relatives, friends and neighbours) who were in a position to help, provided only 146 instances of regular help with the whole range of child care and household tasks. Figure 3 shows the abysmally small proportions of relatives, friends and neighbours who helped with a range of individual tasks. Many of these people lived within walking distance of the families and visited frequently, but practical help was neither expected nor offered. In the light of the emphasis laid on neighbourhood support networks by some advocates of community care, it is interesting to note that only half of the mothers interviewed said that there was a neighbour on whom they could call for help if necessary, and even these provided little in the way of regular reliable help. Rather, they were people who could be called upon in times of crisis.

The range of tasks considered in this schedule is largely outside the usual accepted sphere of activity of the services. Supportive services are mostly based on the assumption that routine care will be provided by the family. The families in this study were receiving little in the way of supportive services which relieved them of the burden of care, with the notable exception of the children's attendance at school. It is not my

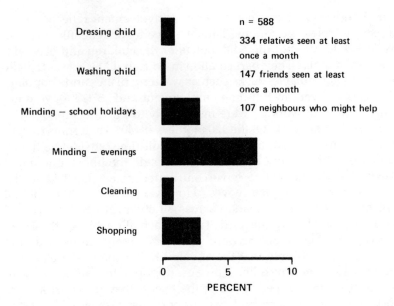

Fig. 3. Proportions of relatives, friends and neighbours helping with selected tasks.

intention to report here on the provision of services, but it is worth noting that no family received the services of a home help, less than half had recent contact with a social worker and only 40% had received short term care for the handicapped child in the preceding year. The limited services that were available were inadequate to meet the needs of the families and, where they were provided, their allocation reflected an orientation to crisis management rather than long-term support.

In addition to its use as a means of assessing the distribution of burden, the 15 child care and household tasks were also used to assess mothers' felt needs for increased support (Fig. 4).

Relatively small proportions of mothers expressed a desire for more help with physical child care tasks and household tasks, perhaps reflecting the fact that they accepted without question the traditional obligations of the maternal role. Thus, to have expressed a need for help would have been, in their terms, an admission of a failure to fulfil these obligations. However, the fact that the proportions who wanted more help were small should not conceal the fact that there were important unmet needs in the families concerned. Much larger proportions of mothers expressed needs for help with child minding at various times, particularly during school holidays. The importance of this type of support was that, had it been available, it would have enabled the mothers to spend time on activities

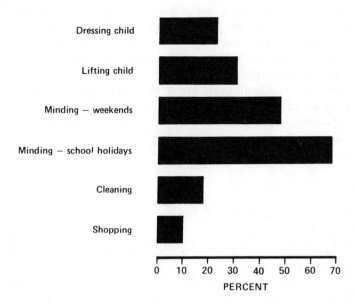

Fig. 4. Proportions of mothers expressing need for additional support with selected tasks.

which they were otherwise unable to do because of the necessity of remaining with the handicapped child.

Discussion

The results obtained using this task oriented approach to the assessment of the distribution of the burden of care paint a very different picture of community care from that provided in other studies and in statements of policy in Britain. Whilst the approach has many limitations and is, in its present form, relatively unsophisticated, it nevertheless provides a much more explicit description of the day to day realities than is available from most studies of community care. It treats the mundane domestic routine as problematic and therefore worthy of study. The main limitation of the method used is that all assessments are relative to the burdens experienced in each family. Thus it cannot, in its present form, be used to measure the extent of burden. However, as a measure of the distribution of burden there is evidence to show that it is a reliable and valid instrument. Further development of the approach should concentrate on the problem of devising procedures for weighting individual items according to their relative importance in particular family situations.

194   D. Wilkin

The results of this study lead one to question whether a framework of social roles and expectations geared to the needs of the majority of families can adapt to the requirements of an increasingly large number of families in which the care of dependent individuals places excessive demands on the family's resources. Modern industrial societies with high standards of living and health care are producing increasing numbers of chronically sick and disabled individuals who must be cared for in communities whose social organization may not be adapted to meet the needs of such people.

References

Bayley, M. (1973). *Mental Handicap and Community Care*. Routledge and Kegan Paul: London.
Carr, J. (1974). The effect of the severely mentally subnormal on their families. In: Clarke, A.M. and Clarke, A.D.B. (eds): *Mental Deficiency: The Changing Outlook*. Methuen: London.
Hewett, S. (1970). *The Family and the Handicapped Child*. George Allen & Unwin: London.
Jaehnig, W.B. (1974). The Mentally Handicapped and their Families, Unpublished PhD. Thesis, University of Essex.
Kew, S. (1975). *Handicap and Family Crisis*. Pitman: London.
MacKeith, R. (1973). The feelings and behaviour of parents of handicapped children. *Dev. Med. Child Neurol.* **15**, 524–7.
McMichael, J.K. (1971). *Handicap: A study of Physically Handicapped Children and their Families*. Staples: London.
Oakley, A. (1974). *The Sociology of Housework*. Martin Robertson: London.
Plant, R. (1974). *Community and Ideology*. Routledge and Kegan Paul: London.
Seebohm Report: Report of Committee on Local Authority and Allied Personal Social Services (1968). London: H.M.S.O. Cmnd 3703.
Titmus, R. (1961). Community care: fact or fiction. In: Titmus, R. (ed.): *Commitment to Welfare*. Unwin: London.
Wilkin, D. (1979). *Caring for the Mentally Handicapped Child*. Croom Helm: London.

Part 6
Assessment and
Evaluation of Special Care

14 Evaluation of services for the mentally retarded in Sweden: a conceptual framework

L. KEBBON

Psychiatric Research Centre, University of Uppsala, Uppsala, Sweden

A short account is presented of the conceptual framework of a project, "Evaluation of integrated services for the mentally retarded in Sweden". The project commenced in 1972 as an assignment from the National Board of Health and Welfare, the intention being to acquire a basis of knowledge for the further development of the services through critical evaluation. Our purpose was to evaluate critically, not in the restrictive sense of drawing up a balance-sheet of the advantages and disadvantages of the existing services, but rather in a more constructive way to make a positive contribution to the ongoing process of development of these services. The following presentation is divided into four sections: model and methods, quantitative aspects, qualitative aspects and critical factors.

Model and methods

The general methodological frame of reference was a goal attainment paradigm, the aim being to evaluate the services in question in relation to certain stated goals. Our main instruments for realizing this objective were what we called "normative models" and "critical factors". Briefly, a normative model is a systematic description of effectively structured and functioning services, as deduced from the stated goals. The function of this model in the project was to enable comparisons to be drawn between such an "ideal" state and the existing reality, in order to reveal essential factors, critical for goal attainment. A critical factor may be positive, implying a necessary condition, or it may be negative, implying an obstacle or constraint.

A normative model was constructed for each of four major aspects of the mentally retarded person's situation; namely, his living conditions, family support, daily activities and leisure time. Schematically the normative model is made up of three components: (1) goals; (2) system description, and (3) evaluative framework.

The function of the *goal analysis* is to establish, analyse and make explicit the goals of the service, based on the special needs of its clients. We tried to cover in this analysis a continuum ranging from general, long-term goals, corresponding to the policy or underlying ideology of the service, to guiding principles for the daily administration and routines. These formulations are then used as criteria in the evaluation.

In the second part of the model, a description of the *existing service system* is given in terms of its essential features: types of unit; forms of residential or other facility; resources and methods of work; relevant figures and statistics. Empirical studies are carried out as part of a general survey of the structure and content of the services. At this stage, factors related to the individual clients are also included: types and degrees of disability, special needs and positive resources of the mentally retarded, as well as the availability of help and support from other forms of agency outside the services for the retarded.

The third stage in the research procedure, corresponding to the third part of the model, is to establish an *evaluative framework*. This is based upon both goal analysis and system description, so that service functioning may be checked against goals in respect of a number of criteria such as quantity and adequacy, accessibility, flexibility and adaptability to individual needs, continuity of care and, above all, therapeutic effectiveness.

Quantitative aspects

Swedish services for the mentally retarded have changed and developed a good deal since the introduction in 1967 of new legislation: the Act on Services and Provisions for Mentally Retarded Persons. The number of persons receiving care provision has increased from about 29 000 in 1966 to 37 000 in 1977. (These numbers correspond to 0·34% and 0·44% respectively of the total population.) Rather more than half the total — 23 000 or 61% — are adults of 21 years or over (Grunewald and Wallner, 1979).

A continuously increasing proportion of mentally retarded children and young persons live either with their families or in foster homes. At the present time, this group comprises some 70% of the total. A further 15% are in boarding schools and the remaining 15% in residential homes or special hospitals. In 1970, no more than 50% were living with their families. It should be noted that all children who are in need have the right to receive special services under the 1967 Act. Parents who care for their retarded children at home are entitled to special contributions from the state, to cover living costs.

Nearly two-thirds of all adults registered as mentally retarded are now living in open forms of residence, as compared with only about 40% in 1970. Characteristic of the development of the services in the past decade has been an increase in the numbers of retarded persons living in their parental homes and to a still greater extent in the numbers living in group homes or in their own apartments. The latter categories have increased from about 3% of the total to 10% and 15% respectively, which means that altogether about one-quarter of adults registered as mentally retarded now live in group homes or in their own apartments; this proportion continues to rise. It should be noted, however, that the proportion living with their parents is still larger and comprises about one-third of the total.

According to the "normalization principle" (Nirje, 1969), separation from the parents and parental home should take place if possible on reaching adult age. A factor of some importancce in this connection is the right of families to receive a pension and additional contributions for living costs for retarded members who continue to live at home. It is also well-established that there is an unmet need for places in group homes.

A high proportion of the mentally retarded are still living in residential homes. The numbers of places in such homes increased continuously up to the middle 1970s, roughly to the same extent as the increase in the numbers of registered mentally retarded persons (Table 1).

An intensive study of the population of registered recipients of services during a 10-year period in one county indicates that the mentally retarded individual when registered usually either remains in his family home, or is taken to a residential home. From the residential homes there is then a slow movement to group homes or to single apartments. Transfer to large, long-stay institutions practically never occurs nowadays. Temporary stay in a residential home may occur, for example, in connection with a change of group home or with some form of family crisis.

This expansion of community-based forms of residential care has affected predominantly the moderately and mildly retarded. Of the profoundly or severely retarded, a little over half live in special hospital or

Table 1   Numbers of registered mentally retarded and of residential home places, 1956–76

Year	Registered retarded persons	Places in residential homes
1956	18 000	7 000
1962	22 000	9 000
1970	29 000	11 000
1976	37 000	11 500

residential homes, about one-third in parental homes and only 4·6% in small group homes. It is nevertheless important to note that a certain number of severely retarded persons do manage to live in such group homes, although of course they require a good deal of supervision and personal support. It is our conclusion that, given proper organization and resources, the great majority of all mentally retarded persons should be able to move to forms of living-group that are integrated in the community.

As regards the composition of the group of retarded persons now living in parental homes (all age-groups), in round figures one-third are mildly, one-third moderately and one-third severely retarded. A separate analysis of adults living in parental homes reveals a different distribution: the mildly retarded now account for only 20% suggesting that some of this group are able to move away as they become adult. The moderately retarded predominate with 45–50%, while the proportion of severely or profoundly retarded remains constant at about one-third among adults and children.

The daily activities of practically all the children and young persons (up to 21 years) are built around the different forms of special school or pre-school kindergarten. Of the adults, rather more than half are occupied at special day activity centres: two-thirds of these are at day centres linked with residential homes and the remaining one-third at community-based day centres. About 18% work in sheltered workshops or in open industry, roughly half in each. While the past decade has been characterized by an expansion of community-based day centres, the total numbers of retarded persons attending day centres of all kinds has remained fairly constant, because of a decrease in the number of places in centres attached to residential homes.

The proportion of retarded individuals working in sheltered workshops or in open industry has remained unchanged over the past ten years, which implies that in this respect expectations have not been entirely fulfilled. One important reason is the generally unfavourable situation of the labour market, leading to increasing rates of unemployment.

Qualitative aspects

The changing pattern of services for the mentally retarded, described above in quantitative terms, has its counterpart in a qualitative change. Evidence of such change is to be found in a general "normalizing" trend within the residential homes, for example in the attainment of higher physical standards and in sub-division into smaller units, developments which cannot be described in detail here.

Our own studies have focused more particularly on the quality of care provided by the "integrated" — i.e., community-based — services. In general, it may be said that integration into the community has been achieved in a *physical* sense for the 60% of the mentally retarded who are now living in some form of small group within the community, and for the 30% who have an organized daily activity under integrated conditions. Housing and occupation have been separated physically, and different groups of personnel are responsible for the services in each of these two main areas of life — a fact which of course in no way precludes the necessary coordination. However, *functional* integration — use of facilities in the neighbourhood such as public transportation, commercial services, etc. — has not yet been realized to anything like the same extent. Observational studies using time-sampling techniques have shown, for example, that persons living in group homes seldom participate regularly in shopping or use public transport to travel from the homes to the day centres. A proportion of the activities organized by the day centres are external, the most common being shopping and errand-going. Another category has a leisure character, such as using public sports grounds or swimming baths. The mentally retarded still participate to only a limited extent in activities in public places — for example, in recreation centres. In general, frequency of participation of the retarded in communal activities is still low.

Social integration, in terms of acceptance and participation in activities with other members of the community, has been achieved to an even smaller extent. Living in the community can thus in a personal sense mean not integration, but rather *isolation*, for the mentally retarded. This form of isolation is experienced, as interview reports have revealed, by retarded persons living in single apartments. Nevertheless, they do not wish to return to institutional care. Furthermore, our studies reveal that most of the social contacts made by retarded persons living in group homes were restricted to other members of the group or to the service personnel. Hence theirs could not be characterized as a normal life situation.

Critical factors

The critical factors for fulfilment of the 'normalization' goal, which we have identified, can be classified on a number of different levels: individual, organizational and social. This can be illustrated by means of a few examples.

A first-order critical factor is the functional disability of the individual which, in combination with the environmental demands upon him, constitutes his handicap. It is important to note that normalization of the life situation presupposes special measures taken to compensate for the handicap. Normalization should not be understood to mean making the handicapped person and his total behaviour-pattern normal, which is manifestly impossible, but rather "making available to all mentally retarded people patterns of life and conditions of everyday living which are as close as possible to the regular circumstances and ways of life of society" (Nirje, 1969). This provision of opportunities should be considered a basic human right. A secondary result may well be some degree of normal modification of behaviour, to a greater extent than would otherwise be possible; but normalization must not be made conditional upon such behavioural change.

There is an implicit risk that measures taken within the services in order to meet the specific needs of the handicapped may actually hinder fulfilment of the general human needs that handicapped persons share in common with other human beings. The use of the normalization principle as a guideline in planning services and in the growth of integrated, community-based forms of care is an expression of the ambition to achieve the best possible balance between specific and general needs.

Mentally retarded persons are individuals and as such have individual needs. In order to fulfil its purpose, a service must be able to adapt to meet individual needs, which in turn presupposes a certain flexibility of organization. Of special importance in this context is consideration of the emotional needs of the retarded, which should be fundamental to all rehabilitation programmes. The emotional capacities of the individual at the same time constitute a positive developmental resource. A critical factor is the presence of at least one of the very few key persons who can serve as an object of identification, thus providing the possibility of emotional contact and continuity in human relations. This factor is often lacking from the retarded person's environment, for basic physical or other practical reasons. Here, the "normalization" principle cannot by itself provide any guarantee that needs will be met; indeed, as we have seen, change to an "integrated" pattern of care may actually lead to increased isolation.

This leads to the question of economic resources, which not unexpectedly constitute an important critical factor. Integration of services must not be considered as a means of reducing the costs of services, but rather as a more adequate and effective use of the available limited resources. Normalization should not be understood to mean liquidation of the existing special services, but rather their adaptation so as to provide the necessary minimum of support needed to achieve normal conditions and opportunities. To attain this goal a differentiated system of services is required, which can be modified according to the needs of individual handicapped persons. Here again, access to resources and flexibility of organization are important. It may even be that in a given situation permanent resources in the form of trained personnel, buildings or organization can be obstacles for the development of effective integrated services.

On a social level, a number of critical factors may be decisive: attitudes of acceptance or rejection towards the retarded person, competition for jobs, political and professional priorities, etc.

These few examples may illustrate our aim to make the evaluation dynamic, to provide means of tracing the causes of success or failure in goal fulfilment and to indicate the most promising directions for further research and further planned change in the services.

References

Grunewald, K. and Wallner, T. (1979). Psykiskt utvecklingsstörda och deras livs-villkor i siffror (Facts and figures on the mentally retarded and their living conditions in Sweden). *Socialstyrelsen redovisar*, **5**.

Nirje, B. (1979). The normalization principle and its human management implications. In: Kugel, R.B. and Wolfensberger, W. (eds.) *Changing Patterns in Residential Services for the Mentally Retarded*. President's Committee on Mental Retardation: Washington.

15 The evaluation of residential services for mentally retarded children

N.V. RAYNES

Hester Adrian Research Centre, University of Manchester, UK

The evaluation of residential services for mentally handicapped children is important for a number of reasons. Foremost is the simple fact that retarded people like all people have a right to humane services. Studies concerned with the quality of life provided in the residential facilities they use are thus valuable in and of themselves. They are a way of monitoring the service as it is provided, irregardless of whether or not the service ultimately results in behavioural growth. Such studies may be further justified by the contribution they can make to a number of other areas. Knowledge of the quality of life provided, the factors affecting this and the impact of quality of life on growth and development permit research workers to assist in the formulation of social policies. There are vogues in the provision of residential services, often based on little sound evidence, yet these vogues shape the lives of clients and their families. Governments spend large sums of taxpayers' money providing services which, as Zigler (1977) has pointed out "the future may inform us were little more than passing fads" (p. 52).

The only antidote to such practices is careful research and evaluation, coupled with the means to disseminate the knowledge gained to inform the decisions of policy makers. Zigler, submitting evidence to the Senate and House Appropriations Committee in the USA to justify the maintenance of federal funding for research in mental retardation, pointed out that it makes little sense to spend large sums of taxpayers' money on residential services currently in vogue, without also spending the considerably smaller sums necessary for research committed to finding out the effects of such services, as well as the actual form they take at the point of delivery.

Knowledge derived from evaluative studies of residential services can also be used by professionals, whose job it is to counsel families trying to determine what is in the best interest of their retarded members. Soundly based knowledge about the merits and demerits of different forms of service could conceivably reduce the distress of families trying to find out how best to care for their children. It should not be forgotten that there are many types of residential service. What is learned from the evaluation of one may further knowledge about another, underlining both similarities and differences.

Evaluative studies of residential services may also contribute to the development of psychological and sociological theory. In the latter case, much can be learnt about complex organizations in which people's work is carried out. A contribution can also be made to developmental psychology and attitude theory. Indeed, many branches of the behavioural sciences may be better informed as a result of studies to evaluate residential services for mentally retarded children.

To me this form of research is potentially very productive and useful, as I have tried to indicate in outlining the several justifications for it. In the past twenty years a considerable amount of knowledge has accumulated from such studies. It is clear from these studies that if evaluative work is to continue to be useful, it must comprehend psychological and sociological factors. It must consider the characteristics of the clients, as well as of the caretaking practices and the caretakers, and the organization of the resources used to run the service. Without a consideration of all these factors, only partial and often misleading knowledge about the efficacy as well as the operation of a service can be gleaned.

Evaluative studies of residential services began with psychological studies of the effects of institutions on the cognitive, behavioural and emotional functioning of institutionalized mentally handicapped people. Birch and Belmont (1961) succinctly identified the weaknesses of these studies. Psychologists continued to work in this area and slowly began to include consideration of gross indicators of various aspects of the institutions in which the client-assessments were made. In the USA Butterfield and his colleagues (1966), for example, included a consideration of overall size, living-unit size, direct-care staff ratios, direct-care staff turnover rates and numbers of professional staff per resident, in their evaluation of the effect of institutions on residents' performance in four institutions. Klaber (1969) in his study of six residential State institutions in three north-eastern States in the USA continued this work. He focused his exploration on the contribution of organizational variables, such as size of unit and staffing ratios, to the actual way in which retarded residents were cared for.

In England, Tizard (1964) pointed to the importance of providing small-group, family-type environments as a means of promoting the functional development of children in residential facilities. His observations led to the famous Brooklands experiment. Here a particular kind of quality of life was sought for the children and a particular kind of organization established to provide it. From this quasi-experimental study Tizard conceived the importance of identifying and measuring sociological features of the residential environment in an attempt to understand better which features were responsible for which effects on the children. In 1963, Roy King and I, both sociologists, joined with him in a comparative study of different forms of residential services mainly for mentally handicapped children (King et al., 1971). The theoretical starting-points and hence the major areas of concern of the study — organizational structure and caretaking practices — were sociological.

Since the mid-60s, a number of research groups have carried out studies which have included consideration of both psychological and sociological factors in residential settings. Attention has not been focused exclusively on traditional institutions; evaluative studies have also been carried out in small, community-based residences (Jones et al., 1975; Kushlick, 1975; McCormick et al., 1975; McLain, 1975; O'Connor, 1976; Udall and Corbett, 1976; Baker et al., 1977; Pill et al., 1979; Raynes et al., 1979). Most recently the clients' perspective has also been investigated, usually in studies in which a small number of other variables have been considered (Campbell, 1968).

Ironically, despite an impressive accumulation of data on structural variables, demographic and personal characteristics of the staff and cognitive and functional levels of the residents, we still cannot say which is the best kind of residential environment for which type of child, even though it may be possible, by means of psychologically sophisticated assessment techniques, to define clearly his or her needs at a given point in time. In this context, longitudinal studies are required. Zigler and Balla (1977) have recently begun such a study in the USA. Another study, reported in several publications by Kushlick (1975) and his colleagues, has been carried out in England. These studies are expensive and time-consuming research endeavours but they are necessary. Two are not enough. Indeed, given the relatively high level of sophistication we have achieved in the past 20 years in measuring organizational and other sociological aspects of residential services, as well as in psychological assessment, a strong case could now be made out for setting up cross-national comparative studies of different types of service in countries such as England and Germany. Studies which began 15 years ago were not equipped with research tools of the kind now available. Our physicist or biochemist colleagues would not expect to make headway with research techniques that were current 20 years ago. Why in evaluative research we tend to ignore methodological advances (except to some extent in statistics) is a question perhaps for students of the philosophy of science or the politics of mental retardation.

The studies which have so far been completed have not only produced methodological advances but enable us to identify areas of consistency in research findings, particularly with regard to specific features of the organisational structure, characteristics of residents and direct-care staff and their relationship to the quality of life. These advances have important implications for future research.

We can summarize the position so far reached as follows:

(1) First, techniques are available to enable fine-grained comparisons of different forms of residential provision to be made.

    (a) Instruments are available to measure aspects of the caretaking process. For example, the Revised Resident Management Practices Scale has been used in a number of studies (Holland, 1973; McCormick et al., 1975; McLain et al., 1975; Raynes et al., 1979).

    (b) Instruments to measure aspects of the structural and ideological characteristics of the residential facilities have also been developed. Millham and his colleagues, for example, have developed techniques for studying the roles of residential organizations. Raynes et al. (1979) have likewise developed techniques to measure the extent of staff autonomy, and King et al. (1971) to measure role-diffusion in the division of labour.

These techniques are less well-established than those which measure facets of caretaking per se. It would be useful if further work were done to test existing measures of autonomy, for example, that of Raynes et al. (1979) and the more widely applied measures developed primarily for use in non-residential complex organizations by Pugh and his colleagues (1969).

(2) Secondly, research tools exist for assessing the cognitive, behavioural and emotional characteristics of the clients. Those developed by Kushlick (1973) and Wing and Gould (1978) have been widely used. In addition, there are the well-established patterns of IQ tests, the AAMD Adaptive Behavioural Scale (1969), the Vineland Social Maturity Scale (Doll, 1953) and the PAC Manual (Gunzburg, 1972), to mention only a few.

(3) It is clear that assessments of the effects on clients' behaviour of their residential experience will also need to take into consideration their pre-institutional experience.

(4) Identifiable and measurable features of the organizational structure and characteristics of residential staff are known to affect care-giving practices; e.g., goals, task analysis and division of labour.

(5) Identifiable characteristics of clients are known also to affect care-giving practices. Raynes et al. (1979) and McCormick et al. (1975) have clearly demonstrated that lower IQ levels are associated with custodial patterns of care.

In the USA studies funded by the Federal Department of Health, Education and Welfare have recently been completed which collate existing client-assessment methods (Mayeda, 1977) and techniques for evaluating facilities (Johnson, 1978). The existence of these useful compendia, which contain information about the nature of each instrument, its construction and measures of its reliability and validity, underlines the point that a wide range of techniques both for client assessment and for evaluating service facilities are now available.

This is not the place to summarize the evidence on associations between staff and resident characteristics, organizational structure or caretaking practices and residents' functioning. It is, however, evident that there are several areas in which research findings of different workers are consistent. Indeed, some findings have been replicated (McCormick *et al.*, 1975; Raynes *et al.*, 1979). For example, most studies looking at organizational characteristics have identified the involvement of direct-care staff in decision-making about daily events as an important factor determining the quality of residential care. There is increasing agreement about the effect of functional grouping on care-taking practices but considerably less, for example, on staff resident ratios. Recent work (Raynes *et al.*, 1979) has identified some of the features involved in the institutionalisation of direct-care staff in these settings, a process hitherto studied almost exclusively as it affects patients and clients in other kinds of residential service.

It seems to me that we have arrived at a point in the development of knowledge about residential services for the mentally handicapped, and their effects, which call for two kinds of studies, neither of which correspond to the comparative, descriptive and correlational studies which have been the source of our knowledge to date; namely, experimental and longitudinal studies. We need first, experimental studies to clarify our understanding about certain aspects of institutional life about which the available data are inconsistent, such as the effect of client mix or staff ratios on care practices. Such studies are also necessary to ascertain the feasibility of effecting change to improve services. Since it has proved possible, for example, to demonstrate that certain structural factors do contribute to the development of resident-oriented care, research findings may help in the planning and design of new facilities. Without experiment, however, we are likely to assist only in failure where attempts are made to change existing service patterns. Secondly, we need longitudinal studies to assess the effect of various types of care on client growth and development.

If Tizard's early work is to bear further fruit, we must capitalize on the natural experiments which are under way in most industrialized societies. Currently, a wide range of different types of residential services is provided for mentally handicapped citizens. To my mind, it is extraordinary that this situation has not been used to compare the relative merits, that is to say the differing effects on client functioning, of these different services. We also have enough information to identify areas in which experimental manipulation is essential to assess the effect of particular characteristics on care-taking practices and to identify blocks to effecting change. Such experimental studies are harder to mount than the longitudinal ones which I have argued are also necessary. They are not impossible but they require careful design and close collaboration with service providers. Research workers do not often seem very skilled in working with service providers. Perhaps this is because they lack humility and in consequence generate hostility towards themselves. It is not impossible to establish goodwill and to identify ways of collaborating to carry out such studies. Perhaps a research worker is most effective in such endeavours when he or she is willing to identify alternative strategies for service providers, rather than adopt an "action research" role.

To summarize, two types of studies are now essential if we are to advance any further in identifying the determining features of residential life and the ways in which these influence behaviour and development. As Tizard and his colleagues pointed out (1975) if we do this "we can begin to make rational choices between different ways of running institutions" (p. 1.). We can assist planners and policy makers, clients and their families. We have gone some way to doing this with comparative evaluative studies of institutions for mentally handicapped children; we can go further with experimental and longitudinal studies.

References

Baker, B.L., Seltzer, G.B. and Seltzer, M.M. (1977). *As Close as Possible.* Little, Brown: Boston.
Birch, H. and Belmont, L. (1967). The problem of comparing home rearing versus foster home rearing in defective children. *Pediatrics* **70**, 956–61.
Butterfield, E.C., Barnett, C.D. and Bensberg, G.J. (1966). Some objective characteristics of institutions for the mentally retarded: implications for attendant turnover rate. *Amer. J. ment. Defic.* **70**, 786–94.
Campbell, A.C. (1968). Comparison of family and community contacts of mentally subnormal adults in hospital and in local authority hostels. *Br. J. prev. soc. Med.* **22**, 165–69.
Castell, J., Cooke, M. and Pill, R. (1979). *A Real Home Life:* the study of purpose-built residential units for mentally handicapped adults. Report submitted to the Welsh Office. University College of Swansea, Wales.
Doll, E.A. (1953). *Vineland Social Maturity Scale.* Manual of Directions. Published for the Educational Tests Bureau. Division of the American Guidance Services, Inc. Minneapolis, Minnesota.
Gunzburg, H.C. (1972). Progress Assessment Charts (P.A.C.) Manual. SEFA Publications: Birmingham.
Holland, T. (1973). Organizational structure and institutional care. *J. Hlth. soc. Behav.* **14**, 241–51.

Johnson, T.Z. (1978). *Annotated Directory of Environmental Assessment Instruments*. Pomona, California: Neuropsychiatric Institute Research Group at Pacific State Hospital.
Jones, K. (1975). *Opening the Door: study of new policies for the mentally retarded*. Routledge and Kegan Paul: London.
King, R.D., Raynes, N.V. and Tizard, J. (1971). *Patterns of Residential Care*. Routledge and Kegan Paul: London.
Klaber, M.M. (1969). *Retardates in Residence*. University of Hartford Press: West Hartford, Conn.
Kushlick, A., Blunden, R. and Cox, G.R. (1973). A method of rating behaviour characteristics of use in large-scale surveys of mental handicap. *Psychol. Med.* **3**, 466–78.
Kushlick, A. (1975). Epidemiology and evaluation of services for the mentally retarded. In: Begab, M.J. and Richardson, S.A. (eds.): *The Mentally Retarded and Society. A Social Science Perspective*, pp. 325–43. University Park Press: Baltimore, Md.
Mayeda, T. (1977). *Performance Measures of Skill and Adaptive Competencies in the Developmentally Disabled*. Neuropsychiatric Institute Research Group at Pacific State Hospital: Pomona, Ca.
McCormick, M., Balla, D. and Zigler, E. (1975). Resident-care practices in institutions for retarded persons: a cross-institutional, cross-cultural study. *Amer. J. ment. Defic.* **80**, 1–17.
McLain, R.E., Silverstein, A.B., Hubbell, M. and Brownlee, L. (1975). The characterization of residential environments within a hospital for the mentally retarded. *Ment. Retard.* **13**, 24–27.
Nihira, K., Foster, R., Shellhaas, M. and Lelan, J. (1969). *Adaptive Behaviour Scales: Manual*. American Association on Mental Deficiency: Washington, D.C.
O'Connor, G. (1976). *Home is a Good Place*. American Association on Mental Deficiency: Washington, D.C.
Pugh, D.A., Hickson, D.J. and Hinings, C.R. (1969). An empirical taxonomy of structures of work organizations. *Adm. Sci. Q.* **14**, 115–26.
Raynes, N.V., Pratt, M.W. and Roses, S. (1979). *Organisational Structure and the Care of the Mentally Retarded*. Croom Helm: London.
Tizard, J. (1964). *Community Services for the Mentally Handicapped*. Oxford University Press: London.
Tizard, J., Sinclair, J. and Clarke, R.V.G. (1975). *Varieties of Residential Experience*. Routledge and Kegan Paul: London.
Udall, E.T. and Corbett, J.A. (1976). *A Home To Go To*. Institute of Psychiatry: London (Unpublished).
Wing, L. and Gould, J. (1978). Systematic recording of behaviours and skills of retarded and psychotic children. *J. Autism Child. Schizo.* **8**, 79–97.
Zigler, E. (1977). Twenty years of mental retardation research. *Men. Retard.* **15**, 51–53.
Zigler, E. and Balla, D. (1977). The social policy implications of a research programme on the effects of institutionalization on retarded persons. In: Mittler, P. (ed.). *Research to Practice in Mental Retardation*. Vol. 1. Care and Intervention, pp. 267–74. University Park Press: Baltimore, Md.

16 The short-term residential care of mentally handicapped children

MAUREEN OSWIN

Thomas Coram Research Unit, Institute of Education, London, UK

This chapter considers some aspects of the short-term residential care provided for mentally handicapped children in the United Kingdom, as a form of relief and support for their parents. It is based on the preliminary findings of a three year research study into short-term care services, undertaken by the Thomas Coram Research Unit.* The work is now nearing completion and the final report will be ready for publication in 1981.

The background to the research study

The long-term placement of mentally handicapped children in mental handicap hospitals should be avoided, because these institutions do not provide normal childhood experiences of family life and neighbourhood living, and because the "putting away" of handicapped children often results in their losing contact with their families. Large institutions also fail to attract specialist staff so that the children will be unlikely to receive the special help they require, such as physiotherapy, speech therapy and paediatric cover.

The emotional and physical deprivations suffered by children in long-stay hospitals have been repeatedly referred to in research reports (Tizard, 1964, 1966; Morris, 1969; King, Raynes and Tizard, 1971; Oswin, 1971, 1978; Jones, 1975) and in the Government reports of hospital "scandals" (Ely Hospital, 1969; South Ockenden Hospital, 1974; Normansfield Hospital, 1978). The National Development Group Report (1978) on mental handicap hospitals referred to the problems of providing appropriate care for children in institutions and Shearer's (1980) well-documented history of residential care policies for handicapped children points out how far their residential needs have not received the same

* With financial support from the King's Fund, London.

legislative protection as that afforded to normal children who live away from their own families. Voluntary organizations and pressure groups for handicapped children have also drawn attention to this problem; foremost among the campaigners have been the Spastics Society, MIND, the National Society for Mentally Handicapped Children, Campaign for Mentally Handicapped People and EXODUS.

Central and local government have made every effort over the last decade to prevent the long-term admission of young children into mental handicap hospitals and the numbers of hospitalised children aged under sixteen years of age dropped from 7000 in 1969 to just under 4000 in 1979. This drop in numbers was not achieved by the whole-scale *discharge* of children but by avoiding the admittance of under-sixteens and the fact that many of those who were in the children's statistics of the early 1970s are now in the long-term *adult* statistics, having literally grown up in the hospitals.

One means of keeping children out of hospitals has been the development of short-term residential care as a form of family relief. Such care may be provided in local authority hostels, mental handicap hospitals, voluntary society homes, holiday homes, private homes, the children's wards of general hospitals, hostels run by local education authorities or short-term "foster" families. This research study began in 1977 with the aim of obtaining a general view of short-term care provision and of how such a service might be meeting the needs of parents and children. Between 1977 and 1980 short visits were made to fifty different residential units and approximately 90 families using short-term care were informally interviewed. Information was obtained on the handicaps, ages and family background of approximately 500 children who were, or had been, using some form of short-term care provision. Observational visits of between two to three months were made to four areas, each of which was providing a different form of short-term care support: one area had developed a short-term foster scheme, another had opened a new purpose-planned local authority social service department hostel, a third had a new mental handicap hospital which provided short-term care as well as long-term care, the fourth was using an ex-paediatric sick children's ward which had been converted into a short-term care unit.

Preliminary findings of the study

Families

By 1980 the family interviews and visits to units had been completed and it was possible to draw some broad conclusions based on personal experience in the field. In particular, it seemed clear that short-term residential care is an important form of family help which may not only prevent or delay the admission of a child to long-term care but may even prevent marital and sibling stress and the likelihood of family break-ups.

From the interviews with parents it became clear that short-term care should be locally based and allow flexible use. Small hostels within two to three miles of their own homes, which can be used in a very flexible manner all the year round, are preferred to "holiday homes" or hospitals which may be twenty or more miles away, require forward-booking of perhaps six months or even a year ahead and permit only two to three weeks stay each year.

When parents spoke about flexibility they meant two things which were very important to them. First, they meant being allowed to telephone the hostel or home themselves and make a direct arrangement with the staff about when their child could go in, instead of having to go through a third party such as a field social worker or an administrator in the social service department or hospital. Direct contact with care staff and the knowledge that telephone calls for help would meet a prompt response, including if necessary booking-in of the child at short notice, gave parents a feeling of confidence in the service. Secondly, flexibility meant being able to choose their child's pattern of short-term care. For example, Mrs A. required every Tuesday night free because she went to an evening class on Tuesday; her husband was a long-distance lorry driver, often away from home, and it was impossible to leave her 14-year-old Down's Syndrome daughter alone in the house late at night. Mr and Mrs B. had been using short-term care one night a fortnight for their 12-year-old mentally handicapped son because they had to visit their elderly parents who lived 50 miles away. As it was difficult to take the rather active and demanding boy to the elderly, frail grandparents, the short-term care unit helped by letting him stay every other Friday night and his parents picked him up on their way home on Saturday evening. This arrangement had been going on for over a year.

Changing family circumstances, such as an older sibling starting to study for A-level examinations, an elderly relative having a stroke, a sibling having an accident or a mother becoming pregnant, may mean altering the parents' usual pattern of short-term care; a good service will permit this and will not make the parents feel that they are inconveniencing the staff or other parents. The majority of parents do not misuse or "take advantage of" this flexibility. Indeed, the reverse appears to be true, because the service creates relief and confidence and with this comes a consideration of the needs of other families and of staff. One hostel with a very flexible admission policy found that some parents were getting together and working out how they might arrange their bookings so that children who knew each other and had similar handicaps and interests might all be there at the same time. This would help staff to plan activities, as well as making the children's stay more pleasurable.

Some professionals, especially those in the hospital service, suggest to parents that their children should be admitted for four weeks and then be at home again for six weeks as a continuous form of "phased care" over a period of one, two or three years. However, the majority of parents who were interviewed expressed a preference for "little and often" short-term care, e.g. every other Tuesday or Friday, or one week-end a month or one week every three months.

Typical comments made by parents regarding very long and regular periods of short-term care were: "He'd have forgotten us by the time he came home again" and "She would be confused about where she really did belong". Observations and interviews did, indeed, suggest that too much short-term care could undermine the child's position in his family and might even result in eventual long-term care (this suggestion is supported by the study of long-stay children in mental handicap hospitals published by Oswin in 1978). In addition to worrying about their child being away from home too much, some of the parents felt a sense of guilt and unease about using any short-term care at all even if the child's time away was as little as three week-ends each year. "We feel awful about sending him away" was a frequent remark during interviews. The way in which the idea of short-term care is initially introduced to parents would seem to have some influence on the development of guilt feelings. More attention should be given to this by unit staff, field social workers, community nurses and teachers.

All the parents who were interviewed were asked what complaints they had about short-term care. Four common ones were: (1) loss of children's clothing; (2) difficulty in booking-in during the long summer holidays; (3) children being bored in the units; (4) the mix of children accepted at any one time.

Most parents, including those who had financial problems, were remarkably patient about the problem of lost clothes; it appeared that the need for short-term care was so urgent in some families that the occasional lost cardigan was regarded as a small price to pay. In some units the staff kept a meticulous list of every item of clothing brought in, which was checked out again when the child went home. This meant extra work for the staff — especially since there might be 28 or 30 children going in and out on most Saturdays in the summer — but it was a means of preventing loss of clothes and also had an advantage in demonstrating that unit staff were concerned about the individuality of each child. Hospitals were more inclined than local authority hostels to resolve the problem of losing clothes by putting children into hospital clothing whenever they were admitted for short-term care, but this decision was disliked by most parents as they saw it as "institutionalizing" their child and taking his identity away from him.

The difficulty of booking in to a hostel or hospital during the long school holidays was evidence of the popularity of short-term care. Very dependent or difficult children were often given priority in August and this was usually understood by the parents of more able children. Parents with difficult children sometimes supplemented the amount of care they were getting in one unit by using other units as well. This could mean that during the summer holiday some children would spend two weeks in a local authority social service department hostel, two weeks in a mental handicap hospital ward and only a week and a half at home.

The parents' complaint that their children were bored when they were in short-term care was often justified; observations of the children's day showed that staff tended to over-use television as a means of occupying the children and would just turn the children out into the garden or courtyard during fine weather. Understandably, the larger the group of children accepted at any one time the more difficult it was to organize play activities, especially when the care staff might also have to receive parents, attend to meals, comfort homesick children, check on clothes and even perform domestic chores. Hospital staff, although having fewer responsibilities than local authority hostel staff as regards domestic chores and cooking, still failed to provide really good activities and play for the children. One reason for this lack of constructive activities is characteristic of short-term care; that is, that staff and children do not know each other very well. This is made worse because not only the children, but also the staff are constantly changing (the latter happens in most residential care units, whether long-stay or short-stay, run by local authorities, health services or voluntary organisations). This means that a child who enters a short-term care unit one weekend in six, throughout one year, may see the same member of staff only twice during the whole time.

In the majority of units there was also a marked lack of helpful child-oriented record keeping; for example, notes on his likes and dislikes, his reaction to his stay, his ability to make relationships with staff and with other children and his play needs; also there was no systematic follow-up of the child's relationships and play activities each time he was admitted, which might have lent some quality of continuity to the care.

Complaints about the mix of children occurred because parents worried that active children could tread on the more frail, dependent, cerebral-palsied children. This worry affected equally the parents of the more active children and those of the frail ones, and tended to increase if the parents knew each other personally. Mrs C., the mother of a very active 14-year-old, said, "I'd never forgive myself if Ben trod on Mrs F's little spastic girl or tipped her out of her chair", whilst Mrs F. said, "I worry if my little girl gets hurt by Ben. And it is upsetting for Mrs C. too. I'd feel so sorry for her if my little girl *did* get hurt by her boy, as I know she'd not forgive herself. We both worry the same about this."

The parents' feelings of guilt about using short-term care are increased if they are also worried about whether their children might do some damage to other children or might get damaged themselves. Paradoxically, the more flexible a short-term care unit aims to be, in accepting requests for help, the more likely it is to book in at any one time a group of children with widely differing abilities; this means that active and frail children are mixed together and the staff find it difficult to meet their individual needs. One local authority hostel tried to resolve this problem by having the staff take the more frail children into a quiet room to do special activities. Mental handicap hospitals do not appear to have so many problems in this respect, because they tend to keep to the traditional hospital arrangement of providing separate wards for those children who are active and those who are physically dependent or frail. However, this also creates problems; for example, short-term care children may be categorized as "active" simply because they are very lively and ambulant; though not seriously disturbed, they may be assigned to a "difficult" ward containing long-stay over-active children whose bizarre patterns of behaviour may have been worsened by their long years in the deprived conditions of the mental handicap hospital. Although the parents of the short-term ambulant children worry about them being placed amongst difficult long-term care children, the staff are adamant that they cannot go into the quieter non-ambulant children's wards. Some parents have stopped using hospitals for short-term care because of this way of categorizing children.

Complaints of the four types referred to above might have been lessened if parents had been given some share of responsibility in managing the short-term care units. This might have been organized through parent–staff associations. However, staff seemed to find some difficulty in encouraging parents to become constructively involved in the management of the units and most families were reluctant to involve themselves in matters of policy although they would gladly have taken on fund-raising to buy specific items such as television sets or minibuses; staff-parent contact appeared to be on safer ground if their joint energies were combined to raise funds rather than sitting down together to discuss policy making. Indeed, staff *and* parents tended to have quite traditional attitudes towards short-term care, seeing it as a service which is given by one group of persons and received by another, instead of as a collaborative sharing of the care of children with special needs.

Staff

Care staff in the units showed a certain lack of direction. When asked about their aims in providing a short-term care service they tended to be vague and make very general statements such as "it is a family service" and "we help families to have a break". Whilst nobody would dispute the value of helping families to "have a break" it would seem important for staff to have very clearly defined aims. One of the many recommendations which will be written into the final report of this research study will be that care staff should receive far more help from senior management in formulating their work aims. They need to sort out exactly how they are helping individual families and children, consider the effect of separation on the children and explore ways of involving families more in the management of the unit. It is also important for short-term care staff to look at their role in conjunction with professionals who are involved in the child's care in other services and settings, such as special schools. In some instances there was a marked lack of contact between short-term care units and the children's special schools and even a certain antagonism between the teachers and the care staff, with neither side appearing to understand each other's role in providing a service for children and families.

There was likewise a lack of constructive contact between the field social workers and residential social workers (care staff), the latter saying they felt like poor relations in the professional hierarchy and complaining that the field social workers did not understand the problems of providing a residential service for handicapped children.

The children

The research study tried to look at children's views of short-term care and the likely effects on the children of having periods of separation from their families. As was to be expected, the children's reactions varied according to their ages, abilities, how often they had used the units before, whether they knew the staff, which other children were in at the same time with them, how carefully they had been prepared for their stay and what former experiences they had had of short-term care. The trauma of separation could be eased if new children visited the units with their families beforehand, met the staff and saw where they could eat, sleep and play. Previous planned periods of day care at the units sometimes helped to settle children for their first overnight stay. Some children adapted more easily to the situation if their friends from school were also receiving short-term care at the same time; this shows a need for short-term care units to be locally based, serving a small group of children and working closely with the local special school. Some children, although going fairly regularly for short-term residential care, suffered persistent homesickness and needed constant reassurance that they would be going home after a few days. A major finding of the study is that the problems of homesickness amongst children receiving short-term care is being underestimated or ignored by staff and families (this point will be extensively discussed in the final report).

All the parents were asked what they thought their children liked about short-term care: three common replies were "the space", "the company of other children" and "the chance to make a mess". The parents of a six-year-old ambulant girl said she liked it because she could run about the hostel garden in summer time with other children, play with the hosepipe and make soap bubbles in the bathroom wash-basins. This particular family led a restricted life in an upstairs furnished flat over the premises where the father worked and it was not easy for the little girl to play actively there; so, for her, short-term care meant a welcome freedom to play. One of the units with a minibus took the children out for many trips for picnics on the nearby moors and seashore; this was popular with the children and made their stay seem more like a holiday for them instead of just being a break for their parents.

In working out aims and philosophies of short-term care it would seem important that the child's enjoyment of his stay should have as high a priority as relief for the parents, otherwise the service becomes merely a means of temporarily accommodating the children without much thought to their feelings about the arrangement. As much as parents require relief it would be wrong for it to be obtained at the expense of the child's need for security and happiness. (In some of my visits during the course of the study I was tempted to describe the services I saw as little more than "kennelling" or "garaging" the children, for it seemed as if no thought had gone into the service except to separate temporarily the child from his family: this point will also be referred to extensively in the final report.)

Short-term fostering

This form of care is now being developed in a number of places, having been pioneered by Somerset and Leeds social service departments in the mid-seventies. It is an excellent form of neighbourhood support and those parents who use it have found it very satisfactory. In the initial stages of the schemes being set up, some parents felt reluctant to take part; for them the word "foster" had implications that one was giving one's child to another family because one was a bad or unsuitable parent. However, following careful introductory meetings of parents and foster-parents in each other's houses and explanations about the needs of the handicapped child, the schemes have proved tremendously successful and many of the natural families now look on their short-term foster family as a form of extended family.

One of the many advantages of short-term fostering is that the child goes into an ordinary family home environment which not only has familiar physical features but normal family figures such as father, mother and sibs, so that he is able to retain a feeling of normality; he also receives more individual care than is possible in hostels or hospitals which have constantly changing staff and numbers of children. Three of the complaints referred to earlier (loss of clothes, boredom and a mix of difficult children) do not occur when a child is fostered with an ordinary family.

Short-term foster parents of handicapped children are usually paid a higher allowance than those who foster normal children, and may receive help as necessary from the local services — for example, provision of incontinence pads, special bedding and mealtime utensils for children who have feeding problems; advice from physiotherapists and domiciliary occupational therapists on the physical handling of cerebral palsied children; advice from community nurses on any problems of feeding or medication. The parents themselves, however, provide the most important link between their handicapped child and the short-term foster family, by keeping in close contact with them and explaining their child's routines and likes and dislikes. The schemes are being used by children who have a wide variety of mental handicaps, including those who are very dependent and may need everything done for them, those with severe epilepsy and some very active children who may also show disturbed behaviour.

The foster families need to be carefully chosen and should receive initial training and follow-up opportunities for regular discussion groups about the service they are providing. One conclusion of the study is that great care should be taken to see that they do not overwork or impose emotional burdens on themselves because they have formed a warm and positive relationship with the families they are helping. One disadvantage of the scheme is the problem that arises if for some reason — such as moving house or the illness of a member — a foster family has to stop taking a child. Parents who have learnt to rely on the foster family's help become upset if it is withdrawn, and the foster parents themselves may feel guilty about letting the other family down. This very human problem of attachment between families is unavoidable, because the whole success of the scheme is based on the formation of a trusting relationship;

however, the problem may be lessened, even if it cannot be eliminated altogether, if it is faced from the beginning in discussion groups and if careful plans are made for the change-over of foster family so that the handicapped child and his parents do not have to face changes without preparation.

The financing of short-term care services

The financial aspects of short-term residential care vary according to which body provides the service. Homes run by charitable organisations occasionally have a short-term care bed and some parents make their own arrangements to use this, paying anything from £50 to £100 a week. Local authority social service departments may occasionally subsidize a two-weeks stay for a child at one of these charitable Homes if there is no hospital or local authority hostel available, and if the family circumstances show there is a need for help and the parents are unable to meet the costs themselves.

No reliable information is available on exactly how much private provision exists for the short-term care of mentally handicapped children, but one tentative estimate has suggested that there are probably fewer than 200 beds available in private Homes in the whole of the United Kingdom (personal communication, Headquarters of the National Society for Mentally Handicapped Children, 1980). The charge is anything from £70 to £100 a week for short-term care.

Parents whose children use National Health Service premises do not have to pay anything, because the children come under hospital in-patient statistics and, in accordance with the National Health Service Act 1948, all hospital in-patient care is free at the point of delivery (i.e., the costs are covered from central government funds). The national average cost to the Area Health Authority of having a child or adult in one of its mental handicap hospitals works out at £94.36 a week (DHSS Statistics for 1978–79).

Payment in local authority premises varies according to local government decisions. There is no national ruling on charges, because local authorities are autonomous and central government can only *advise* on their running of local social services; it cannot *force* local authorities to make charges. This means that parents living in some areas are not paying anything for their children's short-term care in local authority hostels, while in other areas parents are charged according to their means, and in others again a child is allowed to have two weeks each year free but his parents are then charged up to £15 a week for any further care. Some local authority hostels which were free when they opened have begun to charge parents in 1980 in order to meet central government directives to cut back on public spending. For example, one hostel which opened in 1977 was entirely free and permitted parents to use it as much as they liked up to, but not exceeding, a maximum of 50% of the year; however, in 1980 this hostel began to charge parents £6.20 a week. Other local authorities have decided to keep their short-term care services free and aim to meet the economies in public spending by cutting back on some other facilities such as services for elderly people.

The cost to a local authority of running a short-term facility is high and becomes exceedingly high if it is under-used. One hostel which has 20 beds and is well used all the year round is estimated as costing its local authority £170 a week per bed; another, which has 16 beds and is grossly under-used, costs its local authority as much as £500 a week per bed.

Short-term foster schemes, for which there is no charge to parents, are not so expensive to provide as care in a hostel or hospital. Local authorities pay short-term foster parents of handicapped children anything from £35 to £56 a week for each child (1980 figures). The payment varies according to local decisions. By 1980 more than a dozen short-term foster schemes had been established in the United Kingdom, the majority of them being funded jointly by the local authority and the Area Health Authority. The joint funding of new schemes was made possible by the National Health Service Reorganisation Act, 1974, and has given rise to many innovative schemes of community care for vulnerable client groups, including persons who are elderly, mentally handicapped or mentally ill. More and more local authorities are now choosing to develop short-term foster schemes for their handicapped children rather than build hostels, because such schemes have proved to be an economical way of providing a satisfactory service. In Somerset, where a well-established foster scheme has been running since 1976, it is estimated that 300 families are now being helped at an annual cost of approximately £11 000.

Main conclusions

Short-term residential care is a helpful form of family support, but it should be locally-based and flexible in nature if it is to meet the individual needs of families. Common complaints refer to loss of clothing, difficulty in booking in children, bored children and the problems of mixing together children who have very different needs. Some parents feel guilty about using short-term care and this feeling is stronger if the service is poor. Complaints and feelings of guilt might be lessened if parents were given more responsibility for the management of the units, but both staff and parents seem reluctant to collaborate in deciding unit policies, and parental involvement tends to be confined to fund-raising activities. Homesickness is a real problem but this fact is not sufficiently acknowledged by either staff or parents. Care staff need to define more clearly their aims in providing short-term care, so that the service meets the needs of the children as well as helping their parents. More positive contact should be developed between unit staff and other professionals working with the children, e.g. special-school teachers. Short-term fostering is a successful form of neighbourhood help and a more normal way of providing residential care than by putting the children into hospitals or hostels. One of the problems of short-term fostering is that a close attachment is often formed between families, and it can be very upsetting if one of the families moves away; however, this type of trauma can be reduced if families are prepared for such an event from the beginning and have opportunities for discussion.

Finally, it must be emphasized that short-term care services will only be of benefit to the majority of mentally retarded children and their families under a system which allows the main bulk of the costs to be paid from public funds, without too many bureaucratic difficulties.

References

Jones, K. (1975). *Opening the Door*. Routledge and Kegan Paul: London.
King, R., Raynes, N. and Tizard, J. (1971). *Patterns of Residential Care*. Routledge and Kegan Paul: London.
Morris, P. (1969). *Put Away*. Routledge and Kegan Paul: London.
National Development Group for the Mentally Handicapped (1978): *Helping Mentally Handicapped People in Hospital*. A Report to the Secretary of State for Social Services. Department of Health and Social Security: London.
Oswin, M. (1971). *The Empty Hours*. Allen Lane, Penguin Press: Harmondsworth.
Oswin, M. (1978). *Children Living in Long-stay Hospitals*. Heinemann Medical Books for Spastics International Medical Publications: London.
Report of the Committee of Inquiry into Allegations of Ill-Treatment of Patients and Other Irregularities at the Ely Hospital Cardiff (1969). HMSO: London.
Report of the Committee of Inquiry into South Ockendon Hospital (1974). HMSO: London.
Report of the Committee of Inquiry into Normansfield Hospital (1978). HMSO: London.
Shearer, A. (1980). *Handicapped Children in Residential Care*. Bedford Square Press: London.
Tizard, J. (1964). *Community Services for the Mentally Handicapped*. Oxford University Press: London.
Tizard, J., King, R.D., Raynes, N.V. and Yule, W. (1967). The care and treatment of subnormal children in residential institutions. *Proc. First Int. Cong. Spec. Educat.*, London, July, 1966.

Part 7
Early Diagnosis and Prevention

17 Sensory defect, impaired awareness and maladaptive parent–child interaction: their assessment and comparison as indicators of mental handicap in unresponsive motor-intact infants

D.M. RICKS

Children's Department, Harperbury Hospital, Shenley, Radlett, UK

In contrast to the usually prompt detection of motor disability, discovering conditions which distort or reduce the infant's awareness of the world around him is often late. Delayed detection of sensory handicap in the motor-intact infant has serious repercussions, since his parents are bewildered by his odd or unresponsive behaviour combined with apparently normal physical development. As a result there may be far-reaching consequences for the development of the child and the emotional stability of his family. Since evidence is accumulating that early parent–child interaction may be crucial for activating receptive skills, it is essential to ascertain as early as possible in what way the unresponsive child is handicapped. This paper reviews some of the various methods available for this process and the problems associated with such methods both in technique and in interpretation.

An obvious initial major problem is the nature of the child himself. He often looks normal but has aroused anxiety, usually because he seems inaccessible or doesn't communicate. He may or may not have had an episode of cerebral insult. Since by definition he is either unresponsive or oddly — i.e. unpredictably — responsive, he will not cooperate in standard normal testing procedures. Since he has little or no motor defect, and is probably in his second year, he will be well-equipped to be uncooperative. So the first requirements of any clinician assessing such a child are patience, the capacity to observe rather than to intervene, and a readiness to watch the child in familiar settled surroundings where he is more likely to perform. This is vital since the emphasis of investigation must be on what a child can do; what he cannot or will not do will be obvious enough. A patiently awaited but convincing positive response is

of the utmost importance, since the absence of response does not necessarily indicate that the child is unable to detect the stimulus but only
perhaps that he is unwilling or disinterested.

Defects which interfere with the response of such a child can be considered as occurring at three levels. At the first level the child's receptors
may be defective and since most of the sensory input used by the motor-
intact infant is auditory and visual, his capacity to see and hear must be
investigated. Obviously his eyes and ears must be examined for end
organ pathology; usually it is absent so the investigation moves on to find
out how efficiently eyes and ears function. The second stage is to try and
evaluate how the brain responds to the information these receptors
provide — testing what may be called visual and auditory awareness.
Two approaches are available for this task; either by electrophysiological
investigation or by observing behaviour in controlled conditions. Both
have their advantages and limitations. A third stage which is as yet little
explored would be to examine as systematically as possible the way a
child interacts with his parents, especially his mother. This rests on the
assumption that we judge the child to be registering sensory information
because he performs particular motor acts, regarded as appropriate by his
mother, persuading her and us that he is aware of her behaviour. A
growing array of research on this topic is emphasising the importance
such inter-action may have on developing the child's awareness so that
early difficulties or distortion in the mother–child interaction, if carefully
assessed, may be a sensitive indication of handicapping conditions in the
child. These various stages of investigation will be discussed in turn.

Sensory defect

Although in most cases the unresponsive infant has no end-organ
pathology, this possibility must be carefully excluded. Examining the
eyes may reveal lens opacities, retinal pathology or a convincingly pale
disc, or the ear may have a blocked external meatus, but these findings are
rare in this broad group of children. Pupil reactions may be intact, indeed
brisk, but the child may neither blink nor follow a light; nor may simple
distraction techniques, however carefully executed, produce a positive
response to sound. The practising clinician must then usually proceed to
patient repeated behavioural assessment, such as the capacity to avoid
obstacles or to aim in reaching and grasping or to cease movement
suddenly in response to sound. However, often no clear evidence is
obtained, particularly with sound stimuli, so that further investigation
calls for electrophysiological methods. In the case of vision, the elec-
troretinogram (ERG) will reveal a functioning eye, whilst obtaining

visual-evoked responses indicates that the signal reaches the visual cortex. The neurophysiologists with whom I work try to obtain an acceptable EEG recording in the same session, since the absence of an occipital pre-alpha rhythm, they believe, suggests in the presence of a positive visual evoked response that the child is not processing the signal arriving at his visual cortex and so should be regarded as visually "unaware". Problems in this procedure are to obtain a clear recording with a lively, uncooperative infant, and to ensure his detection of a supplied visual stimulus unless it is as striking as a flash — which in turn raises doubts of interpretation.

Hearing can be objectively tested with transtympanic cochleography which at least establishes the presence or absence of a responsive discharge in the cochlea nerve to about 10–15 dB of threshold at 3kHz. However, positioning the electrode at the basal turn of the chochlea prevents the reliable detection of chochlea responses to low-frequency sounds of, for example, 500 Hz which, because it is the frequency range of vowels and inflected vocal sounds, is the most significant range of hearing useful to the infant as he is handled, spoken and crooned to by his mother. A further technical problem is the length of time such a procedure may take, remembering that the infant needs to be anaesthetized throughout. Additional responses giving information about the compound action-potential from the cochlea plus the responses from the four nuclei in the auditory pathway up to the inferior colliculus may be recorded during this procedure or independently using surface electrodes. Middle latency responses between 10 and 100 msec., thought to come from the thalamus, are also obtainable under anaesthetic but are less reliable. Assessment of cortical responses to sound is controversial. Though earlier work (Hrbek *et al.*, 1969; Lenard *et al.*, 1969), and indeed current clinical practice outside the UK (Lenard, 1980) would dispute this point, it is the opinion of the author's colleagues that reliable estimates of acoustic cortical responses require an alert, awake child (Gibson, 1978; Hazel and Graham, 1980). Thus although a positive cortical response, even if obtainable, would indicate intact auditory attention, a negative one strengthens suspicions but does not indicate that the child is unable to attend to a sound stimulus. The protracted investigation may thus bring assessment no further forward. The importance of detecting peripheral response to lower frequency sounds is met by measuring changes in acoustic impedance through the stapedius reflex. Responses to frequencies of 500 Hz can be reliably obtained by this method which is non-invasive, but needs a degree of cooperation to ensure that the ear probe is stable enough to register those pressure changes resulting from changes in compliance of the ear drum.

With certain reservations, therefore, the clinician can discover whether the unresponsive child can hear or not. The detection of such defect, particularly if accompanied by evidence of end-organ pathology, is of course no indication of potential mental handicap, since blind or deaf children with intact brains develop normal intelligence. Indeed, it is the confirming of *intact* visual and auditory receptivity which alerts the clinician to the possibility in the unresponsive child of severe retardation.

Investigations by these methods reveal not only that the child can hear, but roughly how well he hears and over which frequencies, whereas such electrophysiological investigations of vision, although confirming that the child sees, do not reveal how well or how badly he does so. Although there is no evidence connecting severe refractive error with intellectual deficit, it is certainly worthwhile attempting to discover such error in an unresponsive child. The diagnosis presents considerable difficulty. With sufficient patience, an experienced ophthalmologist is able to refract or at least to exclude severe refractive error of 3 dioptres or more in uncooperative children. His persistence in this is all the more appreciated since the more convenient method of refracting under anaesthetic can be misleading because of the extreme difficulty in refracting along the child's visual axis when he is anaesthetized. Recently the technique of photo-refraction has been developed at the Infant Vision Unit in Cambridge. The technicalities of this method, although lengthy to explain, are ingenious and quite simple and have been published (Braddick *et al.*, 1979). Gross refractive error may seriously limit the child's visual attention and although not causal may significantly further impair the responsiveness of a suspect child at least to the extent that the pattern of his handling and stimulation should take it into account.

Impaired awareness

Assuming that the child has no demonstrable defect in his receptors, his clinical state will be attributed to an impairment in awareness, generally assumed to result from a cortical defect in the manner in which his brain processes the information his receptors provide. This is of course an enormously complex field, so that we are compelled to use nebulous terms to describe the child's difficulties, such as "he does not attend", "isn't aware of", or "doesn't make sense of" stimuli presented to him. If we are to examine more closely in practice what these terms mean with reference to a suspect handicapped child, two approaches are available: first, electrophysiological studies of changes in his brain arousal associated with various forms of sensory input; secondly, observation of behaviour thought to be responsive to controlled or defined stimuli. These approaches will be discussed in turn.

Electro-physiological studies of brain arousal

There is a great deal of interesting work on the measurement of electrical changes recorded from scalp electrodes which seem to be associated with cerebral activities processing visual or auditory input. Most of this research is concerned with the blocking of rhythms in different sections of the cortex. Thus, an occipital rhythm, often called a pre-alpha rhythm, is blocked when an infant attends visually. If the stimulus is repeated until attention is lost, the blocking can be re-established by a change in the pattern of the stimulus or from some additional alerting signal. Similarly, a "mu" rhythm in the rolandic area is described, which blocks not only with motor acts but with intention to perform them; for example, when a child is asked — and presumably "intends" — to clutch his fist, the rhythm blocks before the motor act occurs. This and early studies, for example by Grey Walter (1969) on contingent negative variation or anticipatory waves, now extended to the measurement of event-related slow potential changes of the EEG in young children (Gullickson, 1973; Schulman-Galambos and Galambos, 1978) all suggest that it would be feasible to detect an absence of "intent" or "interest" by means of electrophysiological methods. These procedures require expensive equipment and highly trained staff; their interpretation is technically complicated and controversial; but above all convincing results depend upon the child's cooperation. Indeed, linking the record with particular cerebral processes we would call "understanding" or "intending" depends as yet on establishing these acts independently, for example by enquiry to check that the child understands the command "close your fist" and intends to carry it out. It could be argued that more extensive data on such EEG changes in response to standardized stimuli in normal children could facilitate the investigation of suspect children in the same standardized situation. However, a major problem even in normals is to establish a reliable resting state producing a recognizable rhythm, since the infant is so susceptible to stimuli around him and this difficulty would be greater in the children we are investigating. Furthermore, a negative result— that is, an absence of blocking— would not distinguish between inability and disinterest: a difference which may be of crucial clinical significance.

Observing responses in a standard situation

Assessing a child's awareness of stimuli from his behaviour is the basis of simple screening tests. In all of them there is a problem of rapidly waning interest, so that the procedures need to be brief. Distraction tests with suitable precautions are thought to indicate, from his turning his head or eyes, that a child listens to a variety of sounds. This kind of testing can be extended by the use of conditional responses to detect his listening to sounds at different pitch or loudness. Using similar simple behavioural guides, Braddick and Atkinson (1977) have developed techniques for assessing visual acuity and discriminating visual interest in infants. They present the infant with a visual display, alternating between two screens at a calculated distance, initially attracting his gaze to a central position between the screens with a vertical array of flashing lights. By presenting a series of grids of various spacing and brightness, balanced against a blank screen of the same luminosity, they record the child's preference for fixating the grating pattern rather than the uniform field. Apart from the screen, the child, sitting on his mother's lap, is surrounded by a uniform grey fabric to avoid distraction. With this method of forced choice, they are able to estimate the limits of contrast sensitivity, its change over the first months of life, how it differs in response to moving the static patterns, and the detection of spatial detail by presenting two pictures of a face, one of which is de-focused. Work of this nature, using simple behavioural responses to carefully structured stimuli, points to screening techniques which more clearly indicate whether the clinically suspect child is "attending". However, judging that the child is using his cortex to register a particular sensory stimulus by behaviour regarded as appropriate can be misleading. A few cautionary examples deserve mention.

If we are to believe that a particular act indicates response to a given stimulus, we must ensure that it is not a response to other incidental events. Normal young children are highly distractable, hence the problem of obtaining a resting state pre-alpha rhythm in their EEG. The clinically suspect child may be regarded as unresponsive simply because he elects to respond to stimuli other than those presented. Although care to reduce distraction is an obvious safeguard, the most effective way of demonstrating selective attention is by procedures that test the child's ability to transfer attention from one signal to another. Stensland Junker (1972) has developed a simple testing technique for such a purpose, to which nearly all children can produce appropriate responses by seven to nine months; failure in the test at, or beyond, this age gives early evidence of attention defect.

Another factor complicating the simple interpretation of any act as an appropriate response to one sensory channel is that the sensation tested may be closely related to and indeed dominated by another. For example, Lee and Aronson (1974) have demonstrated that children readily fall, as if their balance were defective, when the wall alongside them appears to move even though the floor is stable. Their proprioceptive capacity to maintain posture is easily disrupted by visual information. Again, a child's responses are quite early triggered not simply by an effective sensory channel to register them but by their expectations; that is to say, he may respond to one of a combination of sensations which normally occur together, because some cerebral mechanism equips or compels him to do so. This has been ingeniously demonstrated by Aronson and Rosenbloom (1971), who showed that quite young infants expect voices to come out of faces, and by Bower (1974), who showed that they expect seen objects to be tangible. These examples suggest that children are already in infancy using an array of interdependent mechanisms which presumably guide their attention and complicate the apparently simple connection between a sensory stimulus, its reception and an act, called appropriate, which reveals the child's awareness of that stimulus.

If we are unaware of such complications we may interpret particular acts incorrectly and assume too readily that they reveal a child's social awareness, or are developed in response to socially significant stimuli as we understand them. There are many examples of this fallacy. Blind babies not only smile in response to their mothers' voices (in fact, as Freedman (1964) and Fraiberg (1979) point out, their smiling is more selective for the mothers than that of children with sight), but they also orientate towards the mother's face, so that it would be an understandable error to assume they were responding to a visual display. Normal babies, certainly by eight months, develop an array of inflected vocal signals which, it can be experimentally demonstrated, register their response to a standard situation (Ricks, 1972, 1975). Thus, they produce "request" noises in their efforts to reach a desired object, frustrated noises when they cannot achieve it, and a "surprised" noise at a novel, pleasing situation. These vocal signals have two characteristics: they are almost identical between children independently of their language background, and they are equally likely to occur if parents are present or absent. Common sense would suggest that they are signals learned from patterns children hear in the language around them and that they are voiced in order to obtain the appropriate social response. The evidence suggests that neither of these suppositions is true. We do not yet know whether or not deaf children produce these sounds, so they may or may not be evidence of "listening", but they are certainly not an indication of social awareness. If children's vocal output were related to the frequency with which speech sounds occurred— that is to say, that a child used first those sounds he was most likely to hear — they would follow a totally different pattern of phonetic development from that which applies. Fourcin (1978) has demonstrated that the sequence of speech sound contrasts a child masters relates to the acoustic complexity of these sounds and not to the frequency with which they are heard or heeded by the child as he embarks on speech.

In general, to judge a child's awareness by his behaviour responses such as facial expression, turning the eyes or vocal output as being appropriate to a particular stimulating event needs much more caution than is often supposed. The connection between stimulus and response is complicated presumably by an array of cerebral editing mechanisms which we need to know a great deal more about. Quite early in the child's life these mechanisms may be imposing some sort of order which guides the child's attention, but which is constantly being adjusted and modified. The fact that quite young children do not register for example all the acoustic properties of a voice, but divert their attention to what is being said, has been demonstrated by Costello (1965), who showed that three-year-olds were unable to recognize their own voices on a tape-recording when asked to select it from tapes of other children all saying the same thing. Indeed, accurate recognition of voice sounds at that age is a characteristic of severely handicapped autistic children, as revealed by their skilful mimicry (Ricks, 1978). Although normal children cannot recognize their own voices, non-communicating autistic three-year-olds selectively imitate their own vocal output played back on a tape; they ignore the voices of other autistic children or a mimicry of their own supplied by a normal child of the same age. There is no doubt that these children are aware of their own voices, indeed to an extent unequalled in normal children, but their sensitivity seems to deter rather than assist them in acquiring language.

Thus, any clinically suspect child may have no defect in his receptors; the sensory information his brain receives may be adequate for normal functioning and his brain may process that information quite actively, so that we may assume the child is aware of it. Nevertheless, such processing may result in behavioural responses which we interpret as inappropriate or as indicating disinterest. How is behaviour at this early stage fashioned and rendered appropriate? To what extent does the term "appropriate" have social connotations so that we may assume it is modified through interaction with the mother? Certainly, mothers are usually the most sensitive guide to abnormalities in their child. Can we disentangle reliable indications of potential handicap in the child from indications of anxiety in the mother?

Maladaptive parent–child interaction

The role mothers play in enabling their infants to make sense of their world is bound up closely with the development of mutually satisfying communicative exchange. This is an exciting field now being actively studied by a number of researchers, most of whom assume that the child is little stimulated by the inanimate environment but greatly stimulated by what Newson (1974) calls "person-mediated" events. He points out that for the infant the mother has all the qualities to capture his attention; she is mobile, colourful, noise-producing, and in particular phases her own acts in response to his behaviour in ways which capture, prolong and elaborate his awareness of her. The particular qualities of this interaction between mother and baby have been described in detail by Trevarthen (1974), Tronick (1971), Stern (1974) and many others, with respect to mouth movements, facial expression, cooing, smiling, vocal inflection, hand movements and a whole array of other acts. The major point is that a great deal of evidence is accumulating which connects this interaction with the infant's awareness of facial expression and the significance of different inflections of voice, as revealed in his spectacular capacity to control his own posture, vocal output and facial expression closely to imitate that of his mother. It seems that this reciprocal, mutually adapted behaviour between mother and child opens up a child's awareness and enables him to become a communicating individual. Almost all this behaviour is unintentional in the sense that mothers, video-taped in relaxed familiar situations, appear themselves to be behaving quite spontaneously. Indeed, much of the work concentrates on the unselfconscious mutual adjustment of stimulation and response that occurs between mother and child. It is tempting to suggest that this adaptive behaviour between them is necessary for the development of the child's awareness and his capacity to organize his motor acts as socially appropriate. Two cautionary notes are needed here, since it is only a short step from this point to the assumption that, because such mutually adaptive interaction is necessary for normal learning, maladaptive behaviour on the part of the mother may be a common cause of the child's failure to become normally aware, to learn and to communicate. The two cautions are: (1) that we need to know whether it is the mother or her baby who initiates and paces the interaction, and (2) that we also need to know whether the mother's behaviour patterns the skills and child develops or whether it facilitates skills already established. I will examine each of these points in turn.

Kaye and Braselton (1971), in a detailed study of feeding, found that mothers commonly jiggled their babies between pauses in their sucking, in the belief that this speeded up the onset of the next burst of sucking. In fact it delayed it, because the baby began sucking shortly after jiggling had stopped. This the mother learned within two weeks and so shortened her jiggling phases to provide more frequent opportunity to restart sucking, and judged the pause by the baby's readiness to do so. Thus, the mother fitted her behaviour into the baby's natural rhythm; the interaction between the two was paced by the child.

A whole array of similar, carefully studied examples exist, some of which have recently been published in a book edited by Margaret Bullowa

(1979). The evidence suggests that this highly significant, mutually adaptive behaviour is paced by the baby rather than by the mother, although the mother usually believes and acts as if she were initiating the exchange.

The second question is whether such interaction patterns the child's sensory-motor skills or merely facilitates them once they are already established. Two experiments on parents assisting their children to develop skills are interesting in this context. The first concerns an infant's efforts to reach an object. Bower (1974) has demonstrated that up to about five months a baby aims his reach by locating the target visually, locating his hand proprioceptively, computing a trajectory between them and launching his hand along it. He persists in this even if he repeatedly misses when the position he visually fixes on a target is distorted by a prism. A month or two later he will visually track his reach. Kaye (1970) showed how mothers of six-months-old babies taught them to reach round a plexi-glass screen to retrieve an object. Two points in this study are important. First, the strategy the mother used followed various cues given by the infant — her teaching was "baby-paced"; secondly, it was visually mediated so that it depended on the child visually tracking his reach. In other words, it was only effective because it corrected or facilitated a pattern of sensory-motor control already available and developed about a month earlier.

The second experiment concerns the early use of words. In a study of infants about 18 months old (Ricks, 1975), I discovered that their earliest words had a pointing or labelling quality referring to a broad category of often apparently dissimilar objects to which they attached the label word with zeal, usually pointing enthusiastically as they did so. The words they used to label this group of objects seemed often almost accidentally acquired, generated by the child and rarely achieved by imitation of the adult word; indeed, the parents usually adopted the child's word themselves — another example of "baby-paced" interaction. If a recording of this label word spoken by the parents and two other adults was played to the child, he was alerted to the sound and imitated it preferentially in response to his parents' voices. This does not seem remarkable, but becomes so when compared with a previous similar experiment. This was carried out two months earlier before the child had acquired any label words. In it each child was presented with recordings of words like "dada" used at that time to encourage his imitation and again spoken on the tape by his parents and two other adults. In this situation, not only did he imitate the word less but, significantly, there was no greater likelihood of his imitating it in response to his parents' voices than to those of the other adults. Thus, his greater readiness to imitate, to respond to his parents depended on the word offered by them having some labelling quality which he himself had supplied. In other words, although his parents said words to him to encourage his imitation and his capacity to label, i.e. to call them "Mama" or "Dada" he did not at that stage respond to *their* words preferentially. *Their* words became important to him to imitate after he had, apparently independently, endowed a particular word with meaning by applying it to a category of objects. Thus, their encouragement facilitated the skill —use of a label word independently established — it did not generate it.

It would seem that defects in this highly significant, mutually adaptive interaction between mother and infant are unlikely in most cases to be the cause of unresponsive or apparently inaccessible children, since on closer examination the interaction, although monitored closely by her, is neither initiated nor paced by the mother but rather facilitates the practice and elaboration of sensory-motor skills already patterned or programmed independently. However, it is clear that, since an interaction is crucial to the development of the child's sensory-motor skills, its suppression, interruption, or distortion will have serious repercussions. In this context the infant's role in setting the place of the interaction is crucial. If a child, for whatever reason, does not develop normal sensory-motor skills he will not provide his mother with the triggers and cues with which he would engage her in this vital dialogue. Since she is largely unaware of these cues she will initially only vaguely realise their absence, and later will not be able to identify them. But their absence or unusual quality will not merely arouse her anxiety and distort her interaction with her child; there is evidence that her efforts to establish normal interaction may well result in her behaving in ways which reduce rather than refine his awareness and aggravate his disability. This viewpoint has been developed elsewhere (Ricks, 1977).

Faced with a mobile, or at least motor-intact, infant who is unresponsive, the clinician will automatically investigate the child's hearing and vision. Discovering defects in these senses is an obviously justifiable priority in his assessment. Their early detection enables him to equip the child with aids and to recommend management which will help the child's own efforts to compensate for his sensory defects. But many children who later emerge as handicapped by what Wing and Gould (1979) have termed "severe impairment of social interaction", have no demonstrable pathology in ears or eyes. Nevertheless they constitute one of the most severely disabled groups of children and certainly one of the most difficult to help. The contrast between their gloomy prognosis and that of blind or deaf children of normal intelligence is a striking illustration of how much more disabling are defects in those cerebral mechanisms which equip children to utilize the information their senses provide. As yet, defects in these mechanisms are too often virtually dismissed as "retardation" or "psychosis" with the result that such blanket terms are offered as explanations for a distorted or delayed development which may well render the child totally dependent, socially inaccessible and chronically disturbed. The difficulties confronting anyone who, dissatisfied by these evasive terms, attempts to analyse more thoroughly the nature of the defects in a search for helpful intervention have been made clear in this chapter. Clearly there is much to learn about how even normal infants acquire those simple developmental skills which depend on their being aware and attentive. However, we should not rely too confidently on such normal data when attempting to assess or, more particularly, to help the progress and improve the management of the young mentally handicapped child (Ricks, 1980). But alongside these cautions may be set the exciting prospects offered by improving electrophysiological techniques, experimental ingenuity and sensitive observation of parent–child interactions.

References

Aronson, E. and Rosenbloom, S. (1971). Space perception in early infancy: perception within a common auditory-visual space. *Science (N.Y.)* **172**, 1161–1163.

Atkinson, J., Braddick, O. and Moar, K. (1977). Infant detection of image defocus. *Vision Res.* **17**, 1125–1126. Pergamon Press: Oxford.

Bower, T. (1974). Development of infant behaviour. *Br. med. Bull.* **30**, 175–178.

Bower, T., Broughton, J. and Moore, M. (1970). The coordination of visual and tactual input in infants. *Percept. Psychophys.* **8**, 51–53.

Braddick, O. and Atkinson, J. (1977). Development of contrast sensitivity over the first three months of life in the human infant. *Vision Res.* **17**, 1037–1044. Pergamon Press: Oxford.

Braddick, O., Atkinson, J., French, J. and Howland, H. (1979). A photorefractive study of infant accommodation. *Vision Res*. Pergamon Press: Oxford.

Bullowa, M. (ed.) (1979). *Before Speech*. Cambridge University Press: Cambridge, UK.

Costello, A. (1965). Medical Research Council, Family Research Unit, London (unpublished).

Fourcin, A.J. (1978). Acoustic patterns of speech acquisition. In: Waterson and Snow (eds.): *The Development of Communication*. John Wiley: New York.

Fraiberg, S. (1979). Blind infants, their mothers and the sign system. In: M. Bullowa (ed.): *Before Speech*, pp. 149–169. Cambridge University Press: Cambridge, UK.

Freedman, D. (1964). Smiling in blind infants and the issue of innate versus acquired. *J. Child Psychol. Psychiatry* **5**, 171–184.

Gibson, W.P.R. (1978). *Essentials of Clinical Electric Response Audiometry*, pp. 48–51. Churchill-Livingstone: London.

Gullickson, G.R. (1973). CNV and behavioural attention to a glidetone warning of interesting non-moving kaleidoscopic visual or auditory patterns in 2 and 3 year-old children. In: McCallum, W.C. and Knott, J.R. (eds.): *Event-related*

Slow Potentials of the Brain, pp. 145–150. Elsevier: Amsterdam.

Hazel, J. and Graham, J. (1980). Royal Ear Hospital, University College Hospital, London. Personal Communication.

Hrbek, A., Hrbkova, M. and Lenard, H. (1969). Somato-sensory and visual evoked responses in newborn infants during sleep and wakefulness. *Electroencephelogr. Clin. Neurophysiol.* **26**, 597–603.

Kaye, K. (1970). Maternal participation in infant acquisition of a skill. Unpublished dissertation. Harvard University.

Kay, K. and Brazelton, T. (1971). Mother-infant interaction in the organisation of sucking. Unpublished.

Lee, D.M. and Aronson, E. (1974). Visual proprioreceptive control of standing in human infants. *Percept. Psychophys.* **15**, 529–532.

Lenard, H. (1980). Kinderklinik, Städtische Krankenanstalten, Mannheim. Personal Communication.

Lenard, H., von Bernuth, M. and Hutt, S.J. (1969). Acoustic evoked responses in newborn infants: the influence of pitch and complexitiy of the stimulus. *Electroencephalogr. Clin. Neurophysiol.* **27**, 121–127.

Newson, J. (1974). Towards a theory of infant understanding. *Bull. Br. Psychol. Soc.* **27**, 251–7.

Ricks, D.M. (1975). Vocal communication in pre-verbal normal and autistic children. In: O'Connor, N. (ed.): *Language Cognitive Defects and Retardation*, pp. 75–80. Butterworths: London.

Ricks, D.M. (1972). The beginning of vocal communication in normal and autistic children. Unpublished thesis, University of London.

Ricks, D.M. (1977). Bringing up disabled children. *Proc. R. Soc. Med.* **70**, 28–30.

Ricks, D.M. (1978). Making sense to make sensible sounds. In: Bullowa, M. (ed.): *Before Speech*, pp. 245–268. Cambridge University Press: Cambridge, UK.

Ricks, D.M. (1980). Promoting basic developmental skills in severely retarded children: the need for research into normal models and their values. In: Lader, M. (ed.): *Priorities in Psychiatric Research*. Mental Health Foundation: London (In press).

Schulman-Galambos, C. and Galambos, R. (1978). Cortical responses from adults and infants to complex visual stimuli. *Electroencephalogr. Clin. Neurophysiol.* **45**, 425–435.

Stensland Junkler K. (1972). Selective attention in infants and consecutive communication behaviour. *Acta Paediatr. Scand.* **320**.

Stern, D. (1974). Mother and infant at play: the dyadic interaction involving facial, vocal and gaze behaviours. In: Lewis, M. and Rosenblum, L. (eds.): *The Effect of the Infant on its Caregiver*. Wiley: New York.

Trevarthen, C. (1974). Conversations with a two-month-old. *New Scientist* **62**, 230–235.

Tronick, E. (1971). Stimulus control and the growth of the infant's visual field. *Percept. Phychophys.* **11**, 373–6.

Tronick, E., Als, H. and Adamson, L. (1971). Structure of early face-to-face communicative interactions. In: Bullowa, M. (ed.): *Before Speech*. op. cit. (pp. 349–372).

Walter, W.G. (1969). The contingent negative variation as a cortical sign of attention in man. Discussion in: Evans, C.R. and Mulholland, T.B. (eds.): *Attention in Neurophysiology*. Butterworths: London.

Wing, L. and Gould, J. (1979). Severe impairments of social interaction and associated abnormalities in children: epidemiology and classification. *J. Autism Dev. Disorders* **9**, 11–29.

18 Prevention of mental retardation

J.A. CORBETT

Hilda Lewis House, Bethlem Royal Hospital, Shirley, Croydon, UK

Introduction

One of the most commonly quoted indices of health in early infancy is the perinatal mortality rate; that is, the death rate per thousand still births and live births between the 28th week of gestation and the end of the first week of life. This rate has fallen rapidly in the past fifty years, in England and Wales, from over 60/1000 in 1933 to less than 15/1000 in 1979 (Chamberlain, 1979). The fall has been parallelled in all Western countries for which statistics are available. There is some evidence that the incidence of handicap tends to parallel this fall (Hagberg *et al.*, 1977), although the relationship is a complex one and may not hold when the perinatal mortality rate is low (British Medical Journal, 1980). Furthermore the causes of infant death have changed in their frequency; congenital disease now accounts for 25–30% of all infant deaths and, together with low birth weight and hypoxia, is now one of the commonest determinants of perinatal mortality (Galjaard, 1980).

Although perinatal mortality has fallen steeply, and the incidence of mental handicap may have fallen, there is no clear evidence of any corresponding fall in prevalence rates. For example the overall rate for children 7–14 given in the earliest reliable studies in England and Wales between 1925–7 was 20·9/1000 (Lewis, 1929) compared with 21·2/1000 in children aged 11 in 1965–69 (Davie *et al.*, 1972). The age specific prevalence rate for children with severe mental retardation aged 7–14 was 3·71/1000 in the 1925 study compared with rates of 3·45–5·0/1000 in studies reported more recently (Goodman and Tizard, 1962; Kushlick, 1967; Drillien, 1967; and Wing, 1971).

This discrepancy between the remarkable stability in prevalence rates, on the one hand, and reductions in perinatal mortality and possibly in the incidence of mental handicap, on the other hand, highlights the need to consider not only primary but also secondary and tertiary strategies for prevention. Primary prevention comprises all methods used to stop diseases or handicap occurring in the first place; secondary prevention refers to detection and remedial action at an early stage and tertiary prevention to the limitation of chronic disability and the prevention of the accumulation of secondary handicaps, if chronic intrinsic impairments are unavoidable.

Prevention of mild mental retardation

Although there is evidence of considerable geographical variation in the prevalence of mild mental retardation, in 80–90% (Clarke, 1969) it may be described as subcultural, resulting from an interaction between environmental hazards such as poor nutrition during pregnancy and early infancy, social and educational deprivation and polygenic factors responsible for the inheritance of intelligence.

The primary prevention of subcultural retardation is thus essentially a social and educational problem. We know relatively little in terms of hard facts about the secondary or tertiary prevention of this condition.

Most evidence concerning the possible prevention of mild mental retardation comes from "early intervention" studies in which attempts have been made to compensate for probable environmental and educational deprivation in young children at high risk from such adversity.

Early studies such as those of Skeels (1966) and Skodak (1968) have shown that young children removed from institutions, where they were subject to severe deprivation, made considerable gains in IQ scores over relatively short periods of time. These differences persisted into adult life in similarly deprived children who were adopted and were reflected in the occupational status and adjustment of the subjects.

Similar findings have been reported in isolated case studies of children removed from conditions of extreme isolation and adversity (Mason, 1942; Davis, 1947; Koluchova, 1972, 1976). Many attempts to enrich the environment of culturally deprived children, as in the Headstart programmes reviewed by Bereiter and Englemann (1966), Jensen (1969) and Bronfenbrenner (1975), have foundered because of the short duration and unsystematic nature of the techniques used and the lack of subsequent reinforcement.

An exception which illustrates some of the issues involved in such studies is the Milwaukee Project described by Garber and Heber (1977). In the early 1960s, in what was from the socioeconomic point of view one of the highest risk areas of Milwaukee, it was found that mild retardation was highly concentrated among families where maternal intelligence was low and that 45% of mothers accounted for nearly 80% of children with IQs below 80 (Heber, Dever and Conry, 1968). Following the intellectual development of children born to mothers with different IQ levels they found a marked decline from normal to retarded in the offspring of seriously socially disadvantaged mothers with IQs below 80.

As Kirk (1952) has pointed out, mildly retarded children are difficult to identify in the preschool period, at a time when intervention is likely to be most successful. Heber and Garber overcame this difficulty by utilising their research findings. Taking a maternal IQ of below 75 on the Wechsler Adult Intelligence Scale as their criterion for intervention, they compared the progress of 20 children and their families, who were subject to a six-year intensive intervention programme, with 20 matched controls. The programme for the children included attendance from the age of three months at a special day centre, where they received a highly structured programme of developmental stimulation and compensatory education. At the same time the mothers were involved in a vocational and social education programme which included job training.

The majority of the children have now been followed up until the age of nine years, that is three years after the cessation of the intervention when the children entered school. At the age of six years the mean IQ of the experimental group was 121 and that of the control group 87; at nine years, this difference of over thirty IQ points had been maintained, although there had been some fall off in both experimental and control groups. A number of criticisms have been levelled at this project both in terms of matching of the experimental and control groups (Page, 1972) and on more basic grounds of the design of the experiment (Throne, 1975). Heber and Garber themselves point out that there were considerable individual differences among the families and children both before and after the intervention; for example, not all the control group ended up as retarded and at follow-up only one third had IQs below 75 on the Wechsler Intelligence Scale for Children.

It is nonetheless possible to draw a number of general conclusions from this and other early intervention studies.

(1) There is a need for more and better indicators for intervention if it is to be used economically and effectively with the families in greatest need. These indicators should include better criteria for identifying family risk factors, as well as earlier and more reliable methods for measuring developmental delay. These techniques should be capable of application on an epidemiological basis.
(2) It is of vital importance to involve parents in the intervention programme.
(3) The intervention programmes must be flexible, so as to meet appropriately the needs of individual children and their families.
(4) There must be emphasis on particular aspects of skill development, for example language competence.
(5) Intervention should be based on a clear developmental framework, although not necessarily bound to a particular developmental theory.

(6) Intervention programmes need to be maintained over long periods if early gains are not be dissipated. Caldwell (1975) ends her review of early intervention projects in the USA on a cautionary note and suggests that because of the problems involved we may have to be content with an improvement from such measures of less than 25% in each generation. There is little subsequent evidence to suggest a more optimistic estimate than this.

Primary prevention of severe mental retardation

Before considering some examples of specific conditions which may be amenable to primary prevention, it is relevant to look at the changing patterns of morbidity among the severely retarded.

Firstly Down's Syndrome, which comprises all but a very small minority of severely retarded children with major chromosomal abnormalities, now accounts for nearly one third of the total (Corbett, 1978). In Lewis' study 40 years earlier less than 10% of children with this condition survived to school age (Lewis, 1929). More recently published epidemiological studies give widely varying prevalence rates for Down's Syndrome ranging from 0·6/1000 to 1·85/1000 for children of school age (Drillien, 1966; Birch et al., 1970; Wing, 1971). The higher figures are partly accounted for by increased prevalence rates, local variations in incidence and mortality and differences in case finding. In spite of this there has clearly been striking relative increase in this condition due to increased survival from intercurrent, particularly respiratory, infections.

Another important change has been the virtual disappearance from recent epidemiological studies in which the biological cause for severe mental retardation has been given of conditions such as cretinism, tuberculous meningitis, congenital syphilis and kernicterus due to rhesus incompatibility (Corbett, 1978; Kushlick, 1974). Although occasionally these conditions are still seen they have been virtually totally prevented as causes of severe mental retardation.

Alberman (1979) using data from a study carried out by Laxova and colleagues in Hertfordshire, England, of the different conditions found in a series of severely mentally retarded children born between 1965 and 1967 (Laxova et al., 1977) reports a distribution similar to that found among severely retarded children in Camberwell, South London, aged 0–14 in 1971 (see Table 1) and to that reported by Gustavson and his colleagues in Sweden (Gustavson et al., 1977). Alberman suggests that approximately 20% of cases are potentially preventable utilising present knowledge. This includes 20% of cases of Down's Syndrome if amniocentesis was taken up by all mothers over the age of 40, other genetically

Table 1 Causes of mental retardation in Camberwell children aged 0–4 (IQ <50; N = 140)

Causes unknown	15%
Post infective	14%
Metabolic	4%
Congenital abnormalities	9%
Other inherited conditions	10%
Perinatal injury	18%
Down's Syndrome	26%
Others	4%

determined conditions, cerebral palsy due to perinatal brain damage, meningitis, rubella embryopathy and neural tube defects. It has been argued that this estimate is unduly pessimistic; Hagard and Carter (1976) have suggested that, in economic terms, the "break even" maternal age above which mothers should be screened for Down's Syndrome is 35 years and that this would prevent up to 30% of cases. Such a policy has been in operation in Sweden for over five years (Hagberg, 1979) but it is not clear whether this or a decrease in maternal age have been responsible for a decreased incidence of severe mental handicap. Certainly the uptake of only 20–30%, even in mothers over 40 in Great Britain, of amniocentesis (Forster, 1977; Ferguson Smith, 1979) and the fact that this group comprises little more than 1% of all mothers suggests that alternative strategies need to be explored for the prevention of Down's Syndrome, which must include the search for other indicators for amniocentesis in addition to maternal age.

More complex is the situation where brain damage is caused at or around the time of birth. There is increasing evidence that intensive antenatal surveillance, monitoring for, and immediate relief of, distress during labour, resuscitation at birth and intensive neonatal care will do much to prevent permanent brain damage in a potentially normal infant (Stewart *et al.*, 1978).

The relationship between perinatal morbidity and mortality is however less clear and perinatal mortality rates in most European countries were falling prior to the introduction of such specific measures (British Medical Journal, 1980). The three major determinants of perinatal mortality are congenital abnormalities, hypoxia around the time of birth and low birth weight and these are often interrelated (Chamberlain, 1979). Particular changes in maternal factors which are known to influence perinatal mortality and may have had a more pervasive influence are a trend towards an age-range for child-bearing of between 20–34 years of age, a reduction in parity and a reduction of social class differences in perinatal mortality rates.

Table 2   Secondary handicaps associated with severe mental retardation in Camberwell children aged 0–14 (IQ <50; N = 140)

Additional congenital abnormalities	35%
Epileptic seizures	19%
Cerebral palsy	28%
Severe hearing impairment	17%
Severe visual impairment	9%
Behaviour disorder	47%
Severe behaviour disorder	10%
Severe incontinence	8%

Another general issue in the cost-benefit analysis of primary and secondary prevention of severe mental retardation concerns those strategies which, although perhaps not fully effective in preventing handicap, do substantially reduce the burden of care. Severe deafness and blindness resulting from rubella embryopathy in the first trimester of pregnancy produce one of the most disabling conditions responsible for severe mental handicap. Even though 30–40% of children appear normal at birth they are found to suffer from varying degrees of deafness by the age of six to eight years if the mother suffered from rubella during the first twelve weeks of pregnancy (Peckham, 1972). In Great Britain, immunization with live attenuated rubella vaccine has been offered to schoolgirls between their 11th and 15th birthdays since 1970. It is not possible because of the epidemic nature of the condition to say how effective this immunization programme is although early results are encouraging (Dudgeon, 1976). The low uptake in some areas is a matter for concern and it is relevant that all but one of the five affected children in the Camberwell Study were from immigrant families from countries where rubella is not endemic and who would not have had the benefit of prophylaxis. In the case of phenylketonuria there were two untreated children in the 1967 census of the Camberwell Register, both very severely affected and with seizures. No severely retarded children with phenylketonuria have appeared since that time. This shift of handicap from a very severely affected group to a mildly or non-handicapped group is highlighted by the study of MacCreedy and Jaffrey (1974) comparing the admission of phenylketonuria patients to residential institutions in the USA before and after effective screening programmes had been instituted in different states. This showed that no phenylketonuria patients had been admitted since screening had become effective, confirming the reduction in severe morbidity. There is, however, evidence of an increased rate of behaviour disorders and mild handicap among the treated children on the British

National PKU register (Graham, 1978) and some concern exists about the treated girls who are now reaching child-bearing age.

Tertiary prevention of handicap

The stable or increasing prevalence rates for severe mental handicap mean that particular attention must be given to the tertiary prevention or amelioration of handicap in the severely retarded. It seems probable that there is a rising prevalence affecting the more severely or profoundly handicapped; the low death rate among this sub-group in Camberwell, identified in 1967 and followed to date (9 out of 140), tends to support this belief. In looking at the major secondary handicaps which were seen in the Camberwell study it is clear that any intervention needs to be multidisciplinary.

Early intervention, as with mild mental retardation, has tended to focus on easily identifiable and homogeneous groups, particularly Down's Syndrome (Bricker and Bricker, 1970; Hayden and Haring, 1977), and has involved the training of parents in the use of behaviour modification techniques aimed at increasing skills and imparting techniques of behaviour management. There are now many reported instances of the efficacy of such techniques and it is clear that significant gains can be demonstrated in selected groups compared with matched controls, at least over short periods of time.

So far there has been a failure to establish the efficacy of these techniques on an epidemiological basis or in a clear developmental context. The Portage system evaluated by Revill and Blunden (1979) and others goes some way to meet these criticisms but the problems of maintainence of such programmes within a community service remain.

The other main change has been towards community care with adequate schooling or day care extending into the pre-school period, play groups, clubs and improvements in housing for the families of handicapped children.

In Camberwell since 1967, it has been deliberate policy to avoid admitting children to long term hospital care and since that time only one child under the age of 16 has been admitted to an institution of this type. It is too early to say whether this has reduced the prevalence of secondary behavioural handicap as described by Tizard in the Brooklands Experiment on which this pattern of care is modelled (Tizard, 1960). The majority of children requiring residential care have been provided for in four small children's homes and attend day special schools; only two children are so severely behaviourally disordered as to have been excluded from school.

In spite of these improvements in community services and the provision of a community mental handicap team of psychologists, psychiatrists, paediatricians, community nurses and other therapists to families and schools, the same proportion of children as previously, approximately a quarter of the total, have been found to require residential care.

Similar projects in Great Britain which set out to provide an alternative pattern of community care for severely retarded children also await the results of systematic evaluation, and having established an epidemiological data base this would seem to be the next major task facing case registers. As has been stressed in this symposium the essential prerequisite for such studies is the establishment of common methods of evaluating care and treatment.

References

Alberman, E.A. (1979). Main causes of major mental handicap: prevalence and epidemiology. In: *Major Mental Handicap: methods and costs of prevention*. Ciba Foundation Symposium 59, Elsevier: Amsterdam.

Bereiter, C. and Englemann, S. (1966). *Teaching Disadvantaged Children in the Preschool*. Englewood Cliffs, NJ: Prentice Hall.

Birch, H.G., Richardson, S.A., Baird, D., Horobin, G. and Illsley, R. (1970). *Mental Subnormality in the Community*. Williams and Wilkins: Baltimore.

British Medical Journal (1980). Leading Article. Quality not quantity in babies. *Br. Med. J.* **280**, 347–8.

Bricker, W.A. and Bricker, D. (1970). Toddler Research and Intervention Project. IMRID Behav. Sci. Monogr. No. 20 Nashville, Tenessee.

Bronfenbrenner, U. (1975). Is early intervention effective? In: Friedlander B.S., Sterritt, G.M. and Kirk, G.E. (eds): *Exceptional Infant*, Vol. III, Assessment and Intervention. Brunner/Mazel: New York.

Caldwell, B.M., Bradley, R.H. and Elardo, R. (1975). *Early Stimulation in Mental Retardation*, Vol. V. Brunner Mazell: New York.

Chamberlain, G. (1979). Background to perinatal health. *Lancet* **ii**, 1051–3.

Clarke, A.D.B. (1969). *Recent Advances in the Study of Subnormality*. (2nd edn). National Association for the Mentally Handicapped: London.

Corbett, J.A. (1978). Population studies of mental retardation. In: Graham, P. (ed.): *Epidemiological Approaches in Child Psychiatry*. Academic Press: London.

Davie, R. Butler, N.R. and Goldstein, H. (1972). *From Birth to Seven*. National Child Development Study. Longman: London.

Davis, K. (1947). Final note on a case of extreme isolation. *Am. J. Sociol.* **52**, 432–437.

Drillien, C.M., Jameson, S. and Wilkinson, E.M. (1967). Studies in mental handicap, Part 1. Prevalence and distribution by clinical type and severity of defect. *Arch. Dis. Child*, **41**, 528–38.

Dudgeon, J.A. (1976). Short and long term effects of viral and other infections in pregnancy. In: Turnbull, A.C. and Woodford, F.P. (eds.): *Prevention of Handicap Through Ante Natal Care*. Associated Scientific: Amsterdam.

Ferguson-Smith, M. (1979). Maternal age specific incidence of chromosome aberrations at amniocentesis. In: Murken, J–D., Stengel-Rutkowski, S., and Schwinger, E. (eds): *Prenatal Diagnosis*. Enke: Stuttgart.

Forster, D.P. (1977). The ante-natal detection of Down's Syndrome: some demographic aspects. *J. ment. Defic. Res.* **21**, 263–272.

Galjaard, H. (1980). *Genetic Metabolic Diseases: Early Diagnosis and Prenatal Analysis*. Elsevier: Amsterdam.

Goodman, M. and Tizard, J. (1962). Prevalence of idiocy and imbecility among children. *Br. Med. J.* **1**, 216–219.

Garber, H. and Heber, F.R. (1977). The Milwaukee Project. In: Mittler, P. and deJong, J.M. (eds.): *Research to Practice in Mental Retardation*, Vol. 1, Care and Intervention. University Park Press: Baltimore.

Graham, P. (1978). Personal Communication.

Gustavson, K.H., Holmgren, G., Jonsell, R. and Blomquist, H.K. (1977). Severe mental retardation in a North Swedish County. *J. ment. Defic. Res.* **21**, 161–180.

Hagard, S. and Carter, F.A. (1976). Screening for Down's Syndrome. *Br. Med. J.* **1**, 753.

Hagberg, B., Hagbert, G. and Olow, I. (1977). The panorama of cerebral palsy in Swedish children born 1954–74. *Neuropediatrics* (Suppl. 8) 516–21.

Hagberg, B. (1979). Severe mental retardation in Swedish children born 1959–1970: epidemiological panorama and causative factors. In: *Major Mental Handicap: methods and cost of prevention*. Ciba Foundation Symposium 59. Elsevier: Amsterdam.

Hayden, A.H. and Harding, N.G. (1977). The acceleration and maintainance of developmental gains in Down's Syndrome school age children. In: Mittler, P. and de Jong, J.M. (eds.): *Research to Practice in Mental Retardation*, Vol. 1, Care and Intervention. University Park Press,: Baltimore.

Heber, R., Dever, R. and Conry, J. (1968). The influence of environmental and genetic variables on the intellectual development. In: Prehm, H.J., Hamerlynch, L.A. and Crosson, J.E. (eds): *Behavioural Research in Mental Retardation*. University of Oregon: Eugene, Oregon.

Jensen, A.R. (1969). How much can we boost IQ and scholastic achievement? *Harv. Educ. Rev.* **39**, 1–123.

Kirk, S.A. (1952). Experiments in the early training of the mentally retarded. *Am. J. ment. Defic.* **56**, 692–700.

Koluchova, J. (1972). Severe deprivation in twins: a case study. *J. Child Psychol. Psychiatry* **13**, 107–114.

Koluchova, J. (1976). The further development of twins after severe and prolonged deprivation: a second report. *J. Child Psychol. Psychiatry* **17**, 181–88.

Kushlick, A. and Blunden, R. (1974). The epidemiology of mental subnormality. In: Clarke, A.M. and Clarke, A.D.B. (eds.): *Mental Deficiency: the changing outlook*. Methuen: London.

Kushlick, A. and Cox, G. (1967). Ascertained prevalence of mental subnormality in the Wessex Region. *Proc. Internat. Congr. Scient. Study of Mental Deficiency*. Montpellier.

Laxova, R., Ridler, M.A.C. and Bowen-Bravery, M. (1977). An etiological survey of the severely retarded Hertfordshire children who were born between 1st January 1965 and 31st December 1976. *Am. J. Med. Gent.* **1**, 75–86.

Lewis, E.O. (1929). Report of an Investigation into the Incidence of Mental Deficiency in Six Areas 1925–7. Report of the Mental Deficiency Committee, Part IV. H.M.S.O.: London.

MacCready, R.A. and Jaffrey, N.H. (1974). Admissions of phenylketonuria

250   J.A. Corbett

patients to residential institutions before and after screening programmes of the newborn infant. *J. Pediatr.* **85**, 383–385.

Mason, M. (1942). Learning to speak after years of silence. *J. Speech Hear. Dis.* **7**, 245–304.

Page, E.B. (1972). Miracle in Milwaukee: raising the IQ. *Educ. Res.* **1**, 8–16.

Peckham, C.S. (1972). Clinical and laboratory study of children exposed in utero to maternal rubella. *Arch. Dis. Child.* **47**, 571–577.

Revill, S. and Blunden, R. (1979). A home training service for preschool developmentally handicapped children. *Behav. Res. and Ther.* **17**, 207–214.

Skeels, H.M. (1966). Adult status of children with contrasting early life experiences: a follow up study. *Monogr. Soc. Res. Child Develop.* **31**, 3, No. 105.

Skodak, M. (1968). Adult status of individuals who experienced early intervention. In: Richards, B.W. (ed.): *Proc. First Congress. Internat. Assoc. Sci. Study Ment. Defic.* Michael Jackson: Reigate, UK.

Stewart, A., Turcan, D. Rawlings, C. and Gregory, S. (1967). Outcome for infants at high risk of major handicap. In: *Major Mental Handicap: Methods and Costs of Prevention.* Ciba Symposium **57**. Elsevier, Amsterdam.

Throne, J.M. (1975). The replicability fetish and the Milwaukee project. *Ment. Retard.* **13**, 14–17.

Tizard, J. (1960). Residential care of mentally handicapped children. *Br. Med. J.* **1**, 1041–1046.

Wing, L. (1971). Severely retarded children in a London area: prevalence and provision of services. *Psychol Med.* **1**, 105–15.

Summing Up

B. COOPER

Department of Epidemiological Psychiatry, Central Institute of Mental Health, Mannheim, FRG

The five groups of questions set out in the preface to this volume concern respectively the epidemiology of mental retardation, the nature of the retarded child's handicaps, associated family problems, the evaluation of services and the prospects for prevention. By way of conclusion, each of these topics will be discussed briefly in the light of the foregoing contributions

Case definition and epidemiology

The incidence and prevalence of any given disorder in a population cannot be estimated with confidence unless a satisfactory case definition is available. The definition of mental retardation, however, remains to the present day highly controversial. At the root of the problem lies the fact that none of the advocated criteria — medical diagnosis, low formal intelligence, educational under-achievement or social incompetence — is by itself adequate as a basis for definition or diagnosis, while the agreement between the different criteria is far from perfect.

Because no single measure has proved sufficient, the weight of expert opinion has moved in favour of some kind of definition comprising a number of clauses. There is, however, continuing debate as to whether such a definition should be restrictive or broadly inclusive, as well as about the relative importance of the various components. Some workers have argued strongly that, in order to avoid unnecessary labelling and consequent social disadvantage, terms such as mental handicap should be restricted to a core-group of "true" retardates with established medical diagnoses (Mercer, 1973). Others reject this proposal on the grounds that it reverts to traditional diagnosticism and tends to reinforce the false notion of mental retardation as a biological entity, rather than simply a descriptive term for a loose clustering of developmental problems stemming from a variety of causes (Goodman, 1977).

Since further controversy, arising from conflicts between different theoretical or ideological standpoints, is unlikely to lead to a consensus, it seems more profitable to seek an answer in the findings of scientific research. These suggest that the major parameters of mental handicap – medico-biological, psychological and behavioural — are closely inter-related below a certain level of mental development, corresponding roughly to IQ 50, but become much less so above this level (Kushlick and Blunden, 1974; Cooper *et al.*, 1979). The importance of detecting severe mental handicap and making special provision for those affected out-weighs any negative consequences for the individual due to "labelling". For the milder degrees of handicap, however, the balance is much more finely drawn; the higher the IQ stands above 50, the more dubious are the benefits of being designated mentally retarded.

When case finding is restricted to the severe and moderate degrees of retardation, an impressive measure of agreement is to be found between prevalence ratios reported from many different surveys of school-age children. The table provided by Dupont (p. 4) shows that age-specific ratios found in a number of urban populations cluster between 3.3 and 3.7 per 1000, though there is greater variation among the ratios reported for rural populations. Dupont rightly comments that differential migration rates must be taken into account in seeking to explain these disparities.

A relative uniformity of urban prevalence ratios extending over more than 40 years might seem to indicate that the incidence of severe mental retardation has remained constant in a rapidly changing world, and thus to speak for genetic rather than environmental causation. There are, however, a number of reasons why these data should be interpreted with great caution. Precise comparison of prevalence statistics from different studies is difficult, because of variation in the definitions and methods employed. There may also be a selective fallacy, due to the understand-able tendency of research workers to emphasize the reliability of their findings by pointing to similarities rather than differences in the reports of other workers. It is in any event somewhat risky to treat prevalence ratios for a given age-group as being equivalent to birth prevalence, unless one has information on the effects of differential mortality and migration.

Fryers has taken pains to meet this last objection, by concentrating on the narrow age-band 5–9 years (possible in the U.K., where schooling begins at five) and by collecting supplementary data on infant and early childhood mortality. His finding that prevalence ratios are *not* constant, but have changed significantly over the past three decades, is thus of great interest. Data from the Salford Case Register point to a rise in birth prevalence rates in the 1950s and early 1960s, leading to a peak in the mid-1960s and a subsequent decline. Moreover, ratios for the 5–9 year age-group, drawn from 14 other surveys carried out during this period, appear to fit the Salford trend quite well, suggesting that it does not represent a purely local phenomenon. (Since 12 of these surveys were made in the British Isles and the remaining two in Denmark, we cannot yet say how widespread the change has been.)

It seems that the prevalence of severe retardation in a population at any given time represents a balance in the changing frequencies of a number of disorders with differing aetiologies, some of which are increasing while others are on the wane. The frequency of Down's syndrome, for example, rose markedly in the first half of this century due to improved survival rates; Fryer's Salford data, however, show a decline in the birth prevalence of this condition in the past two decades which, if continued, must result in a greatly reduced frequency in the general population. Over the same period, the birth prevalence of perinatal metabolic disorders, some of which are associated with severe retardation, has been on the upswing. It is thus entirely justifiable to speak of the dynamics of prevalence (Fryers, 1981): a concept of some importance for the long-term planning of services, as well as in the study of environmental causes of retardation. The problem calls for a system of continuous monitoring, which could be achieved partly with the help of local case registers but would also require anterospective studies of birth cohorts.

Assessment of impairments and handicaps

There is as yet no accepted system of classification of handicaps analogous to those which exist for categorizing disease. In social medicine, as Fryers points out, contemporary thinking favours a differentiation of three levels (Lees and Shaw, 1974):

(1) impairment — the basic fault at structural, biochemical or developmental level;
(2) disability — limitation or disturbance of part-function, consequent upon impairment;
(3) handicap — the resulting biological and social disadvantages suffered by the affected individual.

This schema has manifest advantages for analysing the problems of physical handicap associated with, say, amputation of a limb or chronic bronchitis. It is, however, less easy to apply to mental retardation, partly because in many cases the basic underlying impairment cannot be identified and partly because we know so little about psychological part-functions. In this context, the nature of the individual's disabilities and handicaps must in large measure be inferred from the pattern of his adaptive behaviour. It therefore seems realistic, at the present stage of knowledge, to try to assess a retarded child's problems with the help of information from a number of different sources, such as medical investigation, psychometric testing, informant interviews and direct observation of behaviour, whilst at the same time bearing in mind that information from any single source may not correspond neatly to one of the conceptual levels outlined above.

Medical investigation has been directed chiefly to the diagnosis of clinical syndromes, and hence to the identification of specific pathologies. The proportion of cases in which a medical diagnosis can be assigned has increased with the introduction of new techniques – biochemical, chromosomal, radiological, etc — until it is now claimed that, given the opportunity for full investigation, a "medical" aetiology can be established in up to 90% of cases of severe mental retardation. This claim may be somewhat optimistic: in Iivanainen's careful study of severely handicapped hospital patients, for instance, a broad generic diagnosis could be made in 82% and a neurological disorder identified in 72%. Furthermore, the proportion of medical diagnoses among the mildly retarded (IQ 50–70), who today make up more than half the total, is very much lower than this. In practice, therefore, the proportion of all children classed as mentally retarded who have an established CNS pathology or biological deficit that explains their handicaps convincingly is still only of the order of 50%.

Much basic research has yet to be undertaken into the assessment of specific impairments and disabilities among the mentally retarded by means of standardized examination techniques. Tests of motor function, such as the Lincoln-Oseretsky Test (Sloan, 1955), call for a relatively high standard of comprehension and co-operation on the part of the child. Standard procedures for neurological examination, of the kind developed by Touwen and Prechtl (1970), are better in this respect than tests, but still require some modification before they can be used with the severely retarded.

The limitations of normative psychological tests in assessing the cognitive and learning abilities of the mentally handicapped, and in predicting their further development, are now widely recognized (Clarke and Clarke, 1974). This recognition has stimulated a search for complementary methods which, singly or in combination, might improve the accuracy of prediction. One partial solution has been the construction of tests or test-batteries, which are normative only in the sense that they have been standardized on representative samples of mentally retarded persons. Both Liepmann and Eggert (one of the originators of the German Test Battery for the Mentally Retarded–TBGB) note that this approach, while possessing definite advantages over more traditional intelligence

tests, is not of any great help in dealing with the more severely handicapped children and consider, indeed, that the methods of trait psychology can never be wholly adequate in this context.

An alternative strategy, based on the assessment of learning capacity
through comparison of achievement before and after training on specific
tasks, has drawn much attention in recent years. The value of this kind of
quasi-experimental test is greatly enhanced, as Kornmann points out, if
the selected tasks are both of the right order of complexity and directly
related in content to the realities of the child's social environment. Kornmann bases his arguments on an interactionist theory of handicap, but
substantially similar conclusions have been reached by a number of
psychologists in the light of the empirical evidence. Indeed, it has been
forcefully argued that psychological assessment of the mentally retarded
is of limited practical value unless linked to remedial programmes (Clarke
and Clarke, 1974). Clearly, however, the use of "task analysis", as advocated by Kornmann and others, goes well beyond the traditional boundaries of assessment; the logical implication must be drawn that the aim of
such methods is no longer simply to *predict* the child's future, but to
improve it.

Finally, the use of informant interviews, based on standard procedures
such as the HBS Schedule (described here by Wing and discussed by
Liepmann, Bernsen and Ort), moves away altogether from a test paradigm. Here, the objective is a detailed profile of the child's abilities,
handicaps and behaviour, as manifested in his everyday life-situation.
The approach is not normative; strictly speaking no assumptions are
required as to the distribution of abilities in the child population. In the
construction of ordinal scales, however, established norms of child
development have been of great help (Gesell and Amatruda, 1941; Sheridan, 1973); for this reason, the rating of developmental items poses fewer
problems than does that of intrinsically abnormal behaviour.

While a good deal of methodological research has yet to be done, the
early reports of studies using the HBS Schedule are very promising, and
amply justify Liepmann's conclusion that in extensive surveys both
psychometric tests and informant interviews should be carried out
whenever possible.

Family and social background

Attempts to assess the family problems associated with mental handicap
must confront some difficult problems of aim and method. Earlier studies
tended to concentrate on the degree of burden that a handicapped child
represented for his family, the tacit assumption being that the only way of

relieving this burden was to remove the child. Since the drawbacks of prolonged institutional care have become widely acknowledged and— in some countries, at least— the numbers of children "put away" has been falling, the focus of enquiry has shifted to the help that the families need, and the ways in which it might be provided by community-based services. With this development has come, as Wilkin points out, a change of emphasis from the psychological and emotional impact on family members, to practical issues of day-to-day care. Such a shift might seem to favour the prospects of empirical research, and in the long term no doubt will do so; at present, however, research methods are lagging behind. The task-oriented approach to assessment described by Wilkins offers one interesting example of the kind of technique that will have to be developed in this field; a related approach based on a time-budget has recently been employed by Dupont (1980). The findings of this type of investigation may well differ markedly, as Eggert points out, between diagnostic groups such as Down's syndrome, brain-damaged children and the socio-culturally deprived, and will require careful analysis from this point of view.

One special problem that has still to be satisfactorily resolved is the relationship of severe mental retardation to social class. Most population surveys have lent support to the view stated by Kushlick and Blunden (1974) that ". . . in industrial societies parents of severely subnormal children are evenly distributed among all the social strata in the society, whilst those of mildly subnormal subjects are predominantly from the lower social classes." There are, however, some discrepant findings which have not been convincingly explained, notably from studies in Edinburgh (Drillien et al., 1966), Sheffield (Bayley, 1973) and Mannheim (Liepmann, 1979). It may be that the picture is changing as a result of altered survival rates, or for other reasons. Eggert notes, for example, that there was a marked increase between 1965 and 1979, in one area of Germany, in the numbers of children from lower social status groups who were ascertained as mentally retarded. However, Fryers (1980) could find no confirmation for such a trend in the Salford Case Register data. Further research is called for, not only because of possible aetiological implications of such a trend, but also because of the need to establish to what extent non-specific secondary handicaps, related to social class, may be compounding the difficulties of retarded children.

Evaluation of services

Evaluation in the broad sense does not necessarily imply exact measurement. Good descriptive reporting alone can provide us with an adequate basis for reaching certain limited but important conclusions about existing services. One does not require the help of sophisticated measuring instruments to grasp that the situation of handicapped children in some long-stay hospitals, as recounted by Oswin (1978), is a public disgrace that should not be allowed to continue, or that short-stay facilities of the kind described by Oswin in the present volume have some manifest advantages. Yet as soon as we begin to consider possible ways of improving the quality of residential care, or the extent to which the large institutions might be replaced by small, community-based units, controversy begins and the need for scientific evaluation becomes apparent. In a period of growing economic stringency, when the available social-welfare resources must be used to the best advantage, it will become increasingly important to find "best-buy" solutions and, in the words of Raynes, not to spend large sums of taxpayers' money on services, without also spending the much smaller sums on research to test the effects of these services.

Comparative evaluation of any health care system is bound to prove a major task, calling for the measurement of a variety of clinical, epidemiological, social and economic variables. The Wessex project (Kushlick, 1975), for example, compared two contrasting forms of residential care in terms of their relative costs and management problems, as well as of their effects on patients, their families and the local communities. Since a global approach of this kind is rarely feasible, evaluative studies as a rule have pursued more limited objectives. One relatively simple strategy is to assess, on the basis of epidemiological data, the extent to which existing facilities are meeting the need for special provision within a defined population. Thus, statistics cited by Kushlick and Blunden (1974) and by Tizard (1974) suggest that services for the mentally handicapped are required for some 5.4 per 1000 children — predominantly those in the IQ range below 50. In Western Europe at the present time, this rate corresponds to 340–350 children under 18 years in a "standard" area population of 250 000. The need for different types of facility in such a population is more difficult to gauge, partly because it tends to vary both with geographic factors and with the social conditions that prevail. Most surveys, nevertheless, reveal certain wide disparities between need and provision; notably a shortage of residential places within, or in easy reach of, the catchment area population, of day-care places for the severely handicapped and of creches and special kindergartens for children under school age.

More difficult are the problems of method encountered in trying to assess quality of care. To a limited extent, quality can be judged in terms of quantity; for example, the findings reported by Mittler and Preddy, that while nearly half the children leaving special schools for the retarded

in one region of England have language impairments, only one quarter
have contact with speech therapists and less than half with educational
psychologists, tells us something about the prevailing standards. Data of
this kind can be further analysed to reveal the range of variation among
the individual schools and its correlation with social and administrative
indices. They are not, however, adequate as guidance to the best way of
deploying resources, given that these must remain limited in quantity.
For this purpose, some kind of value judgments are necessary.

If differences between a number of existing services can be analysed in
relation to established principles of patient care, it may then be possible to
test for associations, on the one hand with the organizational structure of
these services and on the other hand with clinical and behavioural characteristics of their patients. This approach was adopted by Tizard and his
co-workers in their study of 16 residential units for children (King *et al.*,
1971). Taking as their theoretical starting point Goffman's (1961) concept
of the "total institution", they incorporated a number of its salient features — rigidity of routine, regimentation of the inmates, absence of
personal possessions, etc — into a scale of child management practice,
whose twin poles represented institution-oriented and child-oriented
care respectively. By this means they were able to demonstrate clear
differences between hospital wards and small hostels, which were related
to the staffing structures of the various institutions.

Analogous methods are now being developed to measure the quality of
non-residential, community-based care. The report of a recent WHO
working group (Regional Office for Europe, 1980) lists a number of basic
criteria by which the quality of mental health services can be judged and
points out that it is possible, with the aid of such guidelines, to monitor
and evaluate changes made in individual services. The logical next step,
therefore, will be to compare the merits and disadvantages of changes
introduced into the patterns of extramural care provided in different
areas. It is not an easy step to make. Raynes, in her concise review of
research into residential care, emphasizes that longitudinal and experimental designs will be required and that their implementation is not
straightforward. Kebbon's brief summary of recent Swedish developments hints at the complexities that are involved, including such paradox-
ical effects as the increased degree of isolation of some handicapped
persons who move out of institutions into the community, in accordance
with the principle of "normalization". Such findings reinforce the conclusion that, in the final analysis, the success or failure of any service has
to be gauged in terms of its influence on the frequency and severity of
handicap, rather than of conformity to any set of principles, however
enlightened.

Prospects for prevention

Some years ago, the US President's Committee on Mental Retardation made its famous pronouncement that:

> using present techniques from the biomedical and behavioural sciences, it is possible to reduce the occurrence of mental retardation by 50% before the end of the century (PCMR, 1972).

The main planks of the recommended programme were: (1) full commitment to improved pre-natal care; (2) a health care delivery system that would ensure equality of access for all; (3) continued advancement of knowledge through research, and (4) a nation-wide campaign of public education on this topic (PCMR, 1976).

This admirable report makes somewhat ironic reading today, especially in the light of ecological forecasts provided by another, more recent presidential commission (Global 2000, 1980). It seems clear that in the next generation, the containment— let alone reduction— of the incidence of mental retardation on a world scale will be possible only by means of a systematic and sustained attack on the central problems of malnutrition and environmental damage with which mankind is now confronted.

Such a conclusion is perhaps all the more unpalatable because in the past 40 years we have witnessed a series of advances in biomedical preventive methods, both specific and general, and — in some of the developed, industrial nations at least— a related fall in the incidence of certain causes of severe mental retardation. Tizard's (1964) comparison of his own survey findings with those of E.O. Lewis, a generation earlier, suggested that there had been a drop of as much as one third in the incidence of cases with IQ below 50, though because of the improvement in life expectation of the affected children, no corresponding decrease had occurred in prevalence rates. Reduction in perinatal mortality appears, as Corbett in his review of the subject points out, to be associated with a decline in the incidence of severe handicapping conditions.

In respect of some specific causes, such as tuberculous meningitis, congenital syphilis and cretinism, the major gains have now been made. In other instances, advances in technique are undoubtedly having an impact, though it is not yet clear to what extent this will be reflected in falling incidence rates. Clarke (1977) lists under this heading: (1) use of immunization techniques against illnesses that have neurological sequelae; (2) early diagnosis and compensatory treatment of inborn metabolic errors; (3) improved standards of ante-natal and natal care; (4) genetic counselling and family planning (including early prenatal diagnosis of Down's syndrome, spina bifida and anencephaly); (5) immunization of rhesus negative mothers against Rh sensitisation by rhesus positive foetuses; (6) surgical treatment of some forms of infantile hydrocephalus.

Undoubtedly, these developments contributed greatly to the new mood of optimism which was expressed by the President's Committee. There remain, however, major problems of finance and organization in delivering preventive care to all groups of the population who are at risk. Fryers, on the basis of a comparison of three birth cohorts in an industrial area, concludes that in one respect the picture is rather disappointing, since "the conditions which have diminished are those largely beyond our control, while the potentially preventable conditions have increased". In developing countries, the difficulties of widespread application are immeasurably greater.

Specific biomedical techniques are much more likely to reduce the frequency of severe retardation, associated with major neurological damage, than that of the milder forms of retardation. Insofar as most mild retardation is, in Corbett's words, subcultural, resulting from an interaction between environmental hazards, polygenic inherited factors and socio-cultural deprivation, the role of specific preventive measures must remain a limited one. Of general measures in this field, those which seem to hold most promise for primary prevention are directed towards betterment of the health of women of reproductive age. Wynn and Wynn (1979) provide a masterly overview, based on the health and morbidity statistics of many countries. They affirm that a large part of reproductive casualty occurs too early in pregnancy to be influenced by ante-natal care services, and that "nothing less than improvement in the health of women of reproductive age before entering pregnancy can reduce these casualties" (p. 221). Since the milder grades of retardation occur preponderantly in the lowest social-status groups of the population, particular attention must be paid to health care for child-bearing women in these groups, and to class-related causes of morbidity found among such women.

Finally, the importance of secondary and tertiary prevention of mental handicap is reiterated in many of the contributions to this volume. One of the more encouraging findings of epidemiological research is the extent to which the rates of persons under care for mental handicap fall off in the age-range between 20 and 40, mainly because of the ability of a high proportion of the mildly retarded to lead relatively normal, independent lives. It seems plausible that an improved quality of education and care in the special schools, combined with careful screening and selection for "intervention" programmes of the kind reviewed by Corbett, would do much to increase this proportion. Here, at any rate, is a high priority for evaluative research.

References

Bayley, M. (1973). *Mental Handicap and Community Care. A Study of Mentally Handicapped People in Sheffield.* Routledge and Kegan Paul: London and Boston.

Clarke, A.D.B. (1977). From research to practice (Presidential Address) *In* Mittler, P. (ed.) *Research to Practice in Mental Retardation,* Vol. 1: Care and Intervention, pp. A7–A19. University Park Press: Baltimore, London, Tokyo.

Clarke, A.M. and Clarke, A.D.B. (1974). Severe subnormality: capacity and performance. *In* Clarke, A.M. and Clarke, A.D.B. (eds) *Mental Deficiency: the changing outlook,* 3rd edn, pp. 369–86. Methuen: London.

Cooper, B., Liepmann, M.C., Marker, K. and Schieber, P.M. (1979). Definition of severe mental retardation in school-age children. Findings of an epidemiological study. *Social Psychiatry* **14**, 197–205.

Drillien, C.M., Jameson, S. and Wilkinson, E.M. (1966). Studies in mental handicap. Part I: prevalence and distribution by clinical type and severity of defect. *Arch. Dis. Child.* **41**, 528–38.

Dupont, A. (1980). A study concerning the time-related and other burdens when severely handicapped children are reared at home. *In* Strömgren, E., Dupont, A. and Nielsen, J.A. (eds) *Epidemiological Research as Basis for the Organization of Extramural Psychiatry. Acta Psychiatr. Scand.,* Suppl. 285, pp. 249–57. Munksgaard: Copenhagen.

Fryers, T. (1981). *Severe Mental Retardation. The Dynamics of Prevalence.* (In press).

Gesell, A.L. and Amatruda, C.S. (1941). *Developmental Diagnosis.* Harper: New York.

Global 2000. Report to the President (1980). Council on Environmental Quality and the US State Office. US Govt. Printing Office: Washington, D.C.

Goffman, E. (1961). *Asylums. Essays on the Social Situation of Mental Patients and Other Inmates.* Anchor, Doubleday: New York.

Goodman, J.F. (1977). The diagnostic fallacy: a critique of Jane Mercer's concept of mental retardation. *J. School Psychol.* **15**, 197–205.

King, R.D., Raynes, N.V. and Tizard, J. (1971). *Patterns of Residential Care.* Routledge and Kegan Paul: London.

Kushlick, A. (1975). Epidemiology and evaluation of services for the mentally retarded. *In* Begab, M.J. and Richardson, S.A. (eds) *The Mentally Retarded and Society. A Social Science Perspective,* pp. 325–43. University Park Press: Baltimore.

Kushlick, A. and Blunden, R. (1974). The epidemiology of mental subnormality. *In* Clarke, A.M. and Clarke, A.D.B. (eds) *Mental Deficiency: The Changing Outlook,* 3rd edn, pp. 31–81. Methuen: London.

Lees, D. and Shaw, S. (1974). *Impairment, Disability and Handicap. A Multidisciplinary View.* Heinemann Educational: London.

Liepmann, M.C. (1979). *Geistig behinderte Kinder und Jugendliche. Zeitschrift für Kinder- und Jugendpsychiatrie,* Beiheft 4. Huber: Berne, Stuttgart and Vienna.

Mercer, J. (1973). *Labeling the Mentally Retarded.* University of California Press: Berkeley.

Oswin, M. (1978). *Children Living in Long-Stay Hospitals.* Spastics International Medical Publications, Research Monograph No. 5. Heinemann Medical: London.

President's Committee on Mental Retardation (PCMR) (1972). *Entering the Era of Human Ecology.* DHEW Publication No. (OS) 72–77. Govt. Printing Office: Washington, DC

262   B. Cooper

President's Committee on Mental Retardation (PCMR) (1976). *Mental Retardion. Century of Decision*. Govt. Printing Office, Stock No. 040 000 00343 6. Washington, DC.

Regional Office for Europe (1980). *Changing Patterns of Mental Health Care*. EURO Reports and Studies, No. 25. World Health Organization: Copenhagen.

Sheridan, M.D. (1973). *Children's Developmental Progress*. National Foundation for Educational Research: Windsor, U.K.

Sloan, W. (1955). The Lincoln-Oseretsky motor development scale. *Genetic Psychology Monographs* **51**, 183–252.

Tizard, J. (1964). *Community Services for the Mentally Handicapped*. Oxford University Press: London.

Tizard, J. (1974). Services and the evaluation of services. *In* Clarke, A.M. and Clarke, A.D.B. (eds) *Mental Deficiency: The Changing Outlook*, 3rd edn Methuen: London.

Touwen, B.C.L. and Prechtl, H.F.R. (1970). *The Neurological Examination of the Child with Minor Nervous Dysfunction*. Clinics in Developmental Medicine, No. 38. Spastics International Medical Publications. Heinemann Medical: London.

Wynn, M. and Wynn, A. (1979). *Prevention of Handicap and the Health of Women*. Routledge and Kegan Paul: London.

Index